Recasting Postcolonialism

D1610899

Recent Titles in STUDIES IN AFRICAN LITERATURE

▼▼▼▼▼▼▼▼▼▼▼▼▼▼▼▼▼▼▼▼▼▼▼▼▼▼▼

Recasting Postcolonialism

Women Writing Between Worlds

Anne Donadey

HEINEMANN
Portsmouth, NH

Heinemann
A division of Reed Elsevier Inc.
361 Hanover Street
Portsmouth, NH 03801–3912
www.heinemann.com

ISBN 0–325–07023–7 (Heinemann cloth)
ISBN 0–325–07022–9 (Heinemann paper)

Library of Congress Cataloging-in-Publication Data

Donadey, Anne.
    Recasting postcolonialism : women writing between worlds / Anne Donadey.
        p. cm.—(Studies in African literature, ISSN 1351–5713)
    Includes bibliographical references and index.
    ISBN 0–325–07023–7 (alk. paper)—ISBN 0–325–07022–9 (pbk. : alk. paper)
    1. Djebar, Assia, 1936—Criticism and interpretation.   2. Sebbar, Leïla—
Criticism and interpretation.   3. Algerian literature (French)—Women
authors—History and criticism.   4. Women and literature—Algeria—
History—20th century.   5. Women in literature.   6. Decolonization in
literature.   7. Postcolonialism—Algeria.   8. Algeria—In literature.
I. Title. II. Series.
PQ3989.2.D57 Z66 2001
843'.914099287'0965—dc21   00–063250

British Library Cataloguing in Publication Data is available.

Printed in the United States of America on acid-free paper.

05 04 03 02 01 SB 1 2 3 4 5 6 7 8 9

Copyright Acknowledgments

The author and publisher gratefully acknowledge permission to reprint the following material:

Excerpts from the following books by Assia Djebar: *L'Amour, la fantasia* (Paris: J.-C. Lattès, 1985) and *Ombre sultane* (Paris: J.-C. Lattès, 1987) reprinted by permission of Assia Djebar; *Fantasia: An Algerian Cavalcade*, translated and introduction by Dorothy S. Blair (London: Quartet Books, 1989) and *A Sister to Scheherazade*, translated by Dorothy S. Blair (London: Quartet Books, undated) reprinted by permission of Quartet Books, Ltd.

Portions of early versions of Chapters 1 and 2 previously appeared as "'Une certaine idée de la France': The Algeria Syndrome and Struggles over 'French' Identity" in *Identity Papers: Contested Nationhood in Twentieth-Century France*, edited by Steven Ungar and Tom Conley (Minneapolis: University of Minnesota Press, 1996), pp. 215–32.

Chapter 3 was previously published in slightly different form as "Rekindling the Vividness of the Past: Assia Djebar's Films and Fiction" in *World Literature Today* 70.4 (Autumn 1996): 885–92. The French version, "'Elle a rallumé le vif du passé:' l'écriture-palimpseste d'Assia Djebar," is also available in *Postcolonialisme et Autobiographie: Albert Memmi, Assia Djebar, Daniel Maximin*, edited by Alfred Hornung and Ernstpeter Ruhe, Coll. Textxet: Studies in Comparative Literature 20 (Amsterdam: Rodopi, 1998), pp. 101–15.

Part of Chapter 4 was published as "Assia Djebar's Poetics of Subversion" in *L'Esprit créateur*, 33.2 (Summer 1993): 107–17.

Part of Chapter 6 is revised from "Cultural *Métissage* and the Play of Identity in Leïla Sebbar's *Shérazade* Trilogy," pp. 257–73, in *Borders, Exiles, Diasporas*, edited by Elazar Barkan and Marie-Denise Shelton, with the permission of the publishers, Stanford University Press. © 1998 by the Board of Trustees of the Leland Stanford Junior University.

To my parents,
who will never be able to read this book written in English,
and to my partner,
who had to.

Contents

Preface

Social responsibility must be the basis of any theorizing on postcolonial literature.
                    —Ketu H. Katrak, "Decolonizing Culture" 157

[Theories] are marked and constituted by, even as they constitute, the field of their production.
   —Gayatri C. Spivak, "Imperialism and Sexual Difference" 225

Ne pas prétendre "parler pour," ou pire "parler sur," à peine parler *près de*, et si possible *tout contre*. [Not to claim to "speak for" or, worse, to "speak on," barely speaking *next to*, and if possible *very close to*.]
         —Assia Djebar, *Femmes d'Alger dans leur appartement* 8/2.[1]

While researching and writing this book, I have had ample time to interrogate my own position, to question my (changing) assumptions, and to ponder the implications of my arguments. Traces of this process will no doubt be perceptible throughout the text. As a Western woman, French citizen, and recently naturalized American working in U.S. academia, three risks have been at the forefront for me as I was writing this book. Will my work repeat, rather than displace, Orientalist modes of thought and stereotypes? Even if it does not, will some of my audience read this book in a way that may reinforce Orientalist parameters? And finally, isn't the radical potential of scholarship written in the "West" always already limited by its location in the centers of power? Interestingly, these issues are also very much a concern for the two women writers whose work I investigate here, although I speak from a different location from theirs and use a different medium—criticism rather than fiction.

In a very real and historical sense, my work is rendered possible and intelligible by a tradition of Orientalist scholarship that has taken "the East" as its object of study. Edward Said argued that the Western scholar is caught in the web of Orientalism because of "the gross political fact" of colonization (*Orientalism* 11). My discourse, whether or not I intend it to be, is inscribed within parameters of "uneven exchange" (12). My work is circumscribed both by an Orientalist framework and by a U.S. academic sphere of influence. Not only is my discourse different from that of an Algerian woman, or man; I myself would have written a different book had I been located in the Maghreb (North Africa) or in France; for instance, my introductory chapter reflects the influence on my thinking of intellectual debates in the United States concerning postcolonialism and feminism.

Gayatri Spivak, who cautioned against the risks of "performing the lie of imperialism," advised "vigilance" in feminist scholarship dealing with (post)colonial contexts ("Imperialism" 234–35). I have attempted to remain as vigilant as possible, tiptoeing rather than "dancing through the minefield" (Kolodny 144), negotiating my way through "controlling images" (Collins 67) of the veil, oppressed Arab women, and "despotic" Arab men. I am aware that any discourse has at least one blind spot, and I also recognize that my location as an academic influences what I write about and how I write about it. As Daphne Patai argued, "[W]e are confronted by dual allegiances. On the one hand, we are obligated to our academic disciplines and institutions, within which we must succeed if we are to have any impact on the academy. . . . On the other hand, if we take feminism seriously, it commits us to a transformative politics. In other words, most of us do not want to bite the hand that feeds us; but neither do we want to caress it too lovingly" (138–39).

Such ambivalence has a long tradition in the (post)colonial context. Edward Said saw "Orientalism as a dynamic exchange between individual authors and the large political concerns shaped by the three great empires—British, French, American—in whose intellectual and imaginative territory the writing was produced" (*Orientalism* 14–15). As writers and critics, we are therefore located in particular contexts that constrain, but do not completely determine, what we will say. We go in and out of the Orientalist tradition, as we sometimes oppose it and sometimes reinforce it. There is only so much margin for maneuver, but the margin exists and must be pushed. Indeed, as I argue in the Introduction, the aspect of oppositionality within complicity, and complicity within oppositionality, is a central characteristic of postcolonial writing.

A larger issue is my participation in a condition of "arrested decolonization" (Jeyifo 33), which "has swung the center of gravity of African literary study away from Africa to Europe and America" and therefore automatically grants "non-African scholars of African literature [and, I would add, scholars based in Europe and the United States in general] . . . power over their African colleagues" (40). In this context, it becomes clear that individual self-awareness and vigilance can never make up for the complicity involved in a scholarship located in the centers of power. For Jeyifo, a first step would be to systematically draw attention to the political grounding or situated nature of critical discourse and to recognize "the aporia under which we all, singly or collectively, work today" (45). However, this is hardly likely to effect world change, and at worst it may serve only to alleviate guilt feelings. At best, it will help keep us honest about our motivations.

African literary critic Obioma Nnaemeka ("Bringing" 306–7), African-American cultural critic bell hooks ("Feminist Scholarship" 46–48), and Native American scholar Wendy Rose (416) have suggested that researchers ask themselves the twin questions of *why* and *how* they want to write about postcolonial texts, "Third World" women, or people from nondominant backgrounds. The answers are multiple, and the researcher is, of course, not conscious of all of them. It is now commonplace to say that we read ourselves into those texts that "speak" to us. What first drew me to the writings of Assia Djebar and Leïla Sebbar was their liminal position, in between, on the threshold, participating in different worlds while being unable to fully inhabit either. I was also attracted to their characters' position as (cultural or real) exiles, which is indissolubly linked to their gender as well as to a colonial legacy, and their resulting insistence on building bridges. I am touched by their honesty, their refusal of reductive dichotomies (East-West, man-woman), and the lucidity and beauty of their language in its polyphony.

Part of me strongly identifies with the issues of identity and language that these writers so forcefully bring out. Albeit for different reasons, the experience of feeling like an "inoutsider," in Obioma Nnaemeka's coinage ("Feminism" 81), is not alien to me. Growing up as part of the lower class in one of the richest areas of France, as well as growing up female in the Mediterranean culture of southern France, developed in me an early sense of injustice and marginality, which in turn sensitized me to the intense racism around me.[2] Part of the motivation for this book is a response to my sense of responsibility, as a French person, to address a French legacy of colonialism and racism. As Susan Griffin succinctly put it, "What is buried in the past of one generation falls to the next to claim" (179).

Because of my personal situation of living between two worlds, of being French by birth and American by choice, I experience a certain sense of displacement that may help to attune me to the voices of "inappropriate other[s]" (Trinh, "Not You" 375). I do not mean to erase the very real differences between (voluntary) expatriation and exile. Rather, I am describing what among my experiences helps me connect profoundly with Sebbar's and Djebar's works.

Like my personal positioning, my theoretical location is informed by diverse schools and traditions. I am most influenced by Francophone anticolonial theory (Fanon, Memmi, Césaire) and postcolonial and feminist/ womanist theory (Bhabha, Said, Spivak, Mohanty, King). My introductory chapter maps out this intellectual terrain. Said's suggestions for post-Orientalist research have, in many ways, served as a point of departure and recurrent thread for this book: "Perhaps the most important task of all would be to undertake studies in contemporary alternatives to Orientalism, to ask how one can study other cultures and peoples from a libertarian, or a nonrepressive and nonmanipulative, perspective" (*Orientalism* 24). A starting point, to my mind, is to focus on literary works coming from Maghrebian and Middle Eastern countries, and thereby to study how people represent themselves and to underscore their strategic responses to master discourses. My goal is to have my work participate in the "new kind of dealing with the Orient" that Said calls for (28). At the same time, I acknowledge that political, institutional, and ideological Western traditions may act as a constricting frame for my discourse, even as I attempt to explode that frame. I hope to have written criticism that respects the works being analyzed and the social, cultural, and political contexts in which they arose. It will be up to my readers to decide for themselves to what extent I have succeeded in this endeavor.

Many people deserve thanks for their support in helping me complete this project. The first person I wish to recognize is Françoise Lionnet, whose intellectual stature, teaching, and mentoring skills serve as a model for my own career and who oversaw the first incarnation of this project. Thanks also go to Bernadette Fort, William D. Paden, and Tilde Sankovitch of Northwestern University; Margarita García-Casado, Susan Ireland, Terri J. Nelson, Radhika Parameswaran, Patrice J. Proulx, and Ernstpeter Ruhe; my colleagues at the University of Iowa, especially Laura Donaldson, Mary Lou Emery, Ruedi Kuenzli, Rosemarie Scullion, Jael Silliman, Steve Ungar, and Margery Wolf; Jim Lance, my editor at Heinemann; Lynn Zelem and Nicole Balant at Greenwood; several anonymous reviewers; and, of course, my partner, as always. I am grateful to the University of Iowa for providing me with two summer research fellowships and a semester sabbatical. Among the many graduate research assistants who have seconded me, I am particularly thankful to Prasenjit Gupta for his meticulous editing. Last but not least, my major debt is to the writers who have made my critical work possible. Both Assia Djebar and Leïla Sebbar have been very generous in sharing with me their time, comments, and stories. Beyond their generosity, I am most grateful of all for their writing.

Notes

1. Whenever available, I have used existing English translations and listed them in the bibliography. When two different page numbers are given, the first refers to the French text and the other to the English version. I have often had to modify translations to remain as close to the original text as possible. All other translations are my own.

2. I do not seek to collapse different forms of oppression here, especially since they have very different *histories* and *manifestations*. This is even though, at a general, theoretical level, they may have similar *structures* (a hierarchical, dualistic framework in which one group is viewed as inferior and the other as superior) and *functions* (to justify and ensure the continued dominance of one group over others). There is certainly no guarantee that people who are oppressed on one or more counts will be able to extrapolate from their experience of oppression to that of other groups. However, preliminary research by Hogan and Netzer suggests that white women who have experienced another form of subordination besides that of gender may be more able to develop an antiracist stance than other whites (cited in Feagin and Vera 175–79).

Introduction: Recasting Postcolonialism

This book recasts postcolonialism by analyzing the fiction of a new cast of characters, women writers at the crossroads between Algeria and France. I argue that it is time to move away from a general emphasis on male writers in Anglophone, postcolonial countries and to focus critical attention on gendered studies of literature and culture in specific geographical and historical contexts, such as Algeria. *Recasting Postcolonialism* contributes, both to the growing scholarship on writers from Algeria, and, more generally, to the elaboration of postcolonial feminist frameworks that are both theoretical and analytical.

Most studies of postcolonial literature have focused on male, Anglophone writers and many make sweeping generalizations about different geographic and cultural contexts (a typical example being Ashcroft, Griffiths, and Tiffin's *The Empire Writes Back*). Similarly, much postcolonial theory, while claiming the necessity of paying attention to context, often fails to account for diverse histories of colonization and decolonization (Thomas ix–x). In such theory, the general effects of colonization are indiscriminately applied to various contexts of production. At the same time, gender issues and texts written in languages other than English continue to be marginalized in postcolonial criticism. I propose a recasting of postcolonial literatures that foregrounds the specificity of the postcolonial by "pivot[ing] the center"[1] from male, Anglophone literature to fiction written in French by women in the postcolonial Algerian context.

Algeria has served as a test case of, and a source of much writing on, decolonization and postcoloniality. Its eight-year struggle for independence (1954–1962) was written about (and participated in) by no less a figure in decolonization than Caribbean theorist Frantz Fanon. Its political status as a postcolonial nation is often taken as exemplary of the postcolonial condition. I choose to focus on such an important site rather than extend my analysis of postcolonial literature to disparate geographical contexts. This avoids the totalizing gesture inherent in what Gayatri Spivak called "the combination of effacement of specificity and appropriation that one might call violation" ("Imperialism" 233). This book is not a general literary history of Francophone Algerian literature. Rather, I illustrate broad theoretical points about the nature of postcolonial literatures by exploring the literary, historical, cultural, and political threads woven by two exemplary women writers, Assia Djebar and Leïla Sebbar.

This book engages current debates in postcolonial discourse theory by integrating within it gender issues and feminist theorizing. As Ketu Katrak showed in "Decolonizing Culture," this can best be accomplished by analyzing the artistic production of postcolonial women writers as they situate themselves in dialogue with other colonial, postcolonial, theoretical, and creative texts. The field of Francophone studies is being reshaped by the insights of postcolonial theory, which, if modified to take gender into account, applies particularly well to the literary projects of Djebar and Sebbar.

Recasting Postcolonialism offers an interdisciplinary, comparative examination of the ways in which Djebar's and Sebbar's writings illuminate several crucial postcolonial issues. I first situate their works in the context of debates over Algerian history and historiography. I then focus on their treatment of the Algerian war of liberation (1954–1962), showing how they link it back in time to a long history of resistance to colonization, as well as forward to a continuing struggle against the forces of women's subjugation and French racism. Finally, I analyze their engagement with a multiplicity of intertexts, Arab and French, Orientalist or not, ancient and recent, literary and pictorial. I demonstrate how they both repeat and subvert these intertexts to create for themselves a legitimate space of writing.

Djebar and Sebbar are the leading Francophone women writers originating from Algeria and the only ones whose oeuvres span several decades. In 1996, Djebar received the U.S. Neustadt International Prize for Literature, a prestigious literary award (several previous recipients have gone on to receive the Nobel prize for literature). Both writers were raised in Algeria and have experienced exile in France or elsewhere. They write in French and publish their works mainly in Paris's top publishing houses. They stand between several traditions and cultures—French and Algerian, Arabic and European. However, their positions at the crossroads differ greatly. By paying attention to the similarities, as well as the differences, between their projects, I insist on the importance of contextual analysis in exploring the complexities of the texts' different positions.

Djebar is Algerian (Arab and Berber) and comes from an Islamic background. Arabic is her mother tongue, which she grew up speaking and which links her to a community of Algerian women. However, she does not write well in classical Arabic. Having gone through the French school system—and having succeeded within it to the point of becoming the first Algerian woman ever to enter the elite Ecole Normale Supérieure de Sèvres, where she was trained as a historian—she is aware of the fact that she must carry with her the colonial burden of a French education. Caught between two cultures—two systems of thought whose difference is embodied in the difference between Arabic calligraphy and French writing—she realizes that it is because her father (who, like Sebbar's, taught in a French school) took her to school with him that she escaped being closed in the harem and was allowed to go out unveiled. Female emancipation was thus achieved at the cost of linguistic colonization. For Djebar, in order to break out from the constraints of the French language, it becomes necessary to do violence to it, forcing it into bilingualism, and letting traces of oral Arabic appear through it in order to bring out both the history of her own people and the voices of her silenced Algerian sisters.

Leïla Sebbar calls herself *une croisée* (a cross-breed / a crusader / at the crossroads), thus playing on the polysemy of the word. Born of an Algerian father and a French mother, both schoolteachers, she never really learned to speak Arabic even though she spent her youth in Algeria. For her, French is the mother tongue, and she has said that it was the deprivation of her father's language and country that compelled her to write. Sebbar's works, even more than Djebar's, exemplify *métissage* (cultural and racial mixing). She finds herself in exile, situated between two worlds, the French and the Algerian. Her novels are often set in the *HLM*, the low-income housing projects of the Parisian suburbs, and her protagonists are children of Maghrebian (North African) immigrants, or *Beurs* (originally a Parisian slang term for *Arab*, which these youths then reappropriated). While Djebar has spent most of her life between Algeria and France (and, most recently, the United States), Sebbar has been living in France since she was about seventeen. Although Djebar and Sebbar belong to the same generation (they were born in 1936 and 1941, respectively), their works evince a concern for different generations in different geographical locations. Most of Djebar's fiction focuses on the pivotal generation of people who lived through, and participated in, the war of national liberation in Algeria. Sebbar's novels and short stories usually portray the lives of Beur teenagers born during or after the war, who negotiate a space for themselves between two territories, languages, and cultures.

Unlike Djebar, Sebbar does not usually write in the autobiographical mode. While Djebar's first works coincided with the Algerian war of liberation (1957), Sebbar began publishing in the mid-1970s; both authors continue to write to this day. Both Djebar's and Sebbar's projects also involve a series of novels (a quartet and a trilogy, respectively). As writers of the in between, for whom identity is always problematic, they find themselves constantly straddling boundaries. Their texts show how impossible it is for cultural hybrids to write entirely counterhegemonic narratives and to embrace a simple, unitary identity. Rather, they use mimicry, in the form of repetition with a difference, to rewrite their intertexts from an oppositional perspective.

Djebar's and Sebbar's novels function as historical palimpsests in which they reconstruct their history through the blanks of the Other's discourse (be it the colonizer's or that of the patriarchal tradition). They have recourse to a variety of historical intertexts (Algerian and French), which they rewrite in their novels. They highlight the voices and acts of resistance of Algerian women through this partly erased historical palimpsest. Their own writing inscribes itself on that same palimpsest, as they respond to French accounts of the colonization from a gendered, postcolonial perspective. They interweave Arabic and European accounts, written archives and orally transmitted histories, of the clash between the two cultures over several centuries. The result is, not a happy pluralism of voices, but an encounter that foregrounds violence as conflicting voices vie for control of the fragmented narratives.

This textual violence repeats the violent history of conquest and colonization between the Maghreb (North Africa) and France over the past twelve centuries, a history that culminated in the Algerian war of independence (1954–1962). I examine how Sebbar and Djebar come to terms with, and deconstruct, the violence of Orientalist (literary and pictorial) representations of Arab women. They subvert these intertexts by reappropriating and recontextualizing them, thus initiating a dialogue between women from past and present. At the same time, they recognize their ambiguous fascination with the expression of Orientalist desire in these European works. The complexity of Djebar's and Sebbar's narratives lies in their construction of border positions as sites of negotiation and critique. They inscribe in their works their uneasy relationship to multiculturalism, religion, languages, nationalism, and feminism. To study the intersection of different discourses—different allegiances—is to foreground the plurality and ambivalence of their literary production.

Signposts in a Theoretical Quagmire

The accumulation of academic contributions to the growing field of postcolonial theory and criticism during the 1980s and 1990s has had the effect of stretching the definitions of postcolonial literature to the extent that almost any literature, from any time period and any area of the world, may now be modified by the qualifier *postcolonial*. On the surface, it may seem that my bringing under the umbrella of the postcolonial the study of works by two leading women writers originating from Algeria may contribute to this ever-widening circle. The postcolonial debate has primarily focused on works written in English, and the Maghrebian context is, in many ways, foreign to it, even though there are inescapable intersections. In what follows, I propose a narrowed redefinition of postcolonial literatures that foregrounds the specificity of the postcolonial. My contention is that postcolonial theory is most useful when we keep in mind that it is meant, not to *replace* anticolonial, counterhegemonic discourse, but to point to its ambivalences. Postcolonial theory is an interstitial practice rather than a new theory of the colonial.

Were I located in the space of a Maghrebian or French university, a focus on the postcolonial debates might make little sense as an introduction to a book on women writers at the crossroads between Algeria and France. However, I live and write in the United States, where the "postcolonial" has become a recognized academic category. I might as well, then, try to respond to the exigencies of location and do the impossible: navigate the quagmire of postcolonial theory without sinking, and in this way, provide my own definitions to serve as signposts and entry points into my discussion of the writings of two contemporary women writers at the crossroads. Because, read in the U.S. context, the complex works of Assia Djebar and Leïla Sebbar are now coded as postcolonial, it is important to map out in what respect their works can be called postcolonial, and thus to zero in on the definitions of the term most appropriate to their projects. In this Introduction, I provide elements for a redefinition of anticolonial and postcolonial literatures. Finally, I demonstrate that gender issues, although a blind spot in much postcolonial theory, are actually a crucial component of much postcolonial literature.

Ketu Katrak asked the central question: "How can we, within a dominant Eurocentric discourse, make our study of postcolonial texts itself a mode of resistance?" (158). She suggested that a first step would be to decolonize theory: "We need to find theoretical models that will challenge what Mohanty aptly calls 'a discursive colonization'" (160). As much as postcolonialism has been written about, there still remain a few crucial

areas that have not been theorized adequately, especially an analysis of
whether the categories of colonial, anticolonial, and neocolonial still retain
any meaning at all in a postcolonial framework, on the one hand, and the
relationship between postcolonialism and feminism, on the other. These
two topics will be the focus of the rest of this Introduction.

Anticolonial or Postcolonial?

Part of the difficulty in navigating the quagmire comes from the fact
that one of the stated goals of postcolonial theorists such as Homi K. Bhabha
has been to use poststructuralist insights to deconstruct earlier (Fanonian)
binary oppositions between colonization and decolonization, colonizer and
colonized, to show that ambivalence is always already present on both "sides"
and threatens the opposition between the two. Most of Bhabha's work in
The Location of Culture is dedicated to showing that colonial discourse is
internally structured by an ambivalence that contradicts, subverts, and
undermines the discourse from within its point of enunciation. The power
of Bhabha's formulations is attested to by the fact that many literary critics
have begun to read Fanon "back" through Bhabha and to focus on Fanon's
own ambivalences, a project that may be easier to put in practice in a study
of *Black Skin, White Masks* (with its modified psychoanalytic framework)
than in a study of later texts such as "Concerning Violence" from *The
Wretched of the Earth* (whose theoretical framework is a modified Marxist
one). In the nine years separating the two books, the lived experience of
the Algerian war had the consequence of hardening Fanon's sense of the
Manichean nature of the colonial world.[2]

One way in which to subvert these rigid, binary oppositions is to uncover a different temporality in colonial discourse, namely, to show that
colonial discourse does not follow chronological divisions in any simple
way. Reconfiguring all discourse about colonialism (whether during or after
colonial times) as "colonial discourse" also permits postcolonial critics to
get away from the fraught question of the speaking subject: all writing
dealing with colonization, regardless of its point of origin, its addresser and
addressee, becomes part of colonial discourse. Bhabha's approach provides
a new angle of vision that, in the context of highly polarized binary divisions, points to the interstitial spaces in which the binaries crumble under
the weight of ambivalence.

While I welcome these sophisticated theoretical moves, I am, at the same
time, concerned that they may be reinterpreted as an absolute collapse of
categories such as colonizer and colonized and used to cover up the continuing existence of colonial situations and the need to keep on pursuing

decolonization (see McClintock, "Angel" 292–94). This reinterpretation is all the more likely since Bhabha's style is extremely dense and a postmodern framework has proven relatively easy to reincorporate into dominant capitalistic ideologies. As Kumkum Sangari pointed out in "The Politics of the Possible," "postmodernism . . . deflates social contradiction into forms of ambiguity or deferral" (240). A similar concern has emerged in the works of Abdul JanMohamed, Benita Parry, and Aijaz Ahmad. Both Parry and JanMohamed argue for a renewed focus on the Manichean structures of colonization à la Fanon in order to retain the full force of the political struggle between colonizer and colonized. Like critic Ania Loomba, I am disturbed by some of the implications of both the hybridity and the Manichean approaches: "[I]nquiry . . . cannot be usefully conducted within the parameters of either a theory which insists on the starkness of the colonial encounter, or another where native recipients are entirely conditioned or devastated by the master culture" (Loomba 311).

On the one hand, I fear the loss of agency involved in discourse theory, as exemplified in Michel Foucault and Bhabha. While Bhabha's formulations do not exclude the violence of the colonial encounter, his notions of hybridity, ambivalence, and mimicry leave very little space for a discussion of forms of direct resistance to, and subversion of, the colonial order. For example, in his essay, "Of Mimicry and Man," the desire to unsettle preconstituted notions of the subject creates a fluidity in subject positions that undermines the binary oppositions between subject/object, self/other, and identity/otherness. A consequence of this deconstructive move is that the position of the desiring subject endowed with agency becomes unmarked, since part of Bhabha's point is to show that colonial discourse generates its own oppositional space from within. At the beginning of the essay, when Bhabha mentions mimicry as strategy and desire, I cannot help wondering whose desire and agency are being foregrounded because the principle of unmarked speech usually ends up referring to the dominant (for example, the generic "he"). Chrisman and Williams noted that "colonial discourse analysis" in general "still tends to position colonial/imperial subjectivity as having epistemological and ontological primacy; native or subaltern subjects feature as secondary 'subject-effects' allowed, according to the critic, greater or lesser degrees of oppositional power within the discourse of empire" (16). The desire to embrace ambivalence and hybridity on the part of critics often ends up having the unwitting effect of privileging the ambivalence of the colonizer and foregrounding his or her voice.[3] Loomba noted, "Despite Bhabha's hybridity thesis, the colonial subject in his work is remarkably free of gender, class, caste or other distinctions" (316). Indeed, the subject that Bhabha tries to dispose of invariably returns as male, English or Indian, and upper or middle class. An even more problematic example of the privileging of the colonizer's position is found in Lawson and Tiffin's *De-Scribing Empire*, in which the editors end up concluding that the most hybrid site of colonial discourse is that of the (white) settler subject—namely, they themselves (231)!

A more productive approach, to my mind, would be to remember the constraints that Bhabha himself places on his work. He is less interested in focusing on discourses of resistance than in locating gaps in the fabric of colonial discourse in order to expose its internal incoherence, uncovering interstitial moments that give the lie to monolithic dualisms. He is saying, *not* that such interstitial moments erase and replace the dualisms with a happy pluralism of voices, but rather that they displace and unsettle categories that had become frozen in time and space. The challenge, to me, is to not throw the proverbial baby out with the bathwater.

On the other hand, Ania Loomba makes an important point regarding the dangers of Manichean formulations. Contra Parry and JanMohamed, she argues that "[i]t is difficult to accept that any notion of hybridity will dilute the violence of the colonial encounter" (308). Indeed, many postcolonial writers such as Assia Djebar and Leïla Sebbar find narrative ways of focusing *both* on the violence of the colonial encounter *and* on its resulting hybridity. Loomba also rightly points out that there is a "variegation" of real-life positions under the stark Manichean scenario of anticolonialism (308). In the context of decolonization, Manichean anticolonialism is a political and theoretical move that may well be necessary at a time of conflicting allegiances, in order to incite people to choose sides in the revolutionary struggle. Its limitation (which is also its strength) is its monism, its single-minded goal. In many ways, the blind spots of revolutionary times have deep impacts on the destiny of newly independent nations. It is in response to the messiness and ambivalences of the colonial situation that writers and theorists of independence construct dichotomous models of resistance. After independence, the grand narratives of nation building continue to erase sites of ambivalence and to focus on the two monolithic blocs, the former colonizers and the formerly colonized. The postcolonial realm is the space where contradictions reemerge with full force.

In trying to avoid focusing solely on counterhegemonic struggle or ambivalence, I retain a distinction between colonial, anticolonial, and postcolonial literature, one that may or may not follow the chronological events of decolonization and that recognizes as a starting point that there will always be some amount of ambivalence even in the most colonialist or radical manifesto. Otherwise, if ambivalence is to be the mark of the postcolonial, then every text would, by definition, be postcolonial (in the same way that, if irony and reflexivity are the mark of the postmodern, as Linda Hutcheon argued in "The Post Always Rings Twice," then we may well discover that all discourse is postmodern). McClintock also criticizes too general a focus on ambivalence in *Imperial Leather* (65). I want to retain a way to foreground opposition and agency on the part of colonized or formerly colonized people, but neither should the distinctions I wish to establish be taken as absolutes. I am simply trying to navigate the quagmire, placing signposts for easier travel while knowing that on such uncertain terrain, the posts are sure to shift somewhat, and perhaps even to sink.

What, then, are the elements that can help us make some distinctions between anti- and postcolonial literature? The main difference, to my mind, lies in the move *from Manichean dualism to multiple critique.* Whereas anticolonial literature relies in great part on dualistic (us versus them) rhetoric and calls for revolutionary warfare against the colonial power, postcolonial literature foregrounds a world in which the battle lines are harder to draw and the enemy harder to identify, a world in which dualisms of any sort cannot be sustained easily. The literature underscores the fractures in the grand narratives of decolonization; it begins to effect a slippage away from the (former) colonizer as its main target and instead turns to a multiplicity of struggles: the hopes of nationalism giving way to disillusion and/or corruption, the forces of cultural imperialism and neocolonialism, continuing economic hardships, the spread of religious fundamentalism, and women's issues. The mark of the postcolonial, then, is the blurring of neat, dichotomous boundaries—*which does not mean the end of power differentials or the end of oppositionality.* Postcolonial literature underscores the impossibility of Manichean resistance as well as the necessity for continued opposition to old and new oppressive structures. It foregrounds a mobile, contextual critique, which Chandra Talpade Mohanty calls a process of "dynamic oppositional agency" ("Cartographies" 13) and which serves as a form of consciousness that shuttles between postmodern indeterminacy and colonial overdetermination.

In the aftermath of the "rencontres . . . contre-nature" [unnatural encounters] of colonialism (Sebbar, "Littérature" 27), something else is born out of violence. Postcolonial texts are (and involve the) hybrid; they stage the internal war of fractured history and languages, borrowing from "both sides" and from elsewhere in order to refashion a self that will not be fully present to itself, but rather will be a subject in process, deterritorialized and forever reterritorializing through literature and the imaginary. Postcolonial texts tend to foreground the thickness of the investigator, focusing on his or her unavoidable presence in mediating the voices of silenced others (Spivak, "Imperialism" 229) and ambivalence at the crossroads between resistance and complicity. It is a literature that must, of necessity, account for its own complicity in structures of domination that are imperialist and patriarchal and that often does so with unflinching honesty. Whereas postcolonial theorists Vijay Mishra and Bob Hodge draw a distinction between oppositional and complicit forms of postcolonialism, I contend that postcolonial literature positions itself in a to-and-fro movement *between the oppositional and the complicit*; it foregrounds oppositionality within complicity and complicity within oppositionality (see Mishra and Hodge, 284). It critiques and appropriates, not only colonialism and neocolonialism, but also a variety of other oppressive practices that are all imbricated. It engages multiple discourses of domination, recognizing an attraction to some of them while appropriating parts of others in a critique. More and more writers are *staging* this complicity, giving it a place in their texts with sometimes brutal honesty. The texts enact sites of hybridity, border crossings, in which the "inoutsider" (Nnaemeka, "Feminism, Rebellious Women" 81) is aware of having neither the racial/cultural nor the moral ground of purity. As John Mowitt argued, "What links the phenomena of postmodernism and decolonization . . . is the structure of ambivalence they drive into the very core of every position open to intellectuals" (182).

Anticolonial literature is a more polarized, more directly committed literature, which urges the people to revolt. A perfect example of such texts is Aimé Césaire's *Cahier d'un retour au pays natal* (1939). Anticolonial literature—such as Mohammed Dib's 1957 novel *Le Métier à tisser* and Ferdinand Oyono's *Une Vie de boy* (1956)—tends to focus on the Manichean structures of colonialism and to denounce the abject poverty it creates for colonized people, whereas postcolonial literature explodes the binary oppositions in order to either find a third term or open onto a multiplicity of other terms. As I show in Chapter 4, Djebar repeatedly sets up dichotomies in her works, only to immediately deconstruct and subvert them, in a typically postcolonial move. To use a simple image, anticolonial literature follows a funnel model, in which, to facilitate the political struggle, a variegated situation is distilled into a binary opposition, whereas postcolonial literature tends to follow an inverted funnel model: it starts from the narrow end and explodes neat formulations into complex and variegated positions.

One emblematic postcolonial Algerian text is Mouloud Mammeri's *L'Opium et le bâton*, published barely three years after independence. *L'Opium* goes against a Manichean historiography of the war, as represented in the novel by the figure of the Marxist teacher and freedom fighter Ramdane: "Enfin terminés les à-peu-près, les cas ambigus, toute la foisonnante, la quelquefois déroutante complexité de la vie. Enfin le monde se présentait selon le schéma manichéen qu'il avait toujours aimé et hors duquel, il devait se l'avouer, il perdait un peu pied" [Finally, they were done with approximations, ambiguous cases, and all the abundant and sometimes disconcerting complexities of life. Finally, the world presented itself according to the Manichean schema he had always liked and outside of which he had to admit he was out of his depth] (256–57). This statement matches the Marxist reference of the title (like capitalism, colonialism will both manufacture consent and use force in order to support itself). The certainty of Ramdane's statement is ironically undercut by the rest of the novel, in which, next to committed freedom fighters and violent French soldiers, the reader encounters several characters who function outside of Manichean structures: one of the main characters—Bachir, an Algerian doctor with a French mistress—becomes a reluctant operative for the National Liberation Front (FLN); one of the French soldiers, ironically nicknamed Hamlet, questions his role in the war; and the most cruel character, Tayeb, is an Algerian working for the French military.

The distinctions between anticolonial and postcolonial literature do not necessarily follow a chronological order (in which anticolonial works would be written prior to and during decolonization and postcolonial works, after decolonization). Nonchronological examples of postcolonial novels include Kateb Yacine's 1956 masterpiece *Nedjma*, published at the beginning of the Algerian decolonization struggle, and Daniel Maximin's 1981 *L'Isolé soleil*, which was written within a colonial context (Guadeloupe as a *département d'outre-mer* [Overseas Department] remains in a direct colonial situation with France similar to that of colonial Algeria).

As Anne McClintock pointedly remarked in "The Angel of Progress," one of the dangers of the term *postcolonial* is that it operates a shift from issues of power to the question of time (292). Indeed, we need a theory allowing us to account for the differences between, say, Jacques Roumain's 1946 *Gouverneurs de la rosée* and Maryse Condé's 1976 *Heremakhônon*, two beautiful Caribbean novels whose difference is more than aesthetic, generational, or due to gender issues (although all three factors play a part in the distinctions between the two). It is crucial to refrain from combining all historical and geographical contexts, colonial and postcolonial, because each context requires *different reading strategies*. For example, to read anticolonial texts such as Césaire's *Cahier* with a postcolonial lens is to run the risk of co-opting these texts, of dulling their resistant edge; in other words, of performing neocolonial work on them. Conversely, to read postcolonial texts as being counterhegemonic without qualification is to obscure the complexity and ambivalence, the agonizing awareness of complicity that texts such as *Heremakhônon* showcase.

Postcolonial literature tends to foreground a number of elements that, although they are also constitutive of anticolonial literature, are treated in different ways because of a focus on setting up *and* breaking down dichotomies. Of particular interest to me are the fractures of history and intertextuality, two aspects that will serve as the lens through which I analyze Djebar's and Sebbar's literary production. Postcolonial literature is an attempt to come to terms with several factors: the *fractures of history*; the *physical and sexual violence* of the colonial encounter; and the erasure of that violence from historiography. History, in such a context, can never be a seamless, linear, grand narrative. Instead it is presented as a fractured, painfully reconstructed collage pieced together from a variety of sources—oral and written, historical and fictional—with clashing chronology and viewpoints. Although an engagement with history has been part and parcel of most postcolonial literature, the question of history itself has yet to be adequately addressed in postcolonial theory (with the exception of the Subaltern Studies group of Indian historians such as Ranajit Guha, and Gayatri Spivak). One of the reasons for such absence is probably that postcolonial theory has been trying to provide broad-based, cross-cultural models, which have made it harder to focus on discrete histories.[4]

Cultural, discursive, and "epistemic violence" (Spivak, "Three Women's Texts" 804) is reflected in an explosion of *intertextuality* within postcolonial texts. References from "both" sides (colonizer's and colonized's) soon open up onto a proliferation of perspectives. As I demonstrate in the second half of the book, in Djebar's and Sebbar's works, the violent dialogue between the French/Western and the Arabic/Maghrebian intertexts turns into a triangular, or even multipartite, structure. The "French" intertexts (such as Pierre Bonnard, Eugène Fromentin, Eugène Delacroix, Théophile Gautier, Pauline Rolland, Jean-Luc Godard) and the Maghrebian ones (St. Augustine, Abd el-Kader, Ibn Khaldun, women's testimonies) triangulate with Arabic, Middle Eastern intertexts (Ibn Tabari, *The Arabian Nights*, *The Arab Chronicles*) and open onto other ones: Turkish and British (Mehmet Efendi and Lady Montagu), Indo-Caribbean (V. S. Naipaul), and so forth. At the same time, each set is shown to be intricately connected to the others. Middle Eastern intertexts are also part of Maghrebian history and culture; the French intertexts tend to be Orientalist works that can reveal both an intimate knowledge of Maghrebian culture and recirculate Western stereotypes of that culture; some of the North African and Middle Eastern references have also become Western literary, historical, and philosophical reference points, especially St. Augustine, Ibn

Khaldun, and *The Arabian Nights*. These are sources to which Djebar and Sebbar, for instance, have had access only through French translations. Above all, in both writers' treatment of history and intertextuality, overdeterminations and ambivalences of gender emerge again and again.

The Gender of Postcoloniality

In contrast with many postcolonial literary texts, much postcolonial theory is oblivious to gender. If postcolonial women writers are included in postcolonial theory, it is often as excess, as the element that does not quite fit in the model—which is ironic, since models of postcolonial writing tend to be extremely broad and inclusive. For example, Mishra and Hodge attempt to bring out this issue with the following comment: "[P]ostcolonial women's writing . . . *would* require a different order of theorizing, since postcolonial women are like a fragment, an oppositional system, within an overall colonized framework" (284, italics added). Setting aside the contradictory nature of the pronouncement (that one can be simultaneously a fragment and a system), one should note that many postcolonial women artists have objected in no uncertain terms to being compared to a fragment. Trinh argued that it is precisely a sexist, racist and colonialist discourse that fragments women by forcing them to present only one aspect of their multiple identities at a time (*Woman, Native, Other* 6). In the U.S. context, many "U.S. Third World feminists" (in Chela Sandoval's formulation) such as Audre Lorde have argued along similar lines. The use of the conditional ("would") in the sentence by Mishra and Hodge also implies that they are not interested in providing the "different order of theorizing" required to account for postcolonial women's writing, which will have to content itself with a short paragraph devoted to one early twentieth-century woman writer from India (284–85). It is precisely such theorizing that interests me here, as it has its roots in postcolonial feminist writing itself.

Gender, rather than being peripheral to postcolonial literature, is indeed one of its crucial components. For one, postcolonial women's texts tend to be perfect examples of the ambivalence that is considered by theorists to be the hallmark of postcoloniality. As Ania Loomba observed, "[S]ince 'the colonial subject' is a heterogeneous category, particular positionings (for example, those of different categories of women within nationalist discourses) sharply question the notion of a single master/slave configuration" (314). In other words, the question of gender disrupts Manichean dichotomies. Anne McClintock has traced how "[g]ender runs like a multiple fissure through Fanon's work, splitting and displacing the 'Manichean delirium' to which he repeatedly returns" ("No Longer" 94).[5] It is very difficult for women to wholeheartedly embrace male-centered, Manichean liberation projects that figure them as objects to be protected or as stakes in the struggle and that use them as metaphors for the nation.

The problem with (national) allegories is that they erase the term on which they ground themselves. As Winifred Woodhull and Anne McClintock have shown, even Frantz Fanon, one of the very few (if not the only) early theorists of decolonization to have attempted to address the issue of gender in his work, was not entirely able to escape the allegory of Woman as the Nation.[6] When women are equated to the land, there is no discursive space for them as citizens. When woman stands in for nation, it becomes difficult to present the women of the nation as agents in that nation's constitution because their body image is being activated as the object for which to fight. Ketu Katrak's comments about Lata Mani's work on *sati* in India also apply to the Algerian situation: "[W]omen were simply the *ground* on which debates about tradition were thrashed out; women themselves were not significant as human beings; tradition was" (168).[7] Both Joanne P. Sharp and Elleke Boehmer astutely remarked that in most male nationalist rhetoric, men have a metonymic relationship to the nation (they are seen as being a part of it), whereas women are presented as symbols of, or metaphors for, the nation (Sharp 99, Boehmer 6). "It is the metonymic bond of male citizens who must act to save or promote the female nation" (Sharp 99). Male citizens are the agents who actively create and maintain the nation. Female citizens are erased as agents by being made to serve as symbols of the land and nation: "[N]ationalism does not see women as nationals" (Boehmer 8).

One of the important moves in Sebbar's and Djebar's fiction is to engage the allegory of Woman as Nation, with its concomitant sexualization of the land, and then to destabilize it by foregrounding the presence, voices, and desires of real Algerian women. Many postcolonial feminist texts (written by women or men), such as Djebar's *L'Amour, la fantasia*, Daniel Maximin's *L'Isolé soleil*, and Ousmane Sembène's *Xala* (1973), focus both on national allegory *and* on sexual politics, taking up the discourse equating the land with women's bodies and, at the same time, underscoring women's agency so that the women of the nation are no longer erased from the text. Sembène has always played on the two registers with much finesse, but he has been quite unique in this respect among male writers in his generation.

In the three main regions of Francophone postcolonial literature—the Caribbean, the Maghreb, and Africa—models examining the stages of national literature are usually based only on an examination of male-authored texts.[8] Such is the case with Kwame Anthony Appiah's two-stage formulation of postcolonial African novels: an anticolonial, nationalist, realist phase followed by a phase that is postrealist, postnativist, pan-Africanist, and humanist. The works he considers are all canonical, Francophone novels written by male writers for whom gender issues are not at the forefront. Revealingly, this leads Appiah to ignore the contribution of Sembène, who is not mentioned once (149–55).

In "Sur la culture nationale" ("On National Culture"), Fanon proposed a dialectical model of development of literature in colonized countries: the assimilated stage of mimicry of European literature gives way to a nostalgic, romantic protest stage, to be finally replaced with the revolutionary stage of national literature in struggle (*Wretched* 162–63/222–23). One could add a fourth phase of postcolonial/decolonized literature. Besides the fact that such a model remains caught in chronology, there is also the problem that it is based mostly on men's works. Many other male Caribbean writers have provided blueprints for defining and codifying Caribbean literature, but author Maryse Condé has taken issue with their definitions, arguing precisely for the "different order of theorizing" called for by Mishra and Hodge (284). Condé showed that it is only in reference to a male-centered, Marxist-dominated norm, in which women stand by their men as the men lead the anticolonial struggle, that women's works can appear as marginal, disorderly, and apolitical (Condé, "Order, Disorder"). This comment helps explain why Fanon was so brutal about Mayotte Capécia's works in *Black Skin, White Masks* and why he placed her in the assimilationist phase of literature. Indeed, male critics' reactions to Condé's first novel, *Heremakhônon*, paralleled Fanon's reactions to Capécia's, demonstrating the high personal stakes involved in any confrontation with sexual politics.

The chronology of women's literature often differs from that of men, and it also varies according to the country or region. If one considers Francophone literature in West Africa, for example, the first autobiographies by women were published in the early 1970s and the first fictional texts a few years later; this amounted to a fifty-year gap following the men's works (in Anglophone Africa, women began publishing earlier than Francophone African women). In contrast, in the French Caribbean, both men and women began publishing fiction in the 1920s. In Algeria, the first two novels by women, Djamila Debêche's *Leïla, jeune fille algérienne* and Taos Amrouche's *Jacinthe noire,* came out in 1947, whereas the first novels by men appeared in the 1920s.

Réda Bensmaïa articulates three stages of Algerian literature: a stage of reformism still caught in the framework of "French Algeria"; a counterhegemonic stage in which a unitary myth of the nation is consolidated; and a dissonant stage that interrupts this unitary myth of Algeria by exposing its fictional underpinnings and bringing out the voices of multiple communities ("Nations" 173–76). Women writers have participated in each stage, and some writers (such as Djebar) have moved through two or more stages during their literary careers. Yet it can be argued that such a model, with its privileging of the nation and national consciousness, does not account for certain works by women such as Djebar's first novel, *La Soif* (*The Mischief*) (1957), which was criticized precisely for not taking the war of liberation as its setting (the novel focuses on the life and inner turmoil of a young Algerian woman from the elite class and her friends). The reception of *La Soif*, like that of *Heremakhônon* almost twenty years later, exemplifies the difficulties that women writers encounter when their works fail to correspond to a dominant, masculine framework of national literature.

Postcolonial feminist texts are predictably marked by an emphasis on women. They foreground female characters, ambivalent relationships among women, and sexual politics. Sometimes women are at the center of the text; sometimes they figure in it as an important element in a broader pattern. The style is often extremely literary and fragmented in complex ways, although some works (such as those by Ken Bugul or Fatima Mernissi's autobiographical memoir, *Dreams of Trespass*) can also be deceptively simple and can be read at several levels. They may be authored by women or men (a few male writers, such as Daniel Maximin and Ousmane Sembène, have been able to write from a woman's point of view rather than presenting female characters as subordinate supports for male characters). The characteristics of postcolonial literature I deployed earlier—foregrounding historical violence and intertextuality—are traversed by a focus on the feminine in postcolonial feminist texts, as the rest of the book will elucidate at greater length for the works of Assia Djebar and Leïla Sebbar. What seems to be formative in postcolonial feminist texts is the fractures caused by colonization and gender inequality. My definition of postcolonial feminist literature stems from what I see the texts themselves to be foregrounding. In effect, this book presents itself upside down, beginning with a theoretical framework that could only be developed once the rest of the book had been written.

Organization of the Book

My first chapter establishes the historical framework of the study. I outline historiographical and theoretical debates over the Algerian war and the place of women in that war in order to situate the cultural politics that Djebar's and Sebbar's works both engage and subvert.

The second chapter examines some of the consequences of the Algerian war of independence on French society. Making use of the model of conflicted memory developed by Henry Rousso in *Le Syndrome de Vichy*, I argue that Sebbar's 1984 novel, *Le Chinois vert d'Afrique,* sharply criticizes the cultural politics of racism in 1980s France by linking the French erasure of its violent history, its Algeria syndrome, to the rise of anti-Maghrebian violence in the 1980s. Fifteen years later, in *La Seine était rouge*, Sebbar created a literary anamnesis of an occluded event of the war, the October 17, 1961, massacre of hundreds of Algerians who were demonstrating peacefully in Paris. She thus memorialized the event, piecing it together from diverse testimonies over two generations in order to create a narrative of the massacre that accounts for all its participants and may allow for national reconciliation.

Chapter 3 explores the postcolonial feminist strategies used by Djebar to rewrite in the fictional mode a history partially erased by the colonizer's historiography. My comparative analysis of her novels and films reveals the complex ways in which she foregrounded Algerian women's memory in the project of rewriting history. I examine how she has reconstituted the past using French colonial archives and then destabilized the archives through an appeal to the female, Algerian oral tradition. I trace how she intermingles the experiences of different women, thus highlighting an ongoing history of resistance on the part of Algerian women that legitimates the struggle for emancipation of contemporary women.

In Chapter 4, I analyze the complex system of epigraphs framing Djebar's novels. Epigraphs serve to legitimate her writing at the same time as she manipulates them in order to decenter and decontextualize them in a subversive manner. I specifically explore the relationship between her novels and her historical, literary, and artistic intertexts. I focus on three exemplary sources that belie the binary opposition usually drawn between "East" and "West": fourteenth-century Maghrebian historian Ibn Khaldun's autobiography, the ancient tale of *The Arabian Nights*, and French Orientalist painter Eugène Fromentin's travelogue.

Chapter 5 investigates the role of European painting in shaping a postcolonial feminist consciousness. I begin with an analysis of Djebar's use of French postimpressionist painter Pierre Bonnard to craft her own painterly tableaux and provide a detailed study of the many parallels between their oeuvres. I then develop a comparative analysis of Djebar's and Sebbar's responses to major paintings of the Orientalist tradition that represented male, colonial fantasies of languid Odalisques, especially works by Eugène

Delacroix and Henri Matisse. I foreground their characters' ambivalent responses to the paintings and trace the process of attraction-repulsion at work in their novels.

In Chapter 6, I focus on the hybrid position of Djebar's and Sebbar's protagonists by showing how the works foreground multiple encounters between Algeria and France. I analyze how Sebbar subversively juxtaposes French texts about the "Orient" to Arabic texts on Europeans in her Shérazade trilogy and how the names she gives her protagonists exemplify their hybridity and liminal location. Finally, I examine the many ways in which Shérazade, the title character, engages Orientalist discourse, including subversive strategies of reappropriation and distancing such as anger, derisive laughter, destruction, masquerade, and stealing. The conclusion to this study proposes further avenues for research.

In this Introduction, I have woven an attempt at redefining postcolonial literature in narrower terms, with an argument for gender as a crucial parameter in the definition of postcolonial texts. Gender does not allow for an unproblematic affiliation with male-centered, nationalist rhetoric, and it destabilizes binary oppositions such as colonizer/colonized by foregrounding women's "divided loyalties" (Kandiyoti 380). The remainder of this book elucidates the specific ways in which Leïla Sebbar and Assia Djebar represent historical violence and intertextual negotiations through a gendered perspective.

Notes

1. Elsa Barkley Brown, quoted in Collins 236.

2. In the first fifteen pages of "De la violence" ("Concerning Violence"), the allusions to this Manichean nature appear on almost every page. Some examples include: "La décolonisation est la rencontre de deux forces congénitalement antagonistes" [Decolonization is the meeting of two forces, opposed to each other by their very nature] (*Wretched* 25–26/36); "Le monde colonisé est un monde coupé en deux" [The colonial world is a world cut in two] (27/38); "ce monde coupé en deux est habité par des espèces différentes" [this world cut in two is inhabited by two different species] (28/39–40); "Le monde colonial est un monde manichéiste" [The colonial world is a Manichean world] (29/41). Words derived from "manichéiste" [Manichean] are repeated on five occasions (29/41, 35/50, 36/51, 59/84, 65/93) in the text. For a detailed critique of Bhabha's reading of Fanon, see Benita Parry, Abdul JanMohamed, and Neil Lazarus (especially pp. 86–91). For a discussion of these multiple readings of Fanon as symptoms, see Henry Louis Gates Jr.

3. Anne McClintock raises similar issues in *Imperial Leather*, where she shows how Bhabha's focus on colonialism's internal ambivalence may serve to obscure

the importance of the resistance of the colonized in undermining the colonial project (63).

4. Among many other critics, Anne McClintock ("Angel") and Ella Shohat have criticized postcolonial theory for its ahistoricity.

5. In recent years, several excellent reinterpretations of the problematic of gender in Fanon have appeared. See especially Gwen Bergner, Rey Chow ("Politics"), Mary Anne Doane, Diana Fuss, Marie-Chantal Kalisa, Anne McClintock ("No Longer"), and Winifred Woodhull.

6. See Woodhull 2–3, 16–24, and McClintock, "No Longer" 93–99. In *A Dying Colonialism*, Fanon's chapter on women is titled "L'Algérie se dévoile" [Algeria unveils itself], a clear equation of women and the nation through the synecdoche of the veil. The English translation, "Unveiling Algeria," renders Algeria and Algerian women as passive and the writer/male nationalist (presumably) as the active agent (see John Mowitt 174–76).

7. See also Deniz Kandiyoti. A perfect novelistic example of Woman-as-Nation is Jacques Roumain's otherwise sumptuous novel, *Gouverneurs de la rosée*.

8. I do not discuss Quebec here because its status as a white settler colony under Anglophone Canadian rule, but also a nation established on indigenous peoples' lands, makes it quite different, historically and politically, from the regional contexts mentioned previously. For a cogent discussion of Canada's experience of multiple colonizations, see Daiva K. Stasiulis.

Chapter 1

▼▼▼▼▼▼▼▼▼

Historical Amnesia and the Construction of National Identity

For reasons both personal and political, almost all contemporary Francophone Algerian writers have felt compelled in their writings to come to terms with the 1954–1962 War of National Liberation—what the French used to refer to with various euphemisms such as "les événements d'Algérie" [the Algerian events], "opérations de police" [police operations], "actions de maintien de l'ordre" [actions to maintain order], "opérations de rétablissement de la paix civile" [operations to restore civil peace], and "entreprises de pacification" [pacification undertakings], and what they finally came to call *la guerre d'Algérie* [the Algerian war].[1] In Algeria, that war has been constructed as the great trauma of the birth of an independent nation. Writing about it often functions as a way for writers to have their works legitimated and accepted, especially if they write in French. (A similar phenomenon can be observed in other fields, especially filmmaking.) For instance, Assia Djebar's first novel, *La Soif*, written during wartime, was criticized for not dealing with the war.[2] Djebar's subsequent novels all featured the war as the setting for the action.

For women, this war was to assume a peculiar significance. In a society where space—real and imaginary—was divided along gender lines, women were, for the first time, called on by the male leadership to participate actively in an armed struggle. However, after the war was won, women were sent back to the private space of the home. This is by no means a unique or anomalous event in world history. Rather than rushing to make connections between Islamic culture and the repression of women's rights, it should be remembered that the same phenomenon occurred in Europe and in the United States after World War II. Jean Bethke Elshtain demonstrated that European women's participation in the war did not change their economic status nor society's essentialist beliefs about women's place; moreover, even the small percentage of women who participated in the war effort considered it a response to an exceptional situation and did not necessarily expect to continue working after the war (7).

Djamila Amrane's analysis of Algerian women in the war parallels Elshtain's (Amrane 260–72). During both World War II and the Algerian War of National Liberation, few women actually bore arms. According to Marnia Lazreg, "[T]he FLN's definition of women's tasks in the war was based on a conventional understanding of the sexual division of labor" ("Gender" 767). Amrane adds that women's actual tasks went far beyond those sketched out for them by the male leadership (252–53). Like European women in the 1940s, many Algerian *mujahidat* (women who participated directly in the war) saw their participation as an extraordinary response to an extraordinary situation and expected life to return to "normal" at the end of the war: "[L]e comportement exceptionnel de ces combattantes répond à une situation de crise dans un pays en guerre. L'espoir d'une transformation, suscité par un tel engagement, ne s'est pas réalisé et la société, en période de paix, a retrouvé ses modes de vie antérieurs" [These female fighters' exceptional behavior was an answer to a crisis situation in a country at war. The hope for transformation that had been aroused by such a commitment was never fulfilled, and in time of peace, society went back to its former ways of life] (294).

The gains that could have been expected from women's sanctioned appearance in public life never became reality, because their participation in the war was both rendered mythic and silenced. The mujahidat were extolled as heroines and symbols at the same time that they were hidden in mental hospitals. Djebar's short story, "Femmes d'Alger dans leur appartement," for instance, criticizes that process (*Femmes d'Alger*). For Algerian women writers, foregrounding women's visibility in the war often means claiming a legitimate space for women—including themselves—outside the private sphere at the same time that it gives them the opportunity of dealing fictionally with a violent past. Djebar's treatment of the Algerian past goes back to antiquity in *Vaste est la prison* (1995). In *Fantasia*, she highlights a 132-year history of resistance against French colonization, beginning in 1830.

Colonial Algeria

Territorial boundaries were erased under French colonization as, by 1848, Algeria had been incorporated into French territory and divided into three

French *départements* (the same divisions used within the French *métropole* and within the *départements d'outre-mer* [Overseas Departments]— Guadeloupe, Martinique, Reunion, and French Guyana). It is only since the 1962 independence that we can speak of "Algerian" versus "French" peoples per se. Before and during decolonization, legally there were no "Algeria" or "Algerians," only "French Algeria."

Close to 1 million "French" people, many of Spanish, Italian, or southern French origins, lived in "Algeria" at the time of the war (in the mid-1950s).[3] The French settlers, also called *pieds-noirs*, were a diverse group in terms of socioeconomic class. Some families had been living in "Algeria" since the mid-nineteenth century and considered "France" as a place of vacation and distant origins and "Algeria" as home, much like third- or fourth-generation immigrant Americans in the United States vis-à-vis their land of origin. Most of them were against Algerian independence, although a few did side with the National Liberation Front (FLN). In "France," the population was divided as well, with a few intellectuals and activists supporting the independence movement.

There were approximately 140,000 Jews living in "Algeria" in 1954. Some had been established in the region since the sixth century (prior to the arrival of the Arabs, in the seventh century). Most had come from Spain in 1492, expelled by the Inquisition at the same time as Muslims. At first, Jews were considered by the French to be "indigènes" [natives], like Arabs and Berbers. In the nineteenth century, however, in an effort to increase the numbers of Europeans in the colony, "Algerian" Jews were singled out by the 1870 Crémieux decree and unilaterally granted French citizenship. In 1940, the Vichy government took away their French citizenship, but it was restored to them after World War II.

By the time of the war, about 7 1/2 million Arabs and 1 million Berbers lived in "Algeria" and about 350,000 "Algerians" lived in "France." Several of the independence parties, most notably L'Etoile nord-africaine (but not the FLN, which was going to lead the war of independence) were formed in "France" by "Algerian immigrant" workers. Since 1865, "Algerians'" legal status had been that of second-class citizens who, in order to be considered "French," had to renounce Islam. Sixty-five thousand "Algerian" men were granted the right to vote in 1944, and even then, it took eight of their votes to match one European's vote (in 1947, "Algerian" men living in "France" received the same rights as other male French citizens). "Algerian" women were only allowed to vote in 1958, thirteen years after "French" women, and that only in the hopes of circumventing the struggle for independence by winning "Algerian" women over to the cause of French Algeria. Needless to say, it was too little, too late.

The anticolonial struggle was much more variegated than Fanon's account in "L'Algérie se dévoile" ("Algeria Unveiled") allows. For example, Algerian people were divided with respect to independence. Many people joined or sided with the FLN at many levels, but there were also "Algerian" men serving in the French military forces: about 20,000 were enlisted soldiers, 40,000 were drafted men, and 58,000 others (*harkis*) belonged to special indigenous units. By the beginning of the war in the mid-1950s, there were several movements for Algerian independence as well as reformist civil rights movements, but purges led by the FLN destroyed the other movements and allowed the FLN to emerge as the sole leader of the struggle. Toward the end of the war, when it became clear that independence would be achieved, many last-minute freedom fighters appeared on the scene.

On the French, as on the Algerian, sides, the war caused the internal rifts of a civil war. There were many blurred zones, messy situations that do not fit into the colonizer/colonized dichotomous model of struggle and are therefore glossed over or silenced in Fanon's account, as in the FLN platform. The FLN was made to represent the entire united Algerian people, and many issues, such as the Kabyle (Berber) and the women's issues, were subsumed under the independence struggle. Such questions have proved to be recurring problems for the Algerian nation. In Algeria, more than thirty-five years after the end of the armed struggle, issues of repression, religion, and women's rights have taken center stage in a spiral of violence. I do not mean to obscure the role of France in creating and/or deepening the problems besetting postcolonial Algeria here. Certainly, the current economic difficulties and chronic high unemployment, as well as women's issues, have their roots in colonial and neocolonial policies. Yet it is also important to recognize that official Algerian historiography followed closely the FLN's Manichean interpretation of Algerian history, according to which a unified anticolonial resistance movement began in 1954.

Historian Guy Pervillé commented that because the war is used in Algeria as the source of political legitimacy, writing the history of the National War of Liberation is considered a state matter (309). It is important to note that a major aspect of the national war of liberation has also been covered up in Algeria: the participation of women on *all* of the war's battlegrounds (Amrane 13, 293–94). Benjamin Stora saw a parallel between the Algerian and the French treatments of the war. In Algeria as well, "[L]'histoire officielle a . . . fabriqué de l'oubli" [official history fabricated forgetting] (*Gangrène* 304) by setting up the FLN as the only nationalist force, thus erasing the existence of other, older parties that were in favor of independence and obscuring the violent purges and political murders between the different groups during the war (122, 141–44, 151). The names of war leaders have been erased by an official version that celebrates the united Algerian people fighting on the side of the FLN (162). More dangerously, the war between Algeria and France was also "une double guerre civile, à la fois algéro-algérienne, et franco-française" [a double civil war, both Algerian-Algerian and French-French] (187). In both cases, the civil war aspect was occulted in official versions. The complexities of the war only began receiving more attention, especially from historians, due to the political opening in Algeria after the bloody 1988 demonstrations and due to the thirtieth anniversary of the end of the war in 1992 France.

France's "Algeria Syndrome"

The Algerian war had similar effects in France to those of the Vietnam War in the United States, and the parallels between these two wars (France participated in both) are not lost on Leïla Sebbar, whose title character, "Le Chinois vert d'Afrique" [The green Chinaman from Africa] is a young boy of mixed heritage named Mohamed. His Algerian paternal grandfather and namesake was sent to fight in what was then Indochina; he then returned to France with a Vietnamese wife who gave birth to Mohamed's father, Slim. The Algerian and Vietnam wars were fought mostly in the 1950s and 1960s, and they were the last two major Western colonial wars. Both caused acute violence, followed by collective guilt feelings in the French and American psyches, respectively. Whereas in the United States the shame has been exorcized (notably through film), in France, coverage of the Algerian war never reached the same intensity. Such silencing has contributed to collective amnesia regarding a war that was only officially recognized as such by the French government in June 1999.[4]

Beur writers Azouz Begag and Abdellatif Chaouite, in their *Ecarts d'identité* [Identity Rifts], comment on the French treatment of the war: "*Guerre d'Algérie*: terminée en 1962. Comme l'élève efface un tableau en classe, on a effacé le souvenir de cette guerre de l'histoire de France. D'ailleurs cet épisode est désigné comme 'événement.' Un événement se caractérise comme un 'point de détail'" [*Algerian War*: ended in 1962. Like a pupil erases the classroom blackboard, the memory of that war was erased from French history. Besides, that episode is referred to as an "event." An event can be characterized as a "detail"] (11–12). The reference to the classroom is not accidental. Education is a privileged means

of creating civic consciousness in young citizens, and the teaching one
receives in school, especially where history is concerned, still retains the
central purpose of reinforcing a sense of national identity. At the time
when Begag and Chaouite were going through the French school system
(in the 1960s and 1970s), the Algerian war was not yet being taught in
school.

If, as the nineteenth-century French philologist, historian, and Orientalist
Ernest Renan argued, forgetting specific elements is necessary to the construction of a national identity, then one might surmise that French national identity continues to be built on the following principle: "L'oubli,
et je dirai même l'erreur historique, sont un facteur essentiel de la création
d'une nation, et c'est ainsi que le progrès des études historiques est souvent
pour la nationalité un danger. L'investigation historique, en effet, remet en
lumière les faits de violence qui se sont passés à l'origine de toutes les
formations politiques. . . . L'unité se fait toujours brutalement" [Forget-
ting, I would even go so far as to say historical error, is a crucial factor in
the creation of a nation, which is why progress in historical studies often
constitutes a danger for (the principle of) nationality. Indeed, historical
enquiry brings to light deeds of violence which took place at the origin of
all political formations. . . . Unity is always effected by means of brutality]
("Qu'est-ce qu'une nation?" 891/11).

One can wonder whether the emphasis on World War II in French
public life, the media, education, and on the literary scene over the past
twenty-five years is not due in part to a displacement: what is being silenced (the Algerian war) resurfaces as an excess of speech about a previous
war. As Assia Djebar remarked about the French colonizers' letters and
reports in *Fantasia*, an excess of language can be used to hide the violence
of war: "Le mot lui-même . . . deviendra l'arme par excellence. . . . Toute
une pyramide d'écrits amoncelés en apophyse superfétatoire occultera la
violence initiale" [words themselves . . . will become *the* weapon. . . . The
supererogatory protuberances of their publications will form a pyramid
that will hide the initial violence from view (56/45)].

Historian Henry Rousso, in his book *Le Syndrome de Vichy*, used a
similar argument regarding World War II. He argued that World War
II is one of the "crises profondes de l'unité et de l'identité françaises"
[deep crises in French unity and identity] (14); it is of the same mag-
nitude as the French Revolution, the Dreyfus affair, and the Algerian
war—each of which crises comes to be partially replayed in the subsequent one. He divided what he calls the "Vichy syndrome" into four
phases, charting a movement from amnesia to obsession: the first phase
is one of interrupted mourning (1944–54); the second (1954–71), one

of repression (forgetting and amnesia), with a repetition of the trauma due to the Algerian war; the third (1971–74), a short phase of the return of the repressed and a shattering of established myths about the war; and finally, the last phase (in which we are still engaged), is one of obsession (20–21).

Borrowing this model to explore the question of the French in the Algerian war, I argue that the phase of mourning for the loss of French Algeria was quickly stifled by the repression of the pain and shame created by that war, as France moved into the second phase of its Algeria syndrome. The third and fourth phases of the Vichy syndrome (the return of the repressed and obsession) may have been precipitated by the desire to cover up the double loss caused by the Algerian trauma: the loss of innocence (which had been regained by the erasure of memories of Vichy and the collaboration) due to the widespread knowledge of the Nazi-like methods employed by the French military in the Algerian conflict, and the loss of a land, which signified the end of France's status as an imperial power and thus signaled a crisis in French identity. Rousso suggested this in quoting Krystoff Pomian: "'Une époque révolue . . . se met, quand vient son heure, à fonctionner comme un écran sur lequel les générations qui se suivent peuvent projeter, en les objectivant, leurs contradictions, leurs déchirements, leurs conflits.' C'est ce qui semble s'être passé à l'orée des années 1970 avec le souvenir de l'Occupation" ["When its time comes, a bygone era can function like a screen on which the next generations can project their contradictions, rifts, and conflicts by objectifying them." This is what seems to have happened in the early 1970s with the memory of the Occupation] (15).

Regarding the Algerian war, France was immersed in the second phase of the syndrome, that of repression, until the early 1990s. French efforts to repress the memory of the war created, in Rousso's words, a "rejeu de la faille" [replay of the rift] (87). Just as the Algerian war acted as a replay of the earlier trauma and allowed unresolved issues about it to resurface, the subsequent obsession about World War II, in turn, helped cover up the painful scars of the new conflict. In his article, "Mémoire d'Algérie," Mustapha Marrouchi remarked that while the Algerian war remains partly taboo and in the realm of the unsaid, debates rage about World War II and even the French Revolution. Just as Rousso noted that it took years before historians were allowed access to the Vichy archives, Marrouchi mentioned that the repatriated archives on the Algerian war were still off-limits to scholars in 1990.[5]

In keeping with Renan's thesis and as shown by Rousso, certain aspects of World War II are also silenced: the discourse on the Resistance and

concentration camps has served to cover up French collaboration with the
Germans (Rousso 96). The Germans have been constructed, by an official
historical discourse (taught in schools), as the archenemy (a "colonizer," as
Aimé Césaire would say) so as to make it easier to forget that in reality,
lines of allegiance cannot be drawn that easily and that many French
people indirectly gained from, or participated in, the Occupation and
Holocaust. The deep internal divisions of French society under Vichy were
more threatening to a sense of national identity than the Occupation itself
and were therefore hidden during the second phase of the Vichy syndrome
(Rousso 18).

Similarly, the Algerian war reopened ideological rifts between the
French—splits that came close to turning into a full-blown civil war—
concerning issues such as the use of torture by the French military,
President Charles de Gaulle's 1959 policy change from supporting French
Algeria to favoring Algerian self-determination, and terrorism by the
OAS (pro-French Algeria group) in the early 1960s (Stora, *Gangrène*
74–91, 113; Rousso 94–95). As had been the case after Vichy, these
internal divisions were covered up and excised from the collective
memory during the second phase of the Algeria syndrome. At the end
of their magnificent "picture book," *La France en guerre d'Algérie*, historians Laurent Gervereau, Jean-Pierre Rioux, and Benjamin Stora concluded that "cette guerre, interdite de reconnaissance nationale, ne peut
que revivre doublement, ressassée, inlassable, inclassable, dans les
mémoires de ceux qui en ont souffert à des titres divers. . . . L'enjeu
français, à trente ans de distance du sang et des larmes d'Algérie, est
donc sans doute d'avoir à se pardonner d'avoir tourné une page dont
on savait trop bien qu'elle n'était pas blanche" [this non-classifiable
war, which was refused national recognition, can only be brought back
doubly, incessantly relived in the memories of those who suffered because of it in different ways. . . . What is at stake for the French, thirty
years away from the blood and tears of Algeria, is thus, undoubtedly,
having to forgive themselves for turning over a page that they knew
only too well was not blank] ("Conclusion" 304). The stakes are much
higher than these three historians acknowledge here. The war, rather
than being simply relived through memory, is actually being waged
again and again on French territory through racially motivated incidents and racist discourse. Rather than needing to forgive themselves
for turning over a new leaf, the French need to face the consequences
of the fact that the page was, in fact, never quite turned.

Since the early 1990s, Algeria and its historical past with France
have been covered in the news much more frequently because of cur-

rent events: the success, then repression of the Muslim fundamentalist group Front Islamique du Salut (FIS), the assassination of President Mohammed Boudiaf, the thirtieth anniversary of the end of the Algerian war, and, finally, the ongoing killings of many Algerian intellectuals, foreigners, and even entire villages by fundamentalist sympathizers. This is not to say that no books had been published on the Algerian war by French people between the 1960s and 1980s. Indeed, Philip Dine carefully synthesized this early production in his *Images of the Algerian War*.

Both Djebar and Sebbar use such sources in their novels. For instance, Sebbar mentioned Marc Garanger's collection of photographs titled *Femmes algériennes 1960* in *Shérazade* (220/237). She also wrote the accompanying text for another of Garanger's collections, *Femmes des Hauts-Plateaux: Algérie 1960*. In *Fantasia*, Djebar centered one of her chapters (234–37/208–11) on a 1961 narrative by Pierre Leulliette, *Saint Michel et le dragon*, a book that was censored by the French government when it first appeared (Stora, *Ils venaient* 298). These early works of testimony, according to Dine, attempt to make up individually for the lack of national commemoration of the war: "A failure of French historiography, then, lies behind the telling of so many conflicting tales about what went on in Algeria" (236). Because these are often private writings or testimonials written without much literary ambition, most of them have not been read by a wide section of the French public (Dine 112).

Guy Perville remarked that, although there exist many testimonial and journalistic narratives on the war, very few historical books have been published on the subject in France (308). After thirty years, in July 1992, the French Ministry of Defense finally opened up most of its archival collection on the war to the public (309). This coincided with a time when French historians began to reconsider the war, due in part to the thirtieth anniversary of its end. Several books by Stora, Rioux, and other historians, were published in the early 1990s. Dine himself, who insists on the significance of the written and filmed French production about the war, concluded that, "While the academic and journalistic commemoration, in 1992, of the thirtieth anniversary of the ending of the Algerian war undoubtedly marked the conflict's entry into the mainstream of French historiography, its definitive assimilation into the broader national consciousness is far from obvious" (234).

Rousso noted that, although the number of French films on World War II was never high, tens of thousands of books of all kinds have been published on the subject (254). Although Benjamin Stora asserted

that the fewer than 1,300 books published on the Algerian war between 1955 and 1988 in France constitute a large corpus, this number
remains low when compared to the outpouring of publications on World
War II. Moreover, compared once again to French films on World War
II, few motion pictures dealing directly with the Algerian war have
been released. As of 1989, *La Bataille d'Alger* (1965), one of the most
famous of these films, had never even been shown on French television
(Stora, "La Guerre d'Algérie" 158, 160).

Dine counted a total of fifty films, many of which use the Algerian
war as the background rather than central focus (215). Early on, this
was a result of operating within the strictures of censorship, as was the
case with Alain Resnais's 1963 *Muriel* (Dine 218). Even a film as recent as André Téchiné's 1994 film *Les Roseaux sauvages* [Wild reeds]
followed the pattern of using the war as background for the action.
Few French films have addressed the war as directly and brutally as
René Vautier's 1972 *Avoir vingt ans dans les Aurès* [To Be Twenty Years
Old in the Aures Mountains], which stands alone in that respect (but
was only seen by a small group of militant French people) (Stora,
Imaginaires 204).

Whereas many French films and books focus on the periods immediately before or after the war, Brigitte Roüan's 1990 feature film
Outremer [Overseas] attempted to account for some of the rifts caused
by the war by portraying its effects on three sisters belonging to the
French colonial upper class. Bertrand Tavernier and Patrick Rotman's
1992 documentary film, *La Guerre sans nom*, "could, with justice, be
hailed as doing for the Algerian war what *Le Chagrin et la pitié* . . .
(Marcel Ophuls, 1970) did for the Occupation period" (Dine 112).
All in all, it appears that it was not until around 1992 that France
began to emerge from the second phase of its Algerian syndrome into
the third phase, that of the return of the repressed and the shattering
of established myths about the war. The 1980s were a decade in which
occlusion about the war coincided with an increase in racist hate
crimes. Since Sebbar's book illustrating the second phase of the Algeria syndrome, *Le Chinois vert d'Afrique* (discussed in the next chapter), was published in 1984, what follows is an examination of the
state of French memory in the 1980s, before the work of many scholars began to consistently bring the Algerian war into French history.
Chapter 2 also includes a discussion of Sebbar's participation in the
third phase of the syndrome through an analysis of *La Seine était rouge*,
her 1999 rewriting of the massacre of Algerian demonstrators by the
Paris police on October 17, 1961, which was one of the most cen-

sored events of the war because it occurred in the French capital toward the end of the conflict.

The Algerian War and Anti-Maghrebian Racism in France

A corollary to the cover-up of the Algerian conflict, a war that has remained in a "semiotic twilight zone," could well be seen in the increase of racist rhetoric and racist sentiment in France in the 1980s.[6] In "La Guerre et l'immigration algérienne en France," René Gallissot pointed out that the Algerian war created in France a shift from anti-Semitic nationalism to colonial racism. Colonial racism returned to France from its Algerian setting by being transferred onto immigrants in such a way that "le Nord-Africain devient l'immigré type" [the North African becomes the typical immigrant] (345). At the end of his 1986 book, *L'Identité de la France*, historian Fernand Braudel discussed three main reasons for the so-called "immigration problem" in France: economic, racist, and cultural (185–200). He rejected the first two on rational, factual grounds: the immigrants do not take jobs from the French, but perform tasks that the French refuse to do; even though they may create some economic difficulties because they receive benefits and social services, they also contribute to French economic growth and to an increase in the standard of living (189). As for the question of race, Braudel pointed out that this is a false issue, because Maghrebians are white and the French, with the country's history of immigration, are all of mixed ethnic backgrounds anyway (192). Braudel's analysis of the immigration question thus centers on what he called "cultural" reasons, which appears to be a code word for Islam, not simply as a religion, but also as a way of life (195). The two main problems Braudel singled out are, predictably, the authority of the father and the status of women (196).

Braudel's considerations, however, are conveniently idealistic. He brushes aside widespread, viscerally negative, emotional perceptions of people of Maghrebian origin in France, sidestepping the crucial issue of racism with facile "melting pot" comments. As Maxim Silverman argued in *Deconstructing the Nation*, "[I]deologically constructed differences do not vanish simply by being proved to be of minimal scientific value: 'race' might not exist but racism does" (165). Braudel also neglected to account for the human tendency (analyzed by René Girard in *La Violence et le sacré* [*Violence and the Sacred*]) to look for a powerless scapegoat to blame for problems befalling a group (in the case of France, economic problems triggering a psychological uncertainty about national identity). Although cultural reasons may account in part for the difficult location of people of

Maghrebian descent in French society, blaming Islam as the only obstacle
to Maghrebian "integration" (which is viewed as the ultimate goal by French
governments) is a reductive gesture that not only puts the blame on the
side of the Other, but also conveniently covers up two long-standing French
traditions, patriarchy and racism/anti-Semitism. Braudel's analysis thus inscribes itself in a French, Orientalist discursive tradition that has created
what René Gallissot called a "préjugé d'incompatibilité des cultures" [pre-
judged incompatibility between cultures] (345); in such discourse, Islam
often functions as *the* marker of irreducible difference.[7] Because Braudel is
a historian of *la longue durée* [long-term evolution], his analysis makes no
mention of the Algerian war. Beyond the economic, social, and religious
causes for the current anti-Maghrebian racism, the anger displayed at
Maghrebians for being "different"—for not assimilating as easily as other
groups into the fabric of French life—takes root at a deeper, unconscious
level. The eight years of violence between Algeria and France were almost
completely erased in 1980s France in an attempt at forgetting (in an interesting parallel to their overexploitation in Algeria).

The explosion of racist violence in France in the 1980s could well be
interpreted through the lens of Sigmund Freud's theory of the return of
the repressed. According to Freud, what used to be familiar but has been
subsequently repressed resurfaces through unconscious acts and dreams
and expresses itself in the compulsion to repeat (see "The Uncanny" and
Beyond the Pleasure Principle). The escalation of anti-Arab incidents, together with the generalization of racist rhetoric in that decade, could be
linked to the long repression, first of the violent reality of the Algerian
war, and then of the psychological loss experienced by the French after
1962.

Any analysis of anti-Arab racism and the so-called immigration question in France must take into account the historical and psychological
scars the Algerian war has left on the French collective unconscious. Un-
fortunately, the war is rarely factored into studies on immigration. Moroccan novelist Tahar Ben Jelloun concurred with this in his remarkable 1984
study of racism in France, ironically titled *Hospitalité française*: "Pour certains,
la guerre d'Algérie n'est pas encore terminée. La présence sur le sol français
d'un peu moins d'un million d'immigrés algériens excite leur haine
nostalgique, et lorsqu'ils agressent un Arabe, cela s'inscrit indirectement
dans le deuil impossible et intolérable que l'histoire exige à propos de
'l'Algérie française'" [For some, the Algerian war isn't over yet. The presence on French territory of a little less than one million Algerian immigrants arouses their nostalgic hatred, and when they attack an Arab, this is
indirectly linked to the impossible and intolerable mourning history de-

mands regarding "French Algeria"] (24). Ben Jelloun's analysis intersects with Rousso's, as both use the concept of mourning as key to understanding the situation in France. Ben Jelloun's description of "impossible and intolerable mourning" corresponds to Rousso's concept of "interrupted mourning." Unresolved and repressed feelings about the Algerian war fester and are carried over into new situations, such as the question of immigration in France, a topic so charged that simply to say the word in France nowadays tends to trigger overwhelmingly negative reactions. At least at the unconscious level, racist acts can be seen as a continuation of the repressed, lost colonial war. The nostalgia for "French Algeria" discussed by Ben Jelloun is a sign of such a repression. In *Women and War*, Jean Bethke Elshtain noted the link between the two poles of "forgetting, on one end," and "remembering in nostalgic and sentimental ways, on the other" (223). Memory as the organization of forgetting (Rousso 14) must substitute nostalgic recollections, which serve as "screen memories," for the more painful memories.[8]

The 1992 celebration of the thirtieth anniversary of the end of the Algerian war served both to create a space in which painful memories could be allowed to resurface and heal (through the emergence of new historical research and new representations) and to boost screen memories. French magazine *Paris-Match*'s poll on French people and the Algerian war, for instance, revealed that although the war was deemed the second most important event to have occurred since 1945 (after the May 1968 riots), 44 percent of the people answering the question were against the anniversary celebration because it "fait revivre des souvenirs douloureux" [brings back painful memories]. A large majority of the people polled (67 percent) indicated that they believed Algeria's independence to have been unavoidable. (This may explain why they would rather avoid thinking about a lengthy and bloody war fought for nothing—unless one sees this as an a posteriori rationalization to help them to deal with the loss.) Remarkably absent from these pages, which otherwise make references to *pieds-noirs, harkis,* and the Algerian people, is any mention of people of Maghrebian origin now living in France ("1962–1992" 92–93).[9]

In the survey, many questions were asked about Franco-Algerian relations and the Algerian people; the responses show a lack of knowledge of, and/or interest in, the topic (the majority of answers fall into the categories "neither" or "doesn't know"). Had questions been asked about Algerians and Beurs in France, the answers might have been much more opinionated. Finally, at the bottom of the page, *Paris-Match* offers several old family pictures of famous pieds-noirs in Algeria, titled, "L'Album de la

'Nostalgérie'" [The album of "Nostalgeria"]. The caption accompanying the pictures centers on these pieds-noirs' positive memories of *prewar* Algeria and on their *current* achievements in France. The war itself is never mentioned, in a striking illustration of the role that nostalgia plays in the constitution of screen memories.

The link that *Paris-Match* refused to make between the Algerian war and the current anti-Maghrebian racism in France, so well expressed by Ben Jelloun, was also obvious to Begag and Chaouite:

> D'abord, le temps de la "question" de l'immigration maghrébine n'est pas son temps premier, mais un temps second. Un temps qui fait écho à un autre où l'immigré-visiteur et l'hôte-accueillant se tenaient en position inverse: c'était le "temps des colonies." . . . C'est là le véritable temps premier: celui de l'effraction violente, de la mort d'hommes, au cours duquel les imaginaires ont été marqués pour toujours. Ce premier temps a provoqué des effets bouleversants durables dans le système par son intensité. Il a, d'autre part, amené un deuxième temps, celui du souvenir. Il est réactivé par toutes les énergies et les tensions non liquidées au cours du premier temps. Le temps des discours actuels sur les Maghrébins de France revêt l'allure de cet après-coup de souvenir. (29)

> [To begin with, the time of the Maghrebian immigration "question" is not a first stage, but a second one. A stage that echoes another in which the visiting immigrant and the welcoming host were inverted: such was the "time of the colonies." That was the true first stage, that of violent breaking into and deaths, which marked the imaginary forever. Because of its intensity, that first stage created long-lasting, overwhelming psychological effects. It also brought about a second stage, that of memory. That stage is reactivated by all the energies and tensions that were not settled during the first stage. The time of current discourses on Maghrebians in France takes on the form of that aftermath of memory.]

Begag and Chaouite and Rousso were indeed discussing the same phenomenon. The current anti-Maghrebian racism in France, with its violent rhetoric and actions, is "an aftermath of memory," "a replay of the rift" that was caused in part by French colonization of Algeria and the Algerian war.

In his book *Arabicides*, reporter Fausto Giudice went even further while investigating racially motivated murders in France in the 1970s and 1980s. He not only claimed that such murders restage the Algerian war (106), but also suggested that contemporary French society may have been founded on the general "Arabicide" committed during the Algerian war on both Algerian and French territories (12). He claimed that the memory of that Arabicide "a été sciemment effacée de la conscience historique française" [was knowingly erased from French historical consciousness] (337). Similarly, Pervillé talked about "une volonté officielle d'amnésie" [an official desire for amnesia] (309). Giudice noted that several assailants and murderers of Maghrebians in France between 1970 and 1991 were either Algerian war veterans or children of such men, and he implied that the pardon granted for crimes committed during the Algerian war encouraged the repetition of similar acts in peacetime France (347).[10]

The Fifth Republic's origin lies in the Algerian war and its devastating effects on the *métropole* in the 1950s. This stable régime, of which the French are so proud, was born out of the Algerian-French conflict, a source that the French prefer not to remember (Berstein, *France* 45). As Benjamin Stora remarked in *La Gangrène et l'oubli*, the Algerian war was a founding event, not only of the Algerian nation, but also of the current French Republic (7, 317). Stora suggested that France's deep involvement with the memory of World War II in the 1960s served as a way to cover up the Fifth Republic's shameful origin (Gangrene 222). In the French, as in the Algerian, case, Renan's assessment is confirmed: the war functioned as a deed "of violence which took place at the origin of [these particular] political formations" ("What Is a Nation?" 11).

For writers from Algeria living in France in the 1980s, the strategic need to write about the Algerian war appears all the more intense as their works become "a struggle of memory against forgetting" (quoted in hooks, "Choosing" 147). This is a powerful response to Ernest Renan's argument about forgetting and national identity. Remembering is a crucial act for breaking the cycle of unconscious repetition that results in the violent return of the repressed. Ben Jelloun disagreed with Renan about the use of forgetting: even though France likes to forget certain memories (Ben Jelloun 18), "L'oubli est mauvais conseiller. Quand il s'installe dans l'histoire, il la mutile et la détourne" [Forgetting is bad advice. When it settles in history, it mutilates and misappropriates it] (33). Using the same words as American feminist Adrienne Rich, Ben Jelloun advised us to resist enforced amnesia ("refuser l'amnésie," p. 22). These writers all criticized the construction of a national identity predicated on their own erasure as minorities and/or women. The identity that contemporary women writers on the margins of Algerian and French societies are trying to establish must, of necessity, transcend national boundaries; thus, forgetting is of little strategic use to them. They all call for contemporary society to come to terms with its métissage, considering that French society is rapidly becoming multiracial, especially with the increased numbers and cultural visibility of Sub-Saharan and Caribbean immigrants.

It is precisely this métissage that, like World War II or the Algerian war, is now contributing to another crisis of French unity and identity. Because of unresolved issues carried over from previous crises, many French people feel threatened by the notion that national identities are, by definition, always already in process. This creates what Gérard Mermet called an "obsession identitaire" [obsession with identity] among the French (211). For Stora, the repressed "amputation" of Algeria from France is the cause of a French "gangrene," that is revealed by the crisis of French nationalism (Gangrene 318). Maxim Silverman suggested that "the current obsession with immigration in France itself [is] in-dicative of a crisis in the structures of the nation-state," as the unifica-tion of Europe is beginning to erode the ideology of French sover-eignty (33).

As the national feeling is perceived to be threatened, the repressed re-turns: the population of Arab origin in France is singled out as the scape-goat, the enemy Other, which endangers some essentialist, fixed, and ro-manticized essence of *Francité*. It is precisely at the point at which the static notion of a "true" French identity is no longer valid that so many people feel the need to mobilize around the fight to preserve it. In the words of Herman Lebovics, the discourse of an "authentic" national iden-tity is generally undertaken "at moments of great cultural-political contes-tation; and it is just at those conjunctures that the interpenetration of cultures is most evident" (125).

According to Renan, the construction of the nation props itself up on an original violence that is then repressed. However, the repressed repeatedly returns, endangering the construction it had originally made possible. Such is the paradox of the creation of national identity. For-getting both enables and destabilizes that creation. Ultimately, the na-tion can only keep surviving if it is ready to collectively face its past deeds of violence. Anamnesis becomes the condition of reconciliation and survival. In the case of France and the Algerian war, historical am-nesia contributed to the compulsive repetition of a blocked situation. In this respect, the changes to the French Nationality Code of sum-mer 1993 (these had failed to pass in 1986–1987) were part of an on-going process to legally separate "us" from "them" at a time in which the separations were becoming more blurred (see Silverman 64–65, 107). These changes made it more difficult for children born to foreigners in France and foreign spouses of French nationals to acquire French nationality.[11] The 1993 legislation was fortunately mostly overturned in March and May 1998, when new laws reestablished the *jus solis* [citizenship laws based on place of birth rather than on the parents' nationality] (Naïr 26–31). The fiction of the 1980s and the historical scholarship of the early 1990s were early signs that France was easing into the third phase of its Algeria syndrome, facing the ghosts of the past in order to meet the challenges of the future.

It may perhaps be said that France fully entered this third phase on June 10, 1999, when the Assemblée nationale officially recognized that the actions carried out to "maintain order" in 1954–1962 in Algeria actually constituted a war. After thirty-seven years, then, the Algerian war is no longer a *"guerre sans nom"* [war without a name].[12] The recognition of the Algerian war received scant coverage on national television news and in *Le Monde* the next day. This indicates that France still has a long way to go before nearing the phase of obsession—yet it is well into the phase of shattering the silence. The following two chapters investigate Sebbar's and Djebar's literary rewritings of the history of struggle between Algeria and France. While Djebar's project focuses on bringing the voices of Algerian women into history, Sebbar highlights the different phases of France's Algeria syndrome.

Notes

1. Noted in Benjamin Stora, *Gangrène* 13.

2. See Danielle Marx-Scouras's discussion of this event in "Muffled Screams/ Stifled Voices."

3. I am using the current nations' names to avoid the colonial terminology, but I have placed "Algeria" and "France" in quotation marks to indicate the historical anachronism. The historical facts mentioned here are summarized from Benjamin Stora's book *La Gangrène et l'oubli.*

4. See Berstein, "Une Guerre sans nom"; Stora, *Gangrène* 13–24. Mustapha Marrouchi discusses the different ways in which France and the United States deal with the two wars: "Les Américains exorcisent. Les Français se replient sur un consensus de silence" [Americans exorcize; the French withdraw into silent consensus] (245). The purpose of this chapter is not comparative, but for further discussion of similarities and differences between the Algerian and Vietnam wars, see David Schalk 16–37 and Benjamin Stora, *Imaginaires.*

5. Marrouchi, 245–46, 251–52. In 1991, Amrane noted that the archives of the FLN-ALN and the French army and police were still inaccessible (272).

6. The words are Jean Bethke Elshtain's on the Vietnam War (219).

7. For analyses of French identity and immigration, see Lebovics; Noiriel, *Le Creuset*; Schnapper; and Silverman.

8. Rousso identified the 1945 Liberation as a screen memory used to cover up French wartime collaboration with the Nazis (25).

9. The *pieds-noirs* are French settlers in Algeria who had to move to France after the Algerian victory, often losing everything they owned in the process; the *harkis* are Algerians who fought on the side of France during the war. Those who were not abandoned by the French government in Algeria to be killed as traitors were repatriated to France, where they were, not only ghettoized in camps, but also often ostracized by other Maghrebians.

10. History, if it is repressed, does indeed repeat itself. The 1953 pardon of most Occupation collaborators, legally termed an *oubli juridique* [judicial forgetting], was repeated in the pardon of war crimes committed in Algeria (Rousso 62, 105). As early as 1962, the French government began making provisions for amnesty. A string of amnesties for war crimes in Algeria followed (1964, 1966, 1968, 1974, 1982). Stora suggests that the 1982 complete amnesty and reinstatement of civil servants and military personnel involved in the Algerian conflict was directly responsible for the rise of extreme right-wing groups in politics because it gave them a new legitimacy (the Front National went from .8 percent of votes in 1981 to 14.5 percent in 1988—a sad by-product of President Mitterrand's first *septennat*) (*Gangrène* 215, 281–83, 289).

11. For an excellent discussion of the parallels between this legislation and the Vichy government's 1940 Jewish Statutes, see Rosemarie Scullion.

12. Bacqué. The vote was overshadowed by the news of the end of the war in Kosovo that very same day. As the coincidences of history would have it, June 10 also marked the fifty-fifth anniversary of the World War II Oradour massacre, in which most of the villagers were executed by the Nazis.

Chapter 2

▼▼▼▼▼▼▼▼▼

The "Algeria Syndrome"

What is buried in the past of one generation falls to the next to
claim.
—Susan Griffin, *A Chorus of Stones* 179

Leïla Sebbar, born and raised in Algeria by an Algerian father and a French
mother, remarked that the Algerian war "est chaque fois, malgré moi, dans
les livres que j'écris [is in each book I write, in spite of myself]" (quoted
in Salien 4). In her 1984 novel, *Le Chinois vert d'Afrique*, almost all the
characters have been involved with the war to some degree. Early on in
the Shérazade trilogy, the reader discovers that Shérazade's grandmother
died during that war (*Shérazade* 147/158–59). The protagonists of Sebbar's
novels are most often children of Maghrebian immigrants in France, or
Beurs. They never experienced the Algerian war as a direct trauma. Rather,
the teenagers learn about the war through older Algerians' stories (the oral
tradition), books, and photographs.

Sebbar depicts their lives at the periphery of large French cities, where
the HLM, the low-income housing projects in the suburbs, become a
metaphor for a motley immigrant population ghettoized on the margins of
French society. Living in France makes it doubly difficult for the protagonists to gain more than a fragmented knowledge of the Algerian war,
especially because, until a 1983 decree including decolonization in the
Terminale (last year of high school) curriculum, the history taught in French
schools stopped with the end of World War II (Rousso 285).[1] In her
novels, Sebbar repeatedly presents young Beurs who do not know anything about the Algerian war (*Shérazade* 56, 147, 164/56–57, 158–59,

176). In what follows, I chart how Leïla Sebbar's novels confirm, as well as go beyond, the existence of the Algeria syndrome that I traced historically in the previous chapter.

Literature as a *Lieu de Mémoire*

In *Le Chinois vert d'Afrique*, Sebbar points repeatedly to the link between current French racism and the Algerian (and Vietnam) war(s) by putting the most offensive racist discourse in the mouths of the Frenchmen who fought in these wars.[2] At the same time, she is careful to show that not all war veterans react in the same way: Inspector Laruel and Myra's grandfather, Emile Cordier, are much more open to the young Beur protagonist, Mohamed and what he represents than are the other veterans; for Laruel, it is because of a certain Orientalist fascination, and for Emile, it is due to his leftist politics of solidarity.

Mohamed falls in love with Myra, a young *métisse* (part Moroccan, part Italian, part French) who lives with her grandfather Emile in a lower-middle-class neighborhood (*pavillons de banlieue*) not too distant from Mohamed's housing project. One of their neighbors, Tuilier, exemplifies the most violently racist and classist ideology in the novel.[3] As a young man he fought in Indochina, and he wishes he had been sent to Algeria as well. Tuilier vicariously lives his failed military career through dreams of a neighborhood militia. He sets up a room in his house for target practice and owns a trained police dog named Mao.[4] The young people of Arab descent living in the projects provide him with a live target for war games. Together with a handful of other older, working-class, conservative men, he attempts to set up a militia in an act they call "autodéfense" [self-defense] (233). Taking "justice" into his own hands allows him to give himself more importance and power than he actually has, as he bestows upon himself the mission of "faire des rondes matin et soir avec mon chien Mao. Ça rend service à tout le monde" [patrolling the area morning and evening with my dog Mao as a service to everyone] (137).

The proximity of the housing projects and Mohamed's wanderings around Myra's garden are all that is needed to generate racist hysteria: "Tuilier parle de ses armes, de la guerre, du club de tir, de l'insécurité des banlieues, des voyous, des Arabes qui colonisent la France, de la légitime défense" [Tuilier speaks of his weapons, war, the shooting club, insecurity in the suburbs, hoodlums, Arabs who are colonizing France, justified self-defense] (136). Tuilier's racist discourse is rooted in violence, as he projects his own (real) violence and dreams of a glorious military career onto the (fantasized) violence in the projects, which he associates with Maghrebian immi-grants and their offspring; for him, the jump from "hoodlums" to "Arabs who are colonizing France" is automatic. The equation of people of Arab background with violent and lawless groups brings about the "logical" conclusion, the need for self-protection—in an ironic reversal of reality, for, as we have seen, the 1980s were marked by a rise in racist crime (see Giudice, Ben Jelloun 41). Sebbar's use of reported speech and of the enu-merative device creates an ironic distance between speaker and reader, helping expose the flimsiness of Tuilier's argument.

In these few lines, Sebbar has perfectly encapsulated racist and dema-gogic rhetoric à la Jean-Marie Le Pen. That same racist ideology, which is precisely what historian Fernand Braudel sidestepped so easily in his analysis, has been steadily gaining ground in France, where the Front National, Le Pen's extreme right party, nationally received an estimated 14 percent of votes in the first round of the regional elections in May 1992.[5] The percentages were almost double in some regions, such as the south, where a very depressed economic situation coupled with the presence of large pied-noir and immigrant populations fuels a stronger anti-Maghrebian sentiment. In the first round of the presidential elec-tions of April 1995, candidate Le Pen gathered 15.7 percent of all votes (4,673,000). The two extreme-right candidates together (Le Pen and Philippe de Villiers) swept one-fifth of all votes (20.44 percent), almost as much as Socialist candidate Lionel Jospin (23.3 percent) and much more than the Communist and Trotskyist candidates, who to-gether scored less than 14 percent.[6] In the municipal elections of June 1995, Front National mayoral candidates were elected in three south-ern cities (Toulon, Orange, and Marignane). A former Front National member was elected as the mayor of Nice, one of France's largest cities. It was only in the European elections of June 1999 that Le Pen lost a lot of his electorate, due to internal dissension within the Front Na-tional and the scission of the party into two competing ones, Le Pen's Front National and Bruno Mégret's Mouvement National (Mégret is Le Pen's former second in command). Although the French political class is currently unanimous in distancing itself from the Front Na-tional, Le Pen's rhetoric on immigration has spread to most right-wing politicians and is not being countered very strongly by the Left, either.

Gérard Noiriel, in his book, *Le Creuset français*, defined the racist rhetoric that Sebbar illustrates in her novel: "[L]a force de cette stratégie politique tient à ce qu'elle ne s'adresse pas à la raison, mais à l'*'inconscient*' qui sommeille en chacun de nous . . . le discours xénophobe joue volontiers sur les fantasmes: la peur, l'exotisme. . . .

En martelant constamment les mêmes thèmes, le xénophobe tente de
susciter des associations d'idées et surtout d'images qui peuvent conduire
aux automatismes de pensée qui illustrent fréquemment les propos
racistes" [the force of this political strategy is precisely that it does not
appeal to reason but, instead, addresses the "subconscious" dwelling
within each of us . . . xenophobic discourse readily plays on fantasies
such as fear and exoticism. . . . By constantly hammering on the same
subjects, xenophobic discourse seeks to create associations of ideas and,
especially, of images that can lead to the stereotypical thinking that
usually underlies racist statements] (*Creuset* 275–76/211).

It is no wonder that the rhetoric of Tuilier and his friends in *Le Chinois*
should be so similar to Le Pen's. In *Francoscopie 1993*, Gérard Mermet
noted that—like Tuilier and his cohorts—the Front National's typical con-
stituents are men (71 percent) from the lower and lower-middle classes
who live in large cities (226). In *Le Chinois*, Tuilier's men, who claim to be
"pas des violents, pas agressifs ni rien" [not violent, not aggressive, really],
long for a context of violence legitimated by the colonial wars (233): "Si
on pouvait employer les grands moyens, ils retourneraient tous chez eux,
vite fait. Dommage, c'est loin la guerre d'Algérie, parce que alors là, on
rigolerait pas, balayés, ratissés. On a déjà un ancien d'Algérie dans notre
comité, c'est un dur. . . . Il en a dans le pantalon" [If we could resort to
drastic measures, they'd all go back home quick. It's too bad the Algerian
war was so long ago, because then, there'd be no messing around, they'd
all be swept out, cleaned out. We already have an Algeria vet in our group,
he's a tough guy. . . . He's got balls] (234).

The desire for a revenge over the French failure in Algeria, or rather, the
desire to take up the Algerian war again, this time on French territory and
to the point of French victory, is shown to be one of the driving forces
behind anti-Arab racism. In a psychological fantasy that ignores the factor
of economic power imbalance, the situation of the Algerian war is reversed, the Arabs being now perceived as the colonizer: "[I]ls nous colonisent.
. . . On est colonisé" [They're colonizing us. . . . We're colonized] (236).
This perverse inversion of the historical situation legitimates "les grands
moyens" [drastic measures] (such as the militia) and the racism of the
police force (234). For Benjamin Stora, such a discourse, based on revenge, which perceives the former colonized turned immigrant as a colonizer invading "civilized" territory, reactivates colonial racism and facili-
tates an unproblematic nationalist identification (*Gangrène* 288–90): "La
guerre d'Algérie continue à travers la lutte contre l'islam. . . . La liturgie
d'une France enracinée dans la pureté d'une identité mythique, sans cesse
menacée, voilà ce qui légitime d'avance toutes les mesures de possibles

violences, de 'guerre' pour se défendre des 'envahisseurs'" [The Algerian war continues through the struggle against Islam. The liturgy of a France that would be rooted in the purity of a mythical, constantly threatened identity, legitimates in advance any possible violent measure (or "war") taken to defend oneself from "invaders"] (291).[7] Once again, the Manichean structures of Orientalist discourse exposed by Edward Said are summoned to perpetuate the perception of an alien, external enemy against whom an endangered national unity can be recreated. Ben Jelloun astutely remarked that the problem lies in the fact that "on a omis de décoloniser l'imaginaire d'une grande partie des Français" [there has been a failure to decolonize the imaginary of a large number of French people] (61).

Sebbar shows another driving force behind racism to be machismo and masculinist warrior values. Tuilier himself is the only son of a war widow, and "pour échapper à la tyrannie maternelle, sans le dire à sa mère, il avait choisi de partir pour l'Indochine" [to escape maternal tyranny, without telling his mother, he had chosen to enlist and go to Indochina] (*Chinois* 135). As for Marcel, the Algeria veteran of the militia, his toughness and fearlessness are metaphorically measured through his virility: "Il en a dans le pantalon" [He's got balls] (234). This is literally "proved" to the reader on the next page, a flashback to the Algerian war in which, after seeing dead, castrated young French soldiers, Marcel's company raped the village women and then gathered villagers together and blew them up with grenades: "Un massacre, ce jour-là. Les femmes, les enfants, les jeunes, tout avait explosé, un feu d'artifice" [A slaughter, that day. Women, children, youths, they had all exploded like fireworks] (235).

In this novel, Sebbar foregrounds the links connecting war, hypermasculinity, and sexism, from Tuilier's flight from the maternal to Marcel's company's military exploits as inscribed on the bodies of women and children. I am not arguing that Sebbar condemns *men* as a whole in an essentialist gesture, especially as she depicts men like Emile Cordier in very positive roles, but she does criticize *masculinist*, racist values that place the white man at the top of a hierarchy of values predicated on violence. The acts of raping, setting fire to places and people, and killing express a desire for ultimate power waged through violence. Other people are controlled through the use of a violence that has gone out of control.

Anamnesis and National Reconciliation

Whereas in the mid-1980s Sebbar critically interrogated the continuing second phase of France's Algeria syndrome, in 1999 she participated in its third phase, that of historical rewriting, in a short text published in a collection targeting young adults, *La Seine était rouge*. The novel focuses on the search for historical clues to the October 1961 massacre thirty-five years later. Toward the end of the Algerian war, on October 17, 1961, hundreds of the 30,000 Algerians who were peacefully demonstrating in Paris against the curfew imposed on them by police chief Maurice Papon were brutally massacred.[8] Censorship was forcibly imposed on newspapers, photographers, and publishing houses trying to cover such an unthinkable act of violence. During the attack, the demonstrators were beaten and shot by police, and dozens were thrown into the Seine and left to drown. Over 11,000 men were rounded up in buses and held in stadiums in a move uncannily reminiscent of the *rafle du Vel d'Hiv*, the July 1942 roundup of over 13,000 Jewish men, women, and children arrested by the French police for deportation. Hundreds of Algerians were deported to prison camps in Algeria until the end of the war (Einaudi 80). Because of the general amnesty applied to all Algerian war crimes in France, Papon, like hundreds of others, will never have to answer for his participation in the October 17 massacre.

Sebbar's lengthy dedication inscribes her text in a tradition of re-writing of this repressed page of Franco-Algerian history. The book is dedicated to the Algerian victims of the massacre, as well as to those whose works served as sources for Sebbar's own rewriting. In particular, she mentions four fiction writers, Didier Daeninckx, Nacer Kettane, Mehdi Lallaoui, and Georges Mattei. Before analyzing Sebbar's own contribution to the topic, I will briefly sketch out the seven earlier literary treatments of the massacre, all published between 1982 and 1998. It is important to note that there was a twenty-year silence be-tween the massacre and its earliest literary incarnation, Georges Mattei's *La guerre des gusses*.[9]

Three of the texts refer to the massacre in their opening pages and present it as a landmark event for Algerians living in France. Kettane's 1985 *Le Sourire de Brahim* opens with a chapter titled "Octobre à Paris." The massacre, which was erased from French memory, is presented by Kettane as one of the first examples of racially motivated violence, or "ratonnades," against Algerians living in France (16). The protagonist's young brother is killed during the massacre, and recounting this event at the beginning of the book both provides the basis of the plot and explains the title (Brahim, the protagonist, loses his ability to smile forever after the loss of his beloved brother). A leitmotif in the novel is that anti-Maghrebian violence in the 1980s is directly related to a French desire to continue the Algerian war (58, 74–75, 126, 142). Both Kettane's and Tassadit Imache's texts focus on the childhood and young adulthood of children of Algerian immigrants in France, and both highlight the connections between residual traces of the war and the difficulties these youngsters experience in French society decades later.

Imache, too, opens her 1989 novel, *Une fille sans histoire,* with the protagonist's first memory, that of the October 17 massacre, which occurred when she was three years old. Her Algerian father was arrested during the demonstration and disappeared for three days, and her French mother was interrogated by the police. The title, with its multiple meanings, resonates with this event: part of the young protagonist's malaise is connected to the violent erasure of her history, as a daughter of mixed parents living in France during the Algerian war.

The October 17 massacre is also given foundational status in the autobiographical narrative *Vivre me tue* by Paul Smaïl, a French writer of Moroccan descent (1997). Although he does not begin his narrative with the massacre (unlike Kettane, Imache, and Daeninckx) nor provide a full treatment of it, he mentions it on several occasions and devotes a chapter to it (178–80). The originality of his treatment of the event lies in the fact that the chapter describing the massacre most fully comes right after a description of current racist violence in the 1990s. The transition between the two periods is at first made without any indication of a change in the time frame. Further, this is the only chapter in the entire book that takes place before the narrator's lifetime, thus highlighting its continuing significance. The reader is led to assume that Smaïl's narrator is still describing the recent violence until the date "1961" appears at the end of the first paragraph. Like Kettane, Smaïl argues that there is a link between the events of 1961 and more recent "ratonnades"; both authors explicitly name Maurice Papon as the one who ordered the massacre. In *Vivre me tue,* as in *Le Sourire de Brahim*, the narrator loses a family member in the massacre: his uncle was killed by the French police when he inadvertently ran into the demonstration on his way to work. Farida Abu-Haidar suggests that Smaïl saw the October 17 massacre as a foundational event, not just for Algerians, but for the entire North African immigrant community. The arrests made in 1961 took on a racist nature as the police relied on physical appearance when making arrests and proved unable to distinguish between Algerians, Moroccans, and Tunisians (as citizens of independent nations since 1956, Moroccans and Tunisians were not under curfew regulations). As a result, the Moroccan embassy in Paris had to lodge several formal complaints regarding the mistreatment of its citizens (Einaudi 79).

The interpretation of the October massacre as a foundational event for Maghrebians in France is consistent with Mehdi Lallaoui's presentation in his 1986 novel, *Les Beurs de Seine*. Toward the end of the novel, Kaci, the protagonist, discusses two landmark historical events for Algerians living in France: the first is the May 8, 1945, massacres in Sétif and Guelma (when Algerians demonstrating for their own liberation on the day of France's liberation from German oppression were attacked by the French army), which were a prelude to the war of liberation; the second is the October 17, 1961, massacre, which neither Kaci's southern French girl-friend Katia nor her Beur friend Farida had ever heard of before (158–59). Lallaoui's name figures on the list of people to whom Sebbar dedicated her own literary rewriting of the massacre, *La Seine était rouge*.[10] That the October massacre was a foundational event for the immigrant community is also attested to by the fact that in Algeria, October 17 has, since 1968, been National Emigration Day (Einaudi 293).

The first literary treatment of the October 1961 massacre to have been read widely in France is Franco-Belgian writer Didier Daeninckx's 1984 detective novel, *Meurtres pour mémoire*. Inspired by the then-recent revelations that Maurice Papon had been responsible for the deportation of over 1,500 Jews in World War II Bordeaux, Daeninckx wrote in barely veiled fashion about a killer responsible for both events in his *Meurtres pour mémoire*.[11] The novel opens with the epigraph, "En oubliant le passé, on se condamne à le revivre" [If we forget the past, we are condemned to relive it] (n.p.). Although the novel begins with the perspectives of a few Algerian participants in the peaceful demonstration, the rest of the narrative, which takes place twenty years later, centers only on Franco-French characters. The 1961 massacre is soon obscured by memories of World War II atrocities, and the Algerian characters of the first two chapters disappear.

The plot centers on re-membering Vichy, as the son of a French historian is assassinated in Toulouse twenty years after his father was mysteriously killed during the October 1961 massacre. During his investigation, Inspector Cadin discovers that the Paris prefect of police in 1961, André Veillut, was responsible for the deportation of hundreds of Jewish people in Toulouse (like Bordeaux, a southern French city) during World War II. Both father and son had uncovered Veillut's participation in the Jewish Holocaust and died for this knowledge. Although Daeninckx attempts to make links between the two massacres, in his novel, the Algeria syndrome is covered over by the Vichy syndrome. While participating in the third phase of the Vichy syndrome, that of obsession, the book also enacts the second phase of the Algeria syndrome, even as it attempts to bring it back to memory. While Daeninckx's novel deals with the erasure of French memory, it has little to say about immigrant memory, and thus unwittingly participates in the continued silencing of the October 1961 massacre.[12]

Like *Meurtres pour mémoire*, Georges Mattei's *Guerre des Gusses* (1982) is a fictionalized roman à clef. At the end of this historical novel, Mattei provides a detailed account of the massacre and its place in the Algerian war—most of the narrative deals with a French soldier who becomes a deserter and joins the FLN. The book is framed by the two foundational events mentioned by Lallaoui: the 1945 Sétif and Guelma massacres in Algeria and the October 1961 atrocities. The rest of the book takes place in Algeria in the 1950s. Two major events of the war are foregrounded: the well-known 1957 Battle of Algiers, immortalized by Gillo Pontecorvo's 1965 film by the same name, and the hidden 1961 Paris massacre. Mattei himself was a *porteur de valises* (literally, "suitcase carrier," one of the French who supported the FLN during the war), and he provided historian Jean-Luc Einaudi with FLN archival records of the war when Einaudi was writing his history of the October massacre (Einaudi 14). Significantly, Einaudi, too, took up the parallel Mattei made in his historical novel between the two battles, entitling his 1991 history, *La Bataille de Paris* [The battle of Paris].[13] Mattei's descriptions of the October massacre rely on testimonies culled from FLN records as well as from the few accounts extant in newspapers of the time. Like Daeninckx, his narrator expresses the duty of memory that he experiences: "Je me souviendrai de cette nuit. . . . Je serai mémoire" [I shall remember this night. I shall be memory] (220).

In *La Guerre des gusses*, the identity of the prefect of police is barely disguised: "Marcel Pantobe" bears the same initials and a name sounding quite similar to Maurice Papon's—furthermore, his political trajectory closely resembles Papon's, and Mattei makes direct reference to 1943 Bordeaux. Since the *Canard Enchaîné*'s revelations about Papon's past had occurred only a year before the publication of Mattei's book, readers would have easily been able to identify the character of Pantobe. Moreover, one chapter begins with a quotation from Papon himself, in which he told the Paris police in 1961 that they would be protected no matter what they did (201). These same words are later repeated in the text by Marcel Pantobe (213). Considering Papon's vindictiveness and his predilection for libel suits, this was a courageous act on Mattei's part.[14]

Even before Papon's sordid past was revealed, most accounts drew parallels between the bloody repression of the peaceful Algerian demonstration and Nazi persecutions. Less than twenty years after Vichy, French politicians, Jewish personalities, and porteurs de valises alike denounced French use of the same methods against the Algerians. For example, the Action Catholique ouvrière (Catholic Worker's Action) was censored for making the comparison with Oradour that Daeninckx would take up much later (Einaudi 237). Soon after the massacre, politician Eugène Claudius-Petit asked for an investigation of the police repression, spoke of racism and drew parallels with Nazism (Tristan 116). Claude Lanzmann, who later became famous as the director of the documentary film *Shoah*, wrote a statement, signed by many intellectuals, in which he equated the imprisonment of over 11,000 Algerian men in the Palais des Sports with the internment of Jews at Drancy, the center from which they were deported to concentration camps abroad (Einaudi 225). Mattei draws many parallels between World War II and October 1961 (205, 207–8, 212–14). Daeninckx's Inspector Cadin makes a pithy observation: "Un Oradour en plein Paris" [The Oradour massacre in the heart of Paris] (81), comparing the 1961 pogrom to the infamous killing of 642 Oradour-sur-Glane villagers (men, women, and children) by German SS soldiers in June 1944.

Finally, in Nancy Huston's novel, *L'Empreinte de l'ange* (1998), most events take place in Paris between 1957 and 1962. Besides the numerous references to the Algerian war, the novel also alludes to World War II and the two wars are compared on several occasions. One of the protagonists, a Jewish-Hungarian refugee named András, participates with FLN members in organizing the October 17 demonstration. The day after the demonstration, while searching for him, his German lover, Saffie, witnesses bodies being dredged out of the Seine (287–90). András makes explicit the connections between the curfew imposed on the Algerians by the French and Vichy policies against the Jews: "Un couvre-feu rien que pour les musulmans. *Vingt ans* seulement après le couvre-feu pour les juifs. Pareil! Pareil!" [A curfew just for Muslims! Only *twenty years* after the curfew for Jews. It's all the same! The same!] (274). Huston, of Anglophone Canadian origin, and Sebbar have been friends since their involvement in the Paris feminist movement in the 1970s, and they published their correspondence on exile, *Lettres parisiennes*, in 1986. The convergence of their interests and concerns is as evident in the late 1990s as it was a decade earlier.

Sebbar's own treatment of the massacre in *La Seine était rouge*, which relies on historical and archival documents as well as earlier literary rewritings, is the most detailed in French literature to date. Although all the fiction writers already discussed endowed the massacre with symbolic significance for specific constituencies, none of them used it as the main part of their narratives. Sebbar's novel is the only one so far to focus entirely on the memory of October 1961 or to attempt to include the perspectives of all those involved. In Sebbar's rewriting, anamnesis is shown to be a collective endeavor, which occurs across generations, genders, political persuasions, and ethnic origins.[15] For this reason, her novel presents the points of view of French police officers, harkis, Algerian demonstrators, French porteurs de valises, and other eyewitnesses from various walks of life. Several of her characters insist on the partiality of truth and the unreliability of memory, thus highlighting the need for assembling as many forms of testimony as possible if anamnesis is to take place.[16]

Sebbar pays homage to those who came before her and whose activism and testimony afforded her the historical information that she needed to write *La Seine*. As we will see in detail with respect to Djebar in Chapter 4, Sebbar thus provides the reader with her *Isnad* (the chain of transmission of knowledge), albeit a secular one in this case. Besides naming novelists, she also dedicated her novel to a wide range of other figures interested in the massacre: journalist Paulette Péju, historian Jean-Luc Einaudi, writer Anne Tristan, filmmaker Jacques Panijel, photographer Elie Kagan, and publisher François Maspéro (who helped some of the wounded during the demonstration and whose bookstore appears in Sebbar's novel), as well as the Comité [Committee] Maurice Audin.[17] Without forcing the issue, Sebbar provides her audience with most of the names necessary for further research on the topic. She thus inserts her novel in a four-decades-old tradition of recovery and of bearing witness in the face of censorship and silencing. Indeed, of the texts by authors she mentions in the *dédicace* (dedication) or elsewhere, several were censored and seized by the French government—books by Péju and by the Comité Maurice Audin, books published by Maspéro (including two by Frantz Fanon), Maurienne's *Le Déserteur*, and Jacques Panijel's film *Octobre à Paris* (Stora, *Ils venaient* 297–98; Einaudi 273–74).

The concerns for a young, multicultural audience that Sebbar evinced in the 1980s were still at the forefront for her at the turn of the millennium. The novel takes place thirty-five years after the October 17, 1961, massacre, and its main characters were all born after 1961. Amel, one of the main characters, is a sixteen-year-old girl of Algerian descent whose grandparents and mother (then a seven-year-old) participated in the demonstration. Omer is a twenty-seven-year-old Algerian journalist who had to leave Algeria and came to France illegally because he feared for his life in the current political climate. Finally, Louis, the twenty-five-year-old son of Flora (a former porteuse de valises), is making a documentary film on the massacre. These three central characters are connected through previ-

ous generations of women who all fought for the independence of Algeria:
Amel's mother, Noria, and grandmother, Lalla; Omer's mother, Mina; and
Louis's mother, Flora; all know each other.

In a way, Amel, Omer, and Louis represent the diverse constituencies
(immigrant, Algerian, and French) who have a need for anamnesis regarding both the Algerian war in general and the October 17 massacre in
particular. That the process of anamnesis is fraught with difficulties is
highlighted by the fact that the three characters often clash in their interpretations and over how the event should be memorialized. Tensions arise
between Omer and Louis when Omer uses the word "vous" [you] to refer
to the French in general. Louis, whose parents were considered traitors
during the war for aligning themselves with the Algerian nationalists, is
incensed at Omer's historical oversimplifications (29–30). Later, Omer also
includes Amel in this "vous," eliciting a similarly strong response from her
(83). Indeed, Amel and Omer often argue about issues of politics, identity,
and history (39–40, 54–55, 116–17). In these moments, Omer learns that
simplistic dichotomies (French versus Algerian) cannot fully account for
the events of the Algerian war or for the multiple identities and politics of
people of French nationality.

At the same time, each character brings something different, yet
crucial, to the process of anamnesis. Due to their lack of knowledge
about the October massacre, Amel and Louis set out to unearth information about the past, which Amel's family will not discuss with her:
the book begins with the cryptic sentence, "Sa mère ne lui a rien dit,
ni la mère de sa mère" [Her mother told her nothing, and neither did
her mother's mother] (13). Similarly, Louis's mother is at first reticent
to testify about her political commitment as a former porteuse de valises (26). This personal silence echoes the general lack of public discourse about the Algerian war in France and highlights the necessity of
creating a space for its anamnesis. It is precisely this intergenerational
silence about the war that incites Amel and Louis to begin their search
for information. Louis's contribution takes the form of a film, which is
reminiscent of Jacques Panijel's 1962 documentary on the massacre,
Octobre à Paris. Although Amel's mother will not tell her daughter
about the massacre, she agrees to bear witness in front of Louis's camera. As for Omer and Amel's contribution, it is expressed through graffiti, often a subversive and fragmentary form of self-inscription favored
by the powerless. They write graffiti on well-known monuments to
other historical conflicts, thus creating a palimpsest that provides a
transgressive response to the lack of official commemoration of the
Algerian war in France.

As part of her search, Amel takes Omer on a journey through Paris. Geography features prominently in the process of reconstructing history, as the characters retrace the itinerary of the 1961 demonstration from the Nanterre shantytown where Amel's family used to live to the various places where the demonstration was repressed: subway stations, city intersections, major monuments.[18] The names of these locations, together with the names of people who testify, are used as chapter headings. Already, in her 1982 *Shérazade*, Sebbar had used the Table of Contents to provide a cartography of the title character's identity and inner world. From the Table of Contents on, *La Seine était rouge* presents itself as a multivalent *lieu de mémoire* [site of memory]—the Table of Contents brings together the various memories necessary for national reconciliation through anamnesis. In doing so, Sebbar is also modeling her novel's structure on Einaudi's *Bataille de Paris*, in which, in his methodical description of October 17, he begins each section with the name of the place where specific events happened.

Like other writers, Sebbar draws parallels between the October massacre and events of World War II. One of the people who had been present at the demonstration speaks to Amel and Omer about it for the first time thirty-five years later, saying: "C'est l'affaire Papon qui a remué tout ça" [The Papon affair stirred it all up again] (*Seine* 103). Like other writers before her, Sebbar explicitly names Papon as the party responsible for ordering the repression of the demonstration.[19] In addition, as Amel and Omer criss-cross Paris, they find themselves in front of several historical plaques referring to France's resistance to the Germans during World War II (29, 111). Interestingly, the text of the plaques is never reproduced in its entirety, as there is always something masking part of it (56, 111). That the text is "incomplet" [incomplete] suggests that such memorials only tell a partial truth and can be used to mask other, occluded events of French history (111). As Norindr argues in a different context, official commemoration hides as much as it reveals.

The first plaque that Omer and Amel overwrite is on the wall of the La Santé prison; it read: "En cette prison le 11 novembre 1940 furent incarcérés des lycéens et des étudiants qui à l'appel du Général de Gaulle se dressèrent les premiers contre l'occupant" [In this prison, on November 11, 1940, high school and university students were incarcerated because they were the first to rise up against the occupier at General de Gaulle's call] (29). Next to the plaque, they write in red spray paint, "1954–1962: Dans cette prison furent guillotinés des résistants algériens qui se dressèrent contre l'occupant français" [1954–1962: In this prison, Algerian resistors were guillotined because they rose up against the French occupier] (30). The symmetry of the language used in the two sentences (the dates, the similar syntaxes, the usage of the words, "rose up against," "occupier," and "resistors"—the last, a word usually reserved for the French who fought against the Nazi occupation—to refer to the Algerians) underscores the parallels between the actions of the French against the Algerians during the Algerian war and those of the Nazis against the French during World War II. Omer and Amel's rewriting is all the more subversive since the French are represented as occupiers, even though the October massacre took place in the heart of Paris. The juxtaposition of the graffiti with official commemorations of World War II highlights the metonymic chain between the Vichy and the Algeria syndromes.

In another example, when Omer and Amel find themselves in front of the famous Crillon hotel, they leave behind graffiti that reads, "Ici des Algériens ont été matraqués sauvagement par la police du préfet Papon le 17 octobre 1961" [Here, Algerians were savagely clubbed by Prefect Papon's police force on October 17, 1961] (88). This graffiti is reminiscent of actual graffiti that was painted on one of the Paris bridges a few years after the massacre—"Ici on noie les Algériens" [Here Algerians are being drowned].[20]

The three main characters' contributions to anamnesis are revealed to be interrelated, as well as being dependent on the testimonies of the earlier generation, who witnessed, and participated in, the demonstration. Interdependence is a prominent theme in the novel and constitutes one of its organizational principles. It is Amel's personal search for the past that inspires Omer, while Louis includes Amel's mother's testimony in his film and Amel is comforted in her search by Louis's film. Similarly, as Louis is looking for Amel all over Paris, he comes across the graffiti and includes them in his film. The theme of interdependence is further reflected *en abyme* in Louis's film, which replicates the organizational structure of Sebbar's text, relying as it does on archival documents as well as recent interviews. The structure that divides the story of Amel's mother Noria into six parts, which are juxtaposed with other chapters relating to 1961 and 1996, highlights the dialectical movement between past and present that lies at the heart of anamnesis. Every chapter before a section of Noria's testimony ends with the sentence, "Amel entend sa mère" [Amel hears her mother] or "Amel entend la voix de sa mère" [Amel hears her mother's voice] (32, 40, 57, 83, 111), but before the last installment, the structure of the sentence changes to "*On* entend la voix de *la* mère" [*We* hear *the* mother's voice] (126, italics added). The new formulation of the sentence, with its use of the generic "*on*," highlights the way in which the process of anamnesis has widened to include the community at large. Anamnesis occurs when the generation that lived through an event and the next generation come together to find ways to uncover and memorialize it. Through the shift from "sa mère" [her mother] to "la mère" [the mother], Noria comes to emblematize the mother of all those participating in the process. Sebbar thus suggests that national reconciliation can only occur when the conflicting memories of all those involved in a traumatic event are woven together into a collective narrative of the past deed of violence. By providing a fictional account of the memories of October 17, 1961, Sebbar engages with French historical amnesia once again and helps French memory move into the third phase of the Algeria syndrome.

La Seine était rouge ends in a very open-ended manner with the three young protagonists meeting again in Egypt. Already, in the Shérazade trilogy, Sebbar had moved the action from Paris in the first volume, *Shérazade*; to the rest of France in the second, *Les Carnets de Shérazade*; and to the Middle East (specifically Lebanon) in *Le Fou de Shérazade*. One of the ways in which Sebbar deals with the history of colonial violence in her works is to open her texts to other contexts of violence and war. For example, several of her short stories treat the Bosnian war. Her 1999 collection of short stories, *Soldats* [Soldiers], juxtaposes wars in Algeria, Bosnia, Cambodia, Chechnya, France, Israel/Palestine, and Somalia. The remainder of this chapter will elucidate the role the Middle East plays in Sebbar's literary reconstructions of history, with a specific focus on her 1991 *Le Fou de Shérazade*.

Beyond the Algeria Syndrome

In her novels, Sebbar creates new definitions of French identity based on métissage. *Le Chinois vert d'Afrique* goes beyond a situation blocked by the Algerian/French dualism by pointing to a third focus, Vietnam. Sebbar also makes parallels between the Palestinian situation and the Algerian war as similar colonization struggles (156–57). Since questions of identity and nationalism are often wrestled with through wars, and since these questions are at the heart of Sebbar's concerns, it is not surprising that her texts become a palimpsest of wars overlapping each other. In *Le Fou de Shérazade* (1991), the third installment in her Shérazade trilogy, the Algerian/French conflict is linked to contemporary wars affecting the Arab world, especially in Lebanon and Palestine/Israel. In this way, the Maghreb (the western part of the Arab world) and the Mashrik (the eastern part of the Arab world) are brought together in the text. Beur identity is shown to be part of a larger group identity: it is part of the Arab world as well as French and Algerian, Tunisian, or Moroccan. The *mise en relation* (putting into relation) of different wars, including the one in Vietnam, is generated by what is perceived as a common violence done to different people and expressed in the texts through the repetition of similar violent occurrences.

In *Le Fou de Shérazade*, the link is made between the different wars by insisting on the similarities between fighting men. This creates the feeling that all the wars are pointless, since the enemies look alike and act identically. For instance, in Beirut, Shérazade is taken hostage by an unidentified group of Arab men, who are in turn arrested by a group of Arab enemy militiamen. She changes hands for the first time in what is to be a long series of exchanges, in which she is treated in exactly the same way. Both groups think that she is a spy; they question and threaten her. As in *Le Chinois vert d'Afrique*, the link between war and sexuality is foregrounded in both cases. Two men from the first group want to rape her and leave her in a ditch, saying: "[E]lle est seule, personne la réclamera, les femmes restent à la maison sinon . . ." [She's alone, no one will come asking for her, women stay home, otherwise . . .] (*Fou* 20). This comment points to the symbolic transgression created by the young woman, who is outside, alone, in a country torn by civil war. The man's remark is also used by Sebbar as a direct criticism of the world order for which the guerrillas are fighting, since it indicates how conservative these male revolutionaries are when it comes to sexual politics. Their attitude toward Shérazade casts a doubt over their entire political venture.

As Lebanese writer and critic Evelyne Accad argued in her book *Sexuality and War*, "[S]exuality is centrally involved in motivations to war, and if women's issues were dealt with from the beginning, wars might be avoided, and revolutionary struggles and movements for liberation would take a very different path" (27). With the second militia, the man searching Shérazade takes advantage of the situation to touch her sexually against her will. Sexual violence, from verbal to physical, is structurally shown to be a weapon of war, since it takes place at the same time as the leader is interrogating Shérazade: the episode of sexual violence is framed by two slaps in the face inflicted on her by the leader. Later on, a subsequent jailer will attempt to rape her. After she changes captors for the fourth time, her new jailer alternates between forcefully kissing her and slapping her, then repeats the process. This series of changes that always end up returning to the same state emphasizes the irrationality of a war in which enemy factions behave in similar ways. This, in turn, is reinforced by the parallel established between the different Lebanese militias and the gangs of little boys in the Parisian housing project: the boys are all dressed more or less alike and all look very similar. The narrator asks: "Qui sont les ennemis? . . . Eux savent distinguer l'ennemi" [Who is the enemy? Only they know how to tell friend from foe] (*Fou* 47). Sebbar criticizes the leaders of pointless and brutal wars for acting like young gang leaders (48).

When she is finally freed, Shérazade ends up meeting Jaffar, a young Beur like her.[21] Stopped by more militiamen in Beirut, they are once again treated with disrespect and humiliated. Jaffar makes a parallel between the Lebanese militiamen and French police officers (171). He dislikes the police because, in France, they tend to treat children of immigrants like him violently and in racially motivated ways. The Arab fighters are thus compared to the French police, a force antagonistic to Maghrebians both in contemporary France and in Algeria during the war, when the police participated in the torture of suspected guerrillas. Not only, then, are all Lebanese enemy factions thus collapsed into one, but in a scathing move, they are compared to the French military colonizer in Algeria. From Shérazade's first encounter with the Lebanese soldiers on, Sebbar consistently makes parallels between yesterday's colonizing warriors and today's freedom fighters: Shérazade "ne voit pas tout de suite le soldat debout devant elle, raide, jambes écartées, mitraillette à l'épaule. Elle sursaute à la voix. C'est presque le même soldat, celui qu'elle a regardé souvent dans la vitrine d'un libraire à Paris. Une photographie de la guerre d'Algérie. Le militaire français surveille un enterrement arabe" [doesn't see right away the soldier standing upright in front of her, his legs planted firmly on the ground, with a machine-gun hanging from his shoulder. The sound of his voice startles her. He's almost the exact same soldier as the one she used to contemplate in a bookstore's display window in Paris. A photograph of the Algerian war. The French soldier is keeping watch on an Arab funeral] (17). The scene photographed reinforces the trenchant nature of the parallel between French and Lebanese soldiers: the Lebanese civil war is implicitly condemned as "an Arab funeral." Later on, Shérazade will compare her fourth captor to French paratroopers in Algeria (101).

The photograph of the Algerian war provides the link, not only between contemporary Arab (civil) wars and the Algerian war, but also between the Shérazade trilogy and *Le Chinois vert d'Afrique*. Sebbar likes to weave allusions to previous books into more recent ones to create a feeling of community and belonging in the midst of the fragmentation of exile. In *Le Chinois*, the photograph of the Algerian war is a central element in the formation of the young métis's fragmented identity. He has seen the

picture in the very same bookstore as Shérazade and he also owns a copy
of it, which he religiously keeps in his cabin. Shérazade and Mohamed are
brought together across two different novels through their fascination for
the same object.

In *Le Fou de Shérazade*, the link between sexuality and war is foregrounded
again in the character of Michel Salomon, a Jewish freelance photographer
and reporter covering the Lebanese civil war. Photographing violent war
scenes is sexually exciting for him (129–30). The repetition of the link
between sexuality and war in the words and actions of Arab, Jewish, and
French men places the bulk of the responsibility for wars on the side of
masculinist warrior values.[22] Violence and war, no matter where they origi-
nate or for what purpose, are shown as harmful, and militias, whether in
war-torn Lebanon or suburban France, are exposed as being grounded in a
terrorist use of power.

Just as Djebar foregrounds the formerly erased presence of Algerian
women in the wars (as discussed in the next chapter), Sebbar also insists
on the presence of women on the site of wars, but mostly as agents of
peace rather than as direct participants in the war. The absurdity of the
Lebanese civil war is exemplified by the endless repetitions of the same
blocked situation. Sebbar hints at a possible cause for the problem: the
apparent absence of women around the militias. On several occasions,
Shérazade hopes to be transferred to a place where women would be present
(*Fou* 44), but she never hears a female voice (46). Like Accad, Sebbar
seems to imply that if the sexual politics changed in countries such as
Lebanon, if women's voices were allowed to be expressed and listened to,
the entire political situation might change. And indeed, the women's voices
heard in the text are saying very different things from those of the male
guerrillas.

Apart from Shérazade's presence, the only sign pointing to the hope of
peace in Beirut is the half-destroyed home of an old Lebanese lady who
gives Shérazade shelter. She and her Egyptian maid have chosen not to flee
like so many others but to remain within the confines of her house, refusing the civil war (162). Here, Sebbar follows a pattern that Miriam Cooke,
in *War's Other Voices*, described in the following way: "[I]t was the women
who stayed, and the men who left" in Lebanon during the civil war;
according to Cooke, this pattern then reemerged in Lebanese fiction about
the war (132). The old Lebanese lady's voice and presence mix with those
of another old woman who, for a similar love of peace, engages in an
opposite venture, setting out on a long journey away from her village. For
the film in which Shérazade is to star, an old olive tree from the woman's
village was uprooted and transported into the housing project's courtyard

by a group of male workers whom the old woman had opposed in vain. Accompanied by a young girl and a dove, the old woman sets out on foot to find the stolen symbol of peace and to force the men to bring it back. Her trek parallels Shérazade's own journey.

The novel opens on a single sentence on a separate page, before the first chapter: "Shérazade attend, assise au pied de l'olivier" [Sherazade is waiting, sitting under the olive tree] (*Fou* 7). From the very beginning, Shérazade is presented as ready for peace, waiting for it. On her way to Jerusalem, the city on whose name the word "salem"—peace in both Hebrew and Arabic—is inscribed, she is forced to stop in a place symbolic of war, Beirut. Just as it is difficult for Shérazade to reach Jerusalem, it is very difficult for Jerusalem to find peace, since wars (religious or not) have been fought there for centuries. However, Shérazade's search for peace, like the old woman's search for the olive tree, generates other peace seekers, including some men. For instance, Shérazade's search triggers her pied-noir boyfriend, Julien's, own trip to Jerusalem to find her; in the old woman's village, a little boy is watching over the olive tree's hole for her; and in the housing project, boys, girls, and women participate in protecting the tree when the filmmaker wants to uproot it again. This time, it is the film crew that is unsuccessful, perhaps because now it is opposed, not just by a single old woman, but by a community (105–7). Similarly, toward the end of the novel, in the Palestinian occupied territories, Israeli soldiers come with bulldozers intending to uproot an entire field of olive trees. Palestinian women, together with Shérazade, oppose them through nonviolent resistance, sitting under the trees and waiting, putting their lives on the line (196).[23]

The book progresses from the description of a lone peace seeker (Shérazade under the olive tree in the epigraph, the old woman against the film crew uprooting the tree) to that of community resistance against destruction and violence. It points to the necessity of coalition building in order to successfully oppose war and violence. The women are victorious, since the soldiers never come back (196). The community metaphorically preserves a possibility of peace, neither through surrendering nor through violence, but through a (perhaps utopian) third way—also advocated by Evelyne Accad—that of "nonviolent active struggles" (*Sexuality* 41). For Accad, as for Sebbar, "The alternative to violence is neither reconciliation, love, nor peace, but only a nonviolent struggle aiming at fighting against injustice and oppression" (41).

Sebbar also treats the Palestinian-Israeli war through the character of Yaël, a young Moroccan Jew now living in Israel. Yaël is doing her com-

pulsory military service, but, unlike her brother, says she would desert the
army rather than go to the occupied territories and murder Palestinian
children (*Fou* 65). Yaël, who looks a little like Shérazade, is seen by Julien
as Shérazade's "soeur ennemie" [enemy sister] (64), thus reinforcing the
links between the two women and beyond them, between populations
that have been opposed in recent history.

In the last two pages of the novel, Julien's film is finally being shot. The
scene, taking place in the house of the old woman in Beirut, stages "la
rencontre entre une Palestinienne et une Israélienne, Yaël et Shérazade,
l'Arabe joue la Juive et la Juive l'Arabe, ainsi en a décidé le réalisateur"
[the encounter between a Palestinian woman and an Israeli woman, Yaël
and Sherazade, the Arab woman playing the Jewish woman and the Jewish
one the Arab one, as the director has decided] (202). In the film, which is
a *mise en abyme* of the novel, the Maghreb and the Mashrik, Algeria and
Palestine, are once again brought together through Shérazade.

Reminiscent of the structuring of Djebar's novels, *Le Fou de Shérazade*
had its origin in the weaving together of three different, but related, stories: the film set in the housing project, Shérazade's journey, and the old
woman's trek. They slowly begin to merge as Julien leaves the film set for
Jerusalem in search of Shérazade; the stories converge in the last chapters
of the book, as all the characters make it (back) to the film set. The
constant deferral of the film, due to Shérazade's absence, is what allows the
book to be written. This movement of deferral was already present in the
first part of the trilogy, when Julien began writing the script of that same
film (*Shérazade* 145/156). The scenario evolves with each of Shérazade's
departures and returns. Writing is thereby shown to be a dynamic process
in which both characters participate.

The film's role reversal between Yaël and Shérazade opens up an imaginary space for the beginning of a new conceptualization of peace. In the
script, however, the house is bombed and the three women die. This could
be interpreted as a critique of the role of Western powers in the war and
peace process in the Middle East, since it exposes the peace invented and
imposed by the West as being an illusion based on a simplistic understanding of the situation in the Middle East. The last words of the novel
are those of Meriem, Shérazade's sister. She is comforting her mother, who
did not realize that a film was being shot and thought that Shérazade had
really died: "Shérazade n'est pas morte. C'est le film. . . . Shérazade est
vivante, vivante . . . vivante" [Sherazade isn't dead. It's a film. . . . Sherazade
is alive, alive . . . alive] (203).

If, indeed, Shérazade, like the olive tree, represents the hope for
peace in the novel, then the possibility of peace remains, but perhaps

not on Western men's terms, since it is heralded by a young Beur woman. It is also a peace that will be long in the making, since Meriem and her mother have been waiting to hear from Shérazade since the beginning of the first book of the trilogy (*Shérazade* 35/34). What has been destroyed in the film is, not the real Shérazade, the real possibility of peace, but the staging of both by Western men, perhaps because these men cannot conceive of a peace originating through grassroots, Middle Eastern community movements. In spite of the very negative context of violence, war, and death, the novel ends on a positive note, the reunion of Shérazade and her relatives as a symbol for possible peace in the Middle East and beyond.

Both Sebbar and Djebar foreground a history of violence in their fiction. Sebbar also insists on its corollary: the possibility of a peace brought about by the efforts of a community in which women and children would play a central role. As Djebar tries to (re)construct a dislocated identity by doing violence to her French intertexts, Sebbar attempts to build an imaginary space for a reality that does not yet exist, a utopia. Both writers, through fiction, create "imagined communities" (see Anderson) by foregrounding the experiences of war and suffering.

Notes

1. Sebbar's novel was published the year following the decree. Historian Benjamin Stora noted that 1986 was the first year in which students taking the Baccalauréat [French high school exit exam] in a few regions were asked questions on the Algerian war (*Gangrène* 353).

2. In *Le Sourire de Brahim*, Nacer Kettane also associates racist violence with police and soldiers who had been sent to Algeria during the war (132, 162).

3. The choice of Tuilier's name is extremely interesting, as it reflects a case of fiction prophetically dovetailing with reality. In summer 1986, two years after the publication of *Le Chinois*, a twenty-five-year-old woman of Maghrebian descent was first strangled, and then raped and robbed by two enlisted French soldiers, named Leterrier and Thuillier, who left behind the message, "La France est en guerre contre les Arabes" [France is at war with the Arabs] (Giudice 208). The two were arrested and condemned to life sentences. Fausto Giudice, reporting the incident, concluded that the two young men "se sont trompés d'époque et de territoire. Auraient-ils fait la même chose trente ans plus tôt dans la première mechta venue, ils seraient aujourd'hui de tranquilles pères de famille attendant leur retraite" [got the era and the territory wrong. Had they done the same thing thirty years earlier in any *mechta* (village), they would now be peaceful family men waiting for retirement] (209). This com-

ment uncannily parallels the novel's episode in which the wartime rape and killing exploits of Marcel (now a member of Tuilier's militia) and his company in Algeria are enthusiastically recounted by Tuilier himself (235, discussed later in this chapter).

4. The name is ironic in that it is a tribute to a Communist leader from a conservative man for whom communism is a code word for the loss of law and order. On the other hand, it is significant in that it foregrounds Tuilier's admiration for the kind of strong, totalitarian form of leadership he would like to exercise over his community and against young people like Mohamed.

5. Le Pen, as Rousso mentions, was predictably a supporter of French Algeria (210). In the first years of the war, Le Pen served as a *parachutiste* (paratrooper) in Algeria, an intoxicating experience for him (Rioux 135), which may have included his participation in torture during the (in)famous Battle of Algiers (Stora, *Gangrène* 290). In *Le Chinois*, Tuilier, commenting on the wars in Indochina and Algeria, says that "La France a tout perdu" [France has lost everything], indicating once again a lingering sense of loss about the wars that significantly informs his thoughts and actions twenty years later (135).

6. France 2 evening news, April 24 and 26, 1995.

7. The French comic group Les Inconnus—three young French men, one black, one of Maghrebian origin, and one white—created a powerful satire of this French paranoid tendency in one of their early 1990s skits, "Les Envahisseurs." Ostensibly a parody of the U.S. science-fiction television series *The Invaders*, the skit shows a white Frenchman trying to warn other French people and authorities that "the invaders are among us," only to discover that it is too late: everybody he encounters has already turned into an Arab.

8. Papon's collaboration with the Nazis in sending more than 1,500 Jewish people to concentration camps during World War II was uncovered in 1981; he was found guilty of complicity in a crime against humanity in a 1997–1998 trial. He appealed this judgment to the highest French court, the Cour de Cassation. In October 1999, days before his appeal was to be considered, Papon fled the country (Dumay 1). He was caught in Switzerland and extradited to France. The Cour de Cassation rejected his appeal, and he was incarcerated in the Fresnes prison to begin serving his ten-year sentence.

9. As early as 1967, Claire Etcherelli had mentioned several *ratonnades* (beatings of Arabs) (in her famous novel of the working class, *Elise ou la vraie vie*). However, she did not specifically treat the Algerian demonstration and its brutal repression. Einaudi mentions that for the twentieth anniversary of the massacre, articles about it appeared (in 1980 and 1981) in newspapers such as *Libération*, *Les Nouvelles littéraires*, *Le Monde*, and *Sans frontière* (Einaudi 278–80, 294).

10. Lallaoui also coedited a three-volume book with David Assouline, *Un siècle d'immigration en France*, whose third volume includes a short section on the events of October 1961. He contributed to Anne Tristan's investigative report and picture book on the massacre, *Le Silence du fleuve*

(1991). Tristan's name is also mentioned in Sebbar's *dédicace* (dedication). There is an intertextual reference to *Le Silence du fleuve* in the title of one of Sebbar's novels, *Le Silence des rives*, which was published two years after Tristan's book.

11. See Daeninckx, *Ecrire en contre* 120–21. More than 100,000 copies of his *Meurtres pour mémoire* were sold in the 1980s (Einaudi 282). The book was made into a TV movie of the same title by Laurent Heynemann in 1989 (and was reissued in paperback in 1998).

12. For an excellent (and less critical) analysis of Daeninckx's novel, see Josiane Peltier.

13. The phrase was first used by Pierre Vidal-Naquet (see Hamon and Rotman 363). For details on Mattei's involvement in Henri Curiel's network, see Hamon and Rotman 240.

14. As recently as February 1999, Papon took historian Jean-Luc Einaudi to court for libel after Einaudi used the word *massacre* in a May 8, 1998, *Le Monde* article devoted to the events of October 17. For years, the official number of deaths on October 17 had been three. Papon's libel suit prompted a reopening of the dossier by the government (Papon seems to have been unaware at the time of Einaudi's status as a historian of October 17). Just a few days after photographer Elie Kagan's death, Papon argued at the trial that Kagan's pictures of the 1961 massacre (almost the only pictures of the event to have survived French censorship) were retouched (Benayoun 67). As a response, Jacques Panijel's film, *Octobre à Paris,* was shown at the trial (Sebbar, personal written communication, September 21, 1999). Not only does Kagan's name figure in Sebbar's dedication page, she also mentions him in the novel and describes his pictures, which are featured in the film made by her protagonist, Louis (85–87, 105). Papon lost the suit, and the French government's official number of deaths as of May 1999 is now at least forty-eight (the new report acknowledges the deficiency of some archival documents). FLN estimations run between 200 and 300 deaths (Herzberg, *Le Monde* electronic edition, July 13, 1999).

15. For detailed discussions of anamnesis in the postcolonial context, see Lionnet, *Autobiographical Voices,* and my "Between Amnesia and Anamnesis."

16. See especially pages 17, 26, 29–30, 68–69, 106, 113, 125.

17. See pages 107, 115, 119–20. The story of Maspéro helping a teenage Algerian boy escape the police force is included in Sebbar's book (see Tristan 67; Sebbar, *Seine* 62).

18. In *Les Carnets de Shérazade* (1985), the reader follows a similar itinerary as the protagonist retraces the 1983 march against racism known as the Marche des Beurs.

19. Papon is named several times in the novel (37, 42, 88, 101, 103).

20. A picture of this graffiti is reproduced in several books dealing with the events of October 17, 1961 (Assouline and Lallaoui 19; Tristan 99).

21. Jaffar also happens to be the protagonist of another of Sebbar's novels (outside the Shérazade trilogy), *J. H. cherche âme soeur* (1987).

22. Sebbar once again is not indicting all men, only masculinist values. In the novel, several men participate in peacemaking and community building. Sebbar thus avoids gender dichotomies while still criticizing male war leaders.

23. This episode recalls real-life grass-roots activism such as the highly successful Chipko Andolan (Hugging Movement) in India, in which "poor women who came out of the Gandhian movement have waged a nonviolent land reform and forest preservation campaign" by hugging trees to prevent them from being bulldozed by loggers. "Men have joined this campaign, although it was originated and continues to be led by women" (Ynestra King 132–33).

Chapter 3

Re-Membering Colonial History

[C]'est la mémoire qui dicte et l'histoire qui écrit [Memory dictates and history writes].
　　　　　　　　　　　—Pierre Nora, *Les Lieux de mémoire* xxxviii

Assia Djebar uses the Algerian war of liberation as the setting for several of her early novels and short stories, but it is in her 1985 work, *L'Amour, la fantasia*, that she explores the intersection of war, history, and personal story to the fullest. The novel centers on the history of conquest and violence between France and Algeria. As many critics have noted, Djebar's work follows a trajectory that goes from antiautobiographical writing (*La Soif* 1957) to autobiography (*Fantasia*, followed by *Vaste est la prison* in 1995). Djebar herself has often remarked on the dangerous nature of autobiographical writing for Arab women, especially when done in the colonizer's language. This difficulty, together with a different conception of the speaking subject as well as the feminist project of bringing women back into history, is conveyed through a constant blending of autobiography and history in Djebar's work. Intertextuality, intratextuality, and (individual and collective) memory play a crucial role in her writing, making it an "autobiographie au pluriel" [plural autobiography] (Abdel-Jaouad, "*L'Amour*" 25). As Hafid Gafaiti correctly notes, "[L]a production de Djebar est éclairée par le principe que l'histoire du sujet est un texte inscrit dans le champ général de l'Histoire. . . . le 'je' est porteur d'une expression et d'un message qui ne sont pas seulement personnels mais collectifs" [Djebar's literary production is illuminated by the idea that the history of the subject is a text inscribed within the general field of history. . . . the "I" carries an expression and a message that are not only personal but collective] ("Ecriture" 96–97).[1]

The film *La Nouba des femmes du Mont Chenoua* marks a turning point in Djebar's career. In 1969, when she already was a well-known novelist, she stopped publishing books for a period of about ten years and directed her first feature film, *La Nouba*, in 1977–1978.[2] The film received the grand prize at the Venice film festival in 1979 and was followed by *La Zerda ou les chants de l'oubli*, a 1982 documentary about Maghreb history between 1912 and 1942. In an interview, Djebar explained that it was her experience as a filmmaker that allowed her to go back to writing in French (Le Clézio 242–43). In 1980, she published a collection of short stories, *Femmes d'Alger dans leur appartement*, followed by *L'Amour, la fantasia* in 1985. In that novel, she set out for the first time to write "une préparation à une autobiographie" [a preparation for an autobiography] (Mortimer, "Entretien" 203), whereas beforehand she had viewed writing as a way "to keep as far away from my real self as possible" (quoted in Zimra, "Afterword" 168).

To film *La Nouba*, Djebar went back to the mountains of her childhood, fifteen years after the war of national liberation from the French, in order to interview her female relatives about their day-to-day wartime experiences. Both documentary and fiction, *La Nouba* follows the filmmaker's "alter ego," Lila, as she questions her relatives, thus reactivating her own memory of a war in which she lost many loved ones (Djebar, Comments made at the roundtable). *Fantasia* mixes the personal story of an unnamed female narrator and Algeria's history since the dawn of French colonization in 1830. The film's testimonies are incorporated into the third part of the novel. In *Vaste est la prison* (1995), the third volume of the projected quartet begun with *Fantasia* and followed by *Ombre sultane* (1987), Djebar similarly incorporated personal recollections of the film's shooting into the third part of the novel. In *Fantasia*, she puts the women's testimonies in relation, in dialogue, with the French colonial archives that she uses in the historical chapters of the first two parts of the book. The personal story and the collective history intersect again, since the women she interviews are relatives of hers.

Many parallels can be drawn between the film and the novel, in the movement from sound image to the written word, especially with respect to musical structure, the importance of the gaze, and the weight of history on the couple and on contemporary Algerian society. In this chapter, I focus mainly on one aspect of the links between film and novel, namely, the importance of women's memory in the project of rewriting history. As Djebar herself explained in an interview for the

Algerian newspaper *El Moudjahid,* "le sujet principal [du film] c'est le rôle des femmes dans la transmission orale de l'histoire nationale" [the main topic (of the film) is women's role in the oral transmission of the nation's history] ("Rétablir" 7). The close links between the transmission of that history and the retelling of a personal story are expressed through a series of superimpositions that give Djebar's entire work— and especially the film and the novel—a palimpsestic structure. The superimpositions are visible on at least three levels: the encounter between written, European archives and the oral transmission of history (as well as the insistence on the process of rewriting history through fiction); the multiplication of female voices and the parallels between different female figures; and, finally, the recurrence of temporal superimpositions between different periods of Algerian history.

Overwriting the Palimpsest of Algerian History

Throughout the novel, Djebar establishes a palimpsestic relationship between the French colonial archives and her own writing, between the oral testimonies of women and her autobiographical notes, between the colonizers' writings and the female, Algerian oral tradition. As Patricia Geesey noted, "By juxtaposing the two historical discourses [French archives and women's testimonies] . . ., Djebar recognizes that the common thread between the two is the Algerian woman herself" (161). Djebar reconstitutes the past, using documents that have already rewritten history. She is a historian by training, and the archives she uses as a historical base for her reconstruction of the past were for the most part written in French by military officers who were invading and conquering her country. An illustration of this can be seen in the thirty-seven accounts of the 1830 siege of Algiers: thirty-two are in French; only two are in Arabic; and none were written by women (*Fantasia* 55/44). These reports and letters are not objective or factual accounts; they do not reflect a historical truth. Rather, most of them are examples of the discourse of the military colonizer, which covers up the Algerian people as much as it reveals them. As Trinh T. Minh-ha stated in *Woman, Native, Other,* "[H]istorical analysis is nothing other than the reconstruction and redistribution of a pretended order of things, the interpretation or even transformation of documents given and frozen into monuments. The re-writing of history is therefore an endless task, one to which feminist scholars have devoted much of their energy" (84). For people whose histories have been erased, this rewriting assumes a particular urgency. As Françoise Lionnet explained in *Autobiographical Voices,* women from colonized backgrounds "need to find their past, to trace lineages that will empower them to live in the present, to rediscover the histories occluded by History" (25–26). It is precisely in such a rewriting that Djebar engages.

For Djebar, Algeria is the "prey" of Western military discourse, a discourse she deconstructs/reconstructs as fiction (*Fantasia* 56/45). By placing a colonialist interpretative grid on the Algerians' actions, the Frenchmen created stories ("des histoires") at the same time as a history ("l'Histoire"). As a discourse, history is therefore shown to be very close to fictional narratives. This move is of strategic importance for a people whose history has been distorted and/or erased under a colonizer's discourse. Foregrounding the fictional nature of colonial history empowers the writer to seize fiction as a legitimate means of reconstructing her past: "Her task will be to take on the 'official' record of the French colonial conquest of Algeria, itself a rewriting of historical fact, and to rewrite this rewriting from the perspective of the colonized subject" (Murdoch 75). Djebar expresses a strong desire to insert into history the voices that had been silenced by the lack of a writing: "Or l'ennemi revient sur l'arrière. Sa guerre à lui apparaît muette, sans écriture, sans temps de l'écriture" [But the enemy slips back in the rear. *His* war appears mute, without writing, without time for writing] (*Fantasia* 68/56). The use of the word "enemy" to refer to the Algerians at this particular point in the text foregrounds the mediation/veiling effected by the French archives; it reflects a French standpoint that is unable to account for an Algerian perspective. It is precisely the latter perspective that the novel aims to provide, at the same time as it foregrounds the difficulty of such a project.

Through the opacity of colonial archives, between their silences or abundance of words, the writer/historian scratches the surface in an attempt to decipher and bring to light the traces of the presence of her people. The Frenchmen's writings served to erase and/or distort the Algerian people by (mis)representing and colonizing them. As a writer, Djebar feels that she must reappropriate this discourse, rewrite it, and subvert it by decentering its perspective, operating what Gérard Genette, in *Palimpsestes*, calls a "*transfocalisation* narrative" [narrative *transfocalization*] (285). Nancy K. Miller, in her landmark essay, "Arachnologies," proposed a feminist strategy of "overreading," or "reading woman back in" (292). Djebar "overreads" the colonial archives, reading Algerian women and men back into history, and then *overwrites* their presence by writing over colonial documents, making her fictional text into a palimpsest. As Genette summarized, "Cette duplicité d'objet, dans l'ordre des relations textuelles, peut se figurer par la vieille image du *palimpseste*, où l'on voit, sur le même parchemin, un texte se superposer à un autre qu'il ne dissimule pas tout à fait, mais qu'il laisse voir par transparence" [Within textual relations, this double voicing can be understood through the ancient figure of the *palimpsest,* in which, on the same parchment, one can see a text superimposed onto another one which is not completely hidden but can still be seen through the light] (451).

For Genette, the palimpsest of intertextuality is primarily a question of mise en relation between two texts, two traditions (11). Djebar's novel centers on the double aspect of the mise en relation operated by intertextuality: it can provide a way to survive and bridge the violence of the past at the same time as it carries the possibility of more violence and disintegration. Indeed, using a palimpsest is, of necessity, a violent act, since it has traditionally entailed scraping off a previous inscription to cover it over with another. The palimpsest is a fitting metaphor for colonization, one of whose consequences is the forcible erasure of many traces of a people's history, culture, and way of life in order to replace them with the colonizer's. Successful colonization, like successful use of the palimpsest, would entail complete erasure of what was there before. However, in both cases, such complete erasure is impossible. Just as it is impossible to entirely wipe out a culture, there always remain on the palimpsest traces of the previous writing, even if it may require a special light to decipher them. Djebar provides this special light, a deeper gaze on the palimpsest of Algerian history, and does violence to colonial history by overwriting it from the perspective of the colonized. The traces of the French archives' ornate writing style, for example, were preserved on purpose in the historical chapters, whereas the style of the third part follows the women's oral phrasing (Djebar, Comments made at the Postkolonialismus . . . conference).

One can wonder why Djebar chose to place the first book of her projected quartet under the sign of colonial history. The first historical chapter opens in 1830, with the first written documents of France's conquest of Algiers. The historical loss brought about by colonization is dramatically staged by the lack in the novel of information predating 1830, although traces of a more distant past appear in the epigraphs (Saint Augustine, Ibn Khaldun).[3] In Algeria, it is impossible to start with a clean slate because of the history of colonization. Before one can look to the present and the future, one must come to terms with the scars of the colonial past on the palimpsest of historical discourse. Using 1830 as the novel's starting point is a postcolonial response to the overdetermination of colonial historiography, since French Orientalist historians took pains to make Algeria's history begin in 1830. The writer's task becomes one of exhuming her people's history like a spelaeologist (*Fantasia* 91/77), using fiction to flesh out "la plate sobriété du compte-rendu" [the flat restraint of a military report] (15). Overreading the French documents, Djebar's narrator wonders who will bear witness to what nineteenth-century Algerians, and especially women, thought and felt—who will account for the Algerian memory. In the French reports, Algerians are made invisible, just as on the battlefield, their guerrilla war strategies seem at times to render them invisible to the French army (68/56). Without their own records, Algerians are erased from a history written from the enemy's perspective.

Algerian women, kept in their homes, were, for the most part, invisible to the French soldiers, and because of the veil, they were also rendered invisible to most Algerian men. Their enforced silence cries for a spokes-person: "Qui le dira, qui l'écrira? . . . que se disent les femmes de la ville?" [Who will say it, who will write of it? . . . what are the women of the town saying to each other?] (15–16/7–8). Answering this plea, Djebar searches the archives for traces of the presence of Algerian women throughout the history of conquest and war and recreates missing elements through fiction. She conjures up visions of the ancestors in the fantasia, the horse race in which she mixes love and death. The fantasia is used as a metaphor for two ambiguous relationships, one between the French and Algerian peoples and languages and the other between Algerian women and men. Women, hidden from view, are twice erased by history. Therefore, they must be made doubly present, once from the outside (Djebar centers on the accounts about women in the French narratives) and once from the inside (she insists on female voices and lineage in her autobiographical passages and enters in a dialogue with her female relatives). Women and their presence in the wars are foregrounded (see Mortimer, "Language" 303–5). Djebar insists on the importance of mediation (of archival docu-ments, of fiction), inscribing in the text the impossibility of completely restoring women's voices or, in other words, the impossibility of bypassing one's colonial past.

Under the veiling of the French words, Djebar exhumes "des scories," "des scrofules" [scrofulous excrescences] (*Fantasia* 68/55), "details" that the Frenchmen had unconsciously let slip through and that bear witness to the violence used against the Algerians, especially against women. For instance, in one officer's letter to a friend, she focuses on the casual description of "ce pied de femme que quelqu'un a tranché pour s'emparer du bracelet d'or ou d'argent ornant la cheville" [a woman's foot that had been hacked off to appropriate the anklet of gold or silver] (68/55). Such "details," which do not quite fit with the usual descriptions of the colonial war as a "divertissement viril" [manly sport] (68/55), are the trace of the repressed; they color the rest of the narratives: "Soudain les mots de la lettre entière ne peuvent sécher, du fait de cette incise: indécence de ces lambeaux de chair que la description n'a pu taire" [Suddenly as he inserts these words, they prevent the ink of the whole letter from drying, because of the obscenity of the torn flesh that he could not suppress in his description] (68/56). Djebar centers on this trace, bringing it to light in her rewriting of the historical palimpsest.

For instance, she gives her own version of an episode of the conquest in which the majority of the Ouled Riah tribe was ruthlessly asphyxiated in a cave by Colonel Pélissier. She uses his report to construct her own text, insisting on certain elements and filling in the unsaid blanks. She thus finds herself in the paradoxical position of having to be grateful toward the officers, such as Pélissier, who dared write about the violence inflicted on the Algerian people: "J'oserais presque le remercier d'avoir fait face aux cadavres, d'avoir cédé au désir de les immortaliser. . . . Pélissier, l'intercesseur de cette mort longue, . . . me tend son rapport et je reçois ce palimpseste pour y inscrire à mon tour la passion calcinée des ancêtres" [I am almost tempted to thank him for having faced the corpses, for having yielded to the desire to immortalize them. . . . Pélissier, as the intercessor of this long drawn-out death, . . . hands me his report and I receive this palimpsest on which I now inscribe the charred passion of my ancestors] (92–93/78–79). Using the French report as a point of departure, Djebar retells the story from an Algerian perspective. Without the existence of the report, without the violence that it described, she would not have been able to overwrite this massacre; its violence would have been banished from history and buried with the corpses.

In *War's Other Voices*, Miriam Cooke argued that "[w]ar, the organization of violence against another person, demands to be written. Violence, so that it does not become chaotic and bestial, must be ordered into a narrative sequence" (25). It is such a reconstruction of an initial chaotic experience, borne through the psyches and bodies of the colonized, that Djebar engages in, breaking the concept of chronological, linear historical time into a fragmented, cyclical fictionalized narrative. Telling war, writing war, is a deeply "transformative" process (Cooke, *War's Other Voices* 27), which allows Maghrebian writers, not only to gain some control over a painful experience, but also to foreground a point of view that had been erased by decades of historical writing done by the colonizing other, thus transforming history itself.

Djebar does not use only French documents in her work of reconstructing history. As an Algerian woman, she has access to the richness of an oral tradition transmitted by *les aïeules*, the foremothers. This tradition can be more accurate than the written word when it comes to knowing about one's ancestors. Talking about one of them, the novel's narrator exclaims: "Au-delà d'Oudja, sa trace disparaît dans les archives— comme si 'archives' signifiait empreinte de la réalité!" [Beyond Oudja, there is no longer any trace of him in the archives—as though "archives" meant the imprint of reality!] (201/177). Even though she is using the written medium, Djebar inscribes her work in the female oral tradition, in which she finds her inspiration. The oral tradition is part of Arabic memory, which, with its lapses and accidents, its erosions and traces, is "champ profond pour un labourage romanesque" [a deep field ripe for novels to furrow], as she pointed out in "Le romancier dans la cité arabe" (115). The oral tradition, because it weaves itself through the blanks and gaps of memory, participates in the palimpsestic nature of Djebar's project. It proves to be of utmost importance for the recovery of one's past, especially because the written record has been shown to lie.

Clashes can appear between the documents and the knowledge gained from the oral tradition. As an example, in the nineteenth century, when members of the narrator's family were taken as hostages and exiled, the French written and oral Algerian sources disagreed on the numbers: were there eight or forty-eight (including a pregnant woman)? It is clear which source Djebar chooses to follow as, a few chapters later, she recreates in dialogical form the story of that pregnant woman, filling in the blanks of history by using fiction. This dialogue between two women, between past and present, is also (as Dorothy S. Blair remarked in her Introduction to her translation of *Fantasia*) a dialogue between history and fiction, written and oral traditions: "Je t'imagine, toi, l'inconnue, dont on parle encore de conteuse à conteuse, . . . je prends place à mon tour dans le cercle d'écoute immuable. . . . Je te recrée, toi, l'invisible, . . . aïeule d'aïeule la première expatriée. . . . Je te ressuscite, au cours de cette traversée que n'évoquera nulle lettre de guerrier français" [I imagine you, the unknown woman, whose tale is handed down from storyteller to storyteller . . . now I too take my place in the unchangeable circle of listening. . . . I re-create you, the invisible woman, . . . foremother of foremothers, the first expatriate. . . . I resurrect you during that crossing that no letter from any French warrior was to allude to] (*Fantasia* 214/189). Here, Djebar does violence to her French intertext: she overrides/overwrites its authority with the oral historical tradition of her family. In his study of contemporary Muslim fiction, *Islam and Postcolonial Narrative*, John Erickson examined Djebar's tactics of displacement of master discourses. He assessed *Fantasia* as a text comprising "a multiplicity of equally valid narratives," which I consider a postmodern reading (54). Whereas Erickson sees a convergence between postcolonialism and postmodernism (27–31), he does not focus on the differences between the two and seems to subsume postcolonialism under the rubric of postmodernism. Yet Djebar, while certainly influenced by the postmodern narrative technique of fragmentation, clearly refuses to place all narratives on the same level and privileges nonhegemonic voices such as that of her pregnant ancestor. In this way, her texts enact specifically postcolonial, rather than postmodern, tactics of opposition.

In Djebar's text, the original violence done to the Algerians and to their history resurfaces through the use of the dialogical form. The pregnant ancestor, although brought to light by Djebar, does not speak in her own voice after years of erasure; the narrator addresses her in the second person in an attempt to render her present within her text, to place the past in dialogue with the present while at the same time insisting on the use of mediation necessary in the overwriting process. The use of the second-person pronoun thus bears witness to the violence of historical erasure in the colonial context.[4]

Mediated Dialogues: Women's Voices

In *Fantasia*, as in *La Nouba*, women's testimonies about their own experience of history can only be transmitted to the reader/spectator through a series of external mediations that foreground the aspects of *reconstitution* of such history and the *workings* of memory in the rewriting of a history erased by official versions. The narrator/filmmaker takes her place within the female, oral tradition: "Dire à mon tour. Transmettre ce qui a été dit, puis écrit" [It is now my turn to tell a tale. To hand on words that were spoken, then written down] (*Fantasia* 187/165). Such transmission is effected through the mediation of *translation* (from Arabic to French) and *transcription* (from oral to written words). The narrator constantly insists on the necessity of mediation in the novel, especially in the third (and last) part, with its explosion of narrative voices. Whereas the first two parts of the novel follow a point-counterpoint structure, passing from an autobiographical chapter to a historical one and shuttling between the first and third persons, in the third part, the structure and the use of pronouns become more complex: the women's testimonies are first rendered in the first person, and then taken up again in chapters in which the "I" belongs to the novel's narrator. At first, one does not realize that the "I" in the second chapter of the third part, titled "Voix" [Voice], is not the same as the narrator's in the preceding chapter, "Les deux inconnus" [The two strangers]. Yet the style of these chapters is so different, going from a complex and highly literary language to a voice that maintains itself as close to an oral style as possible, that a certain level of confusion is created in the reader. It is only in the next chapter in italics, "Clameur" [Clamour], that we are made to understand the double referent of the "I": the narrator rewrites and comments in the third person on the story that was just told in the first person, and reveals to us the protagonist's name, Chérifa. Chérifa then continues her narration in the following chapter. The shifts between the different narrative voices suggest both the close link between the varied experiences of women across generations and the complexity of the work of translation and transcription.

A similar technique is used in the film, in which different voices are often superimposed. The narrator's voice—a voice-over in French in the film's French version—often covers over in part that of her relative, who is speaking in the Algerian dialect, using the first-person pronoun to summarize or repeat her words in the other language. In one scene in particular, a woman begins to tell Lila her story; her voice is then covered by Lila's voice-over giving us a summary of what her aunt is saying. From time to time, the voice-over stops and the ongoing dialogue (subtitled in French) between the protagonist and her aunt can then be heard. In general, in the film, the French subtitles—which inherently cannot translate everything and thus leave blanks—create a third layer of mediation in the process of transmitting history. It is as if each voice gave the other the courage to continue to speak up through the means of female polyphony. Djebar has often remarked that it is the presence of anonymous women's whispers that allows her to speak and take up the pen (quoted in Mortimer, "Entretien" 203). Her use of polyphony also foregrounds the violent and dangerous aspect of this means of communication in which a voice invested with narrative authority, the voice-over, will inevitably run the risk of dominating the other voices. Ratiba Hadj-Moussa called this process a relation of "contamination-appropriation" between the two voices (202). Djebar's entire work reflects the impossibility of letting the "other" woman speak outside of the circulation of power, especially in a postcolonial context. Her heightened awareness of this impossibility and her concomitant refusal to "speak for" subaltern women partly explain Gayatri Spivak's interest in her work (see, for example, "Acting," "Echo," and "Examples").

In the novel, women's voices are transmitted, not only from dialectal Arabic to French, but also from oral to written form. The narrator, instead of trying to cover over this double mediation, foregrounds its implications after transmitting the story of Chérifa, a young fighter whose experience also provides the film with a running thread: "Petite soeur étrange qu'en langue étrangère j'inscris désormais, ou que je voile. . . . Ta voix s'est prise au piège; mon parler français la déguise sans l'habiller. A peine si je frôle l'ombre de ton pas!" [Strange little sister whom I henceforth inscribe—or veil—in the foreign tongue. . . . I have captured your voice; disguised it with my French without clothing it. I barely brush against the shadow of your footsteps!] (*Fantasia* 160–61/141–42). The multiplication of narrative voices from one chapter to the next in the novel and the superimposition of these same voices in the film have a double function. They reflect at the same time the desire that Djebar expressed in the overture to *Femmes d'Alger* "[de n]e pas prétendre 'parler pour,' ou pire 'parler sur,' à peine parler *près de*, et si possible *tout contre*" [not to claim to "speak for" or, worse, to "speak on," barely speaking *next to*, and if possible *very close to*] (8/2), and her awareness of the difficulty of such a project in a postcolonial context in which *letting* the other speak also necessarily entails *veiling* her speech: the dialogue between women in Djebar's work inscribes itself precisely in the interstices between sisterhood and appropriation, in the shuttling between "speaking for" and "speaking very close to."[5]

In the film as in the novel, the French language inserts itself between the women, like a veil. In the film, Lila's voice-over was first written in French by Djebar, cotranslated into Arabic, and then taken up again in French in the film's French version (Djebar, comments made at the roundtable). The superimposition, not only of voices, but also of female figures themselves, gives *La Nouba* a palimpsestic aspect. For instance, two central stories, Chérifa's and Zohra's, are repeated in the film (and in the novel as well). Thirteen-year-old Chérifa saw her brother Ahmed, a mudjahid, die in front of her. She spent two nights hiding from the French in a tree, climbing down only to retrieve the body in order to perform the purification ritual (*Fantasia* 136–38/121–22). Zohra, a farmer who had fed the mudjahidin, was punished by the French and her farm was burned down. She and her daughter had to spend the entire night outside, not daring to disturb any of her neighbors. In the film, these women's stories are acted out and replayed in a dream sequence following their narration. Through the medium of the dream, their memories also become Lila's.[6]

In Zohra's story, the use of counterpoint (i.e., the disjunction between sound and image) is to be noted. The story is first narrated by Lila's voice-over. The images shown at that time are from the present (Lila's visit to

Zohra, her relative). The contrast between Zohra and her daughter spending the night outside and Zohra's warm welcome toward Lila is striking.
In the dream sequence that follows, sound and image converge, but do
not merge. Zohra's testimony, in Arabic with French subtitles, now provides the voice-over for the actions being played out on the screen. Zohra
thus goes from the position of witness-storyteller to that of narrator of the
film. Oral dialectal Arabic, like French in the rest of the film, becomes the
language of the voice-over during the dream sequence.

Women's varied personal experiences intermingle without regard for
chronology.[7] A parallel is developed between Lila's and Chérifa's trajectories. For example, after a scene in a barn with her husband, Ali, Lila
tells him, "Je pars" [I'm leaving] before running toward her Jeep. In the
following scene, Chérifa's mother tells Lila: "Ma fille m'a dit, je pars"
[My daughter said to me, I'm leaving].[8] Lila and Chérifa have many
common points. Both have criss-crossed the mountains, be it on foot or
by car; as teenagers, both lost a brother to the war; moreover, we learn
from Lila's voice-over that during the war, both women were jailed in
the same prison. This comment is followed by the sentence, "Ouvrir de
nouvelles prisons" [To open new prisons] as the camera lingers on images of veiled women. Before the scene with Ali, Lila's voice-over had
already mentioned "mes anciens jours de prison. Pour en parler, il faudrait
en être vraiment sortie" [my days spent in prison. To be able to speak of
it, I would have to free myself from those memories]. For Lila as for the
other women, the struggle continues, not only through the memory of
the war of liberation, but also in the struggle for female freedom. In this
context, the fact that Lila's words, "I'm leaving," should echo Chérifa's
takes on a deeper meaning, connecting the national struggle with the
feminist struggle. In the same way, Lila creates a parallel between her
own situation and that of Zohra's daughter. Zohra then becomes her
mother: "Toutes les femmes errantes du passé deviennent ma mère. Et
c'est moi, l'enfant . . ." [All these women wandering in the past become
my mother. And I am the child. . .]. According to Ratiba Hadj-Moussa's
excellent study of *La Nouba*, "[L]a guerre (monumentale) constitue le
référent qui réalise la jonction entre le national et le féminin. Référent
. . . incontournable de la modernité algérienne" [the (monumental) war
constitutes the reference point that allows the junction between the
nation and the feminine, insofar as the war is the inescapable reference
point of Algerian modernity] (200). The many doublings in the film
give Lila the ability, not only to carry out this junction, but also to turn
to genealogy in order to create a bridge with nineteenth-century women's
war experiences.

After a freeze frame ends the dream sequence in which Chérifa's story was being replayed, the camera cuts to a close-up of Lila as a child, thus almost superimposing their two childhood faces. Lila's voice-over comments on the parallel between Chérifa and herself: "C'était elle, c'était moi. Moi, toute petite, dans le lit-cage. Ma grand-mère . . . me racontait, chaque soir, à sa manière, l'histoire de notre tribu" [That was her, that was me. Me, as a little girl, in the crib. Every night, my grandmother would tell me the story of our tribe, in her own special way]. The chain of oral transmission of history is made present, as several old women transmitting their historical knowledge to children appear on the screen. Then, the film shifts to the nineteenth century, with a flashback to the 1871 revolt of the Beni-Menacer. We learn in *Vaste* that, through her maternal grandfather's lineage, Djebar is the great grand-daughter of Malek el-Berkani, the leader who was killed during that large-scale rebellion (321–23). *La Nouba* briefly represents scenes of el-Berkani's insurrection which, although it "n'a eu droit à aucune relation écrite" [was granted no written account], keeps on being transmitted through the female oral tradition (*Vaste* 322). After a few images of horsemen, the film focuses on women running toward a cave in the Dahra mountains and waiting there during the combat. The narrator's voice specifies that "[a]insi, dans l'Algérie muette, toutes les vieilles chaque nuit chuchotaient, et l'histoire contée se répète" [so it was, in a silent Algeria, every night, all the old women would whisper, and the tales would be repeated]. As the images of the 1871 insurrection unfold on the screen, the soundtrack is filled with whispers, emphasizing the creation of a muted but living counterhistory, a subterranean memory, transmitted by the female ancestors. The film thus highlights the process of female transmission.

Lila's voice-over then announces: "Quelque fois, ici, l'ennemi vous enfuma. Vives" [One day, here, the enemy asphyxiated you by fire. Alive]. In the film, this is the only reference to a gruesome event of Algerian history that is central to the novel: "mille cinq cent hommes, femmes, enfants, vieillards" [1,500 men, women, children, elders], almost the entire Ouled Riah tribe, were exterminated by the French in 1845 (*Fantasia* 85/72). Women from the past and present are joined through a similar revolt against colonization, as well as similar loss and suffering. To foreground the similarities, Djebar asked seasonal workers to play the parts of the nineteenth-century women. Not dressed in nineteenth-century costumes but simply wearing their own clothes, they were asked to reenact the same actions and gestures they had performed during the recent war of liberation (Djebar, Comments made at the roundtable). In the film, these women also reappear in Lila's dream. The camera goes back and forth several times from these women dancing in the cave to Lila, alone in the same cave, lighting candles like her ancestors had done earlier. In the film's final movement, "Khlass," Lila, emerging from the cave, sees the women outside. The camera thus allows the superimposition of different eras of resistance in order to create a feeling of continuity between diverse women's struggles. Lila's dream becomes a locus for the work of memory, since it allows a junction between past and present. Like the chain of oral transmission, it creates a connection between different times and different struggles through the process of superimposition.[9]

Djebar explains that "c'est la documentation sonore [les enregistrements des témoignages féminins] qui a servi de point de départ au film. Le son direct de la première prise enregistrée est ce qu'on entend quand les femmes parlent" [it is the soundtrack (the recordings of women's testimonies) that served as a starting point for the film. The sound from the first live recordings is what we hear when the women speak] (Comments made at the roundtable). Djebar's entire work can be understood as an answer to the "regard interdit, son coupé" [forbidden gaze, severed sound] that she perceives as the major problem of Algerian society and that she discusses at length in her postscript to *Femmes d'Alger* (167/133).[10] In *La Nouba*, it is, above all, the sound that guides her work:

> Il s'agit de la mémoire recherchée par la voix. Ma démarche est de partir du son. . . . C'est la même chose dans mes livres. . . . Quand la mère de la fillette dans l'arbre se met à pleurer, il y a un rapport entre voix et mémoire au moment d'un détail de vulnérabilité. Je restitue ce qui est arrivé à la fille dans *L'Amour, la fantasia*. La mère se remet à souffrir, dans le moment, vingt ans en arrière. C'est comme un trou dans lequel entre et s'impose l'image, et donc on revoit la fillette sur l'arbre dans le film. C'est pour cela que le son est le point de départ, à cause des traces de blessures qui restent dans sa mémoire. C'est là qu'il faut restituer, pas forcément au moment le plus caractéristique, ou le plus terrible, mais ce qui vingt ans après continue à toucher dans le vif. (Comments made at the roundtable)

> [It's all about memory sought through the medium of the voice. In this process, I start from the sound. . . . It's the same in my books. When the mother of the girl in the tree begins to cry, there

is a connection between voice and memory during a vulnerable instant. I restore what happened to the daughter in *Fantasia*. The mother begins to suffer anew, thrown back into that moment of twenty years before. It's like a gap through which the image inserts and imposes itself, and that's why we see the girl in the tree in the film. That is why the sound is the point of departure, because of the traces of wounds remaining in her memory. That is what must be restored, not necessarily the most characteristic or most terrible moment, but what, twenty years later, continues to cut to the quick.][11]

The girl in the tree is Chérifa, whose image recurs constantly in the film, like a leitmotiv. This image is present from the very beginning of the film, where it is interspersed with archival images and war sounds. The mother's continuing suffering is the reason for foregrounding this image, thus connecting living memory to the process of making history. As Réda Bensmaïa noted, "*La nouba* may be interpreted as preparation for (the labor of) essential mourning and for anamnesis, both indispensable if we are ever to be emancipated from the past" ("Nouba" 882).

In the book, the image of Chérifa in the tree echoes another story, that of the Agha's daughter in the chapter titled, "La mariée nue de Mazouna" ("The Naked Bride of Mazuna"). This chapter, placed right after the one recounting the asphyxiation of the Ouled Riah, centers on events that occurred a few months before the 1845 massacre. Bou Maza, one of the Kabyle leaders of the resistance in the Dahra mountains, was fighting the Caids and Aghas, who collaborated with the French.[12] Badra, the Caid's daughter, was to marry the Agha's son, but the wedding party was attacked by Bou Maza's men and the Agha was killed. Like Chérifa with her brother, the Agha's daughter witnessed the death. She managed to escape, spending two days and two nights hiding in a tree, only coming down when she saw her brother coming. Although Chérifa and the Agha's daughter belong to two different historical periods and two opposing camps (resistance to, and collaboration with, the enemy), they both go through similar traumas because of the war. In the same way, Badra, the Caid's daughter, and the Agha's daughter suffer similar fates in spite of their different situations. Resistance to varied enemies creates a link between the Algerian women whose lives are restored in Djebar's work. According to Adlai Murdoch, Badra's resistance to Bou Maza (like that of the Agha's daughter) "may be read as a model for the maintenance of female subjective integrity in the face of a patriarchal desire for her subjection" (85). Women thus resist both Algerian and French patriarchal strictures.

A Continuing History of Resistance

The personal story and the country's history are intimately connected. In the film, Lila keeps on repeating the leitmotiv, "[J]'avais quinze ans, j'avais cent ans de douleur" [I was fifteen, with a hundred years of suffering]. In the book, the massacre of the narrator's ancestors by the French becomes her own point of departure, thus linking autobiography and history. She claims, "je suis née en *dix-huit cent quarante-deux*" [I was born in *eighteen hundred and forty-two*] (243/217), the time when the French burned the *zaouia* [religious headquarters] of the Berkani, from whom she is descended. As Hafid Gafaiti noted, she thus creates "la synthèse du 'je' autobiographique et du 'je' historique" [a synthesis between autobiographical and historical "I"] (*Femmes* 174). Four different war periods are superimposed: "la première guerre d'Algérie" [the first Algerian War] in 1842–1845 (*Fantasia* 92/78); the Berkanis' "seconde révolte" [second revolt] in 1871 (201/178); the war of national liberation in 1954–1962; and, finally, the gender wars. This superimposition subverts both French and Algerian official history. In France, traditional historiography tended to divide Algerian history into three parts: a short period of conquest, followed by over one hundred years of French Algeria (supposedly with minimal resistance on the part of the Algerians during that time), and the "Algerian events" that painfully brought the French presence to an end. In Algeria, the war of national liberation is presented as the point of departure of the Algerian nation, thus contrasting sharply with the dark period of French colonialism (Pervillé, Stora). In both countries, the analysis divides history into before and after. Djebar creates a female, postcolonial counterhistory that destabilizes the sharp break between colonization and decolonization by foregrounding the process of continuous resistance and of collaboration (as we have seen in the chapter "La mariée nue de Mazouna"). Djebar contextualizes the nineteenth-century anticolonial wars by placing them in a dialogue with the last war of independence. Likewise, Algerian sociologist Marnia Lazreg saw "a striking symmetry in the history of colonization and decolonization" (*Eloquence* 118) and "an unrecognized continuity in women's participation in the political/military life of their country" (137).[13]

In the third part of the novel (in a passage that has been commented on by Gayatri Spivak, in "Acting," and Denise Brahimi, in *"L'Amour"*), the narrator enters into a dialogue that is an exchange of stories with Zohra. Zohra's story centers on her sons' and her own resistance to the French armed forces during the war of national liberation. French violence and repression affected them directly through physical wounds, repeated house burnings, humiliations, and torture. Her story is emblematic of that of many *musbilat*, or civil militants, as described by Amrane (115, 119, 126). Her participation in the war was a total commitment of herself, her family, and of anything she owned. The kinds of services she performed remained for the most part within the realm of the prescribed female role: cooking and sewing for the mudjahidin, as well as gathering and transmitting intelligence on French troop movements. Her losses, as a punishment for her actions, were not only material but were inscribed on her body and psyche. During one of the house burnings, her hair caught fire, and the scars remained as a reminder of this event. This, combined with torture, caused brain damage, gaining her the nickname "la folle" [the madwoman] (*Fantasia* 184/162).

After listening to Zohra telling her own story, the narrator feels the need to reciprocate by giving her a story through "la médiation de la lecture" [the mediation of reading] (Brahimi, "*L'Amour*" 122). Reading, writing, and oral storytelling mingle into what Spivak called "arabesques" ("Acting" 771). As Zohra's story is translated into French and committed to paper (for a partly Western audience of a book published in Paris), Orientalist painter Eugène Fromentin's written narrative of an Algerian story told to him in 1853 and written down in French is transposed into dialectal oral Arabic and told to an Algerian woman (although the book's audience reads a French written version of this story). The boundaries between French writing and dialectal oral Arabic, between storyteller and writer, lose their rigidity. As Soheila Ghaussy noted, "Djebar's method is inherently paradoxical: it blurs the boundaries of the spoken and the written by emphasizing, precisely through writing, a language that is imagined to be spoken" (458). The oral tradition enters into written history, and the written text inserts itself into the female, oral tradition.

The cruel events of the French colonization of Algeria and their consequences for women echo those of the last war between Algeria and France. Fatma and Mériem, the two nineteenth-century prostitutes of Fromentin's story, are explicitly compared to Khadidja, the prostitute who, like Zohra, was imprisoned by the French and tortured for financially supporting the mudjahidin (*Fantasia* 188/166). Fatma's and Mériem's half-naked bodies recall Zohra's and her female relatives' bodies being stripped by French soldiers (181/159, 189/166). We are also reminded of the bodies of the women whom Chérif Bou Maza had forced to give up their jewelry and finery in 1845 (113–15/97–99). The violent colonial encounter between Algeria and France inscribes itself as a wound whose traces remain on the body and memory of Algerian women, from the beginnings of the French conquest to the final war of liberation. Through the conflation of Fromentin's and Zohra's stories, the 1830 conquest comes to be viewed through the prism of the 1962 victory, as Algerian history becomes a history of continuous resistance.[14] As Danielle Marx-Scouras has shown, the violence of war continues for women during peacetime in Djebar's work ("Muffled" 178).[15]

Contemporary Algerian women's struggle for the liberation of their gaze and voice is no longer marginal to the project of nation building. In Djebar's rewriting, their struggle inscribes itself fully within a national history of resistance and is thus legitimated. Whereas Frantz Fanon, in "Algeria Unveiled," seemed to be considering women's emancipation mostly insofar as it fit into the project of national liberation and tended to ignore the feminist aspect of the issue, Djebar argues that women's liberation cannot solely be a function of national liberation and must be fully achieved on women's own terms.[16]

Djebar's film and novel overwrite a history whose starting point is "the traces of wounds remaining in [women's] memory" (Comments made at the roundtable). Djebar's work *of* and *about* memory allows her to "rallumer le vif du passé" [rekindle the vividness of the past], "écouter la mémoire déchirée" [listen to the painfully torn memories] (*La Nouba*), to prevent the ink from drying (*Fantasia* 68/56), to bring stifled voices and asphyxiated memories back to life and into history.

Notes

1. For a study of *Fantasia* that focuses on the autobiographical aspect of the novel and intersects with my analysis, see Patricia Geesey.

2. The Arabic version of the film with English subtitles is available from Women Make Movies in New York, New York.

3. I discuss these in more detail in Chapter 4. In 1991, Djebar foregrounded earlier history in *Loin de Médine*, a fictionalized rewriting of the lives of women mentioned in early Islamic history. In *Vaste est la prison*, she goes back in time to antiquity (including the Dougga stele, Jugurtha, and Princess Tin Hinan).

4. The use of the second-person singular is characteristic of Djebar's style, as the second book of the quartet, *Ombre sultane*, makes abundantly clear. In the third part of *Fantasia*, the pronouns "I," "she," and "you" alternate. The second-person singular is used when the narrator wonders about her work of transmission and when she initiates a dialogue with the women whose testimonies she is restoring. The presence of these testimonies is crucial to the process of overwriting history. The stakes are high: it is a matter of creating new documents; new "archives" must be developed before the witnesses disap-

pear, in order to produce a history that will account for the Algerians, especially the women.

5. Clarisse Zimra rightly links Djebar's insistence on mediation to the ambiguous position of the intercessor, a term whose recurrence in *Fantasia* she traces in her essay, "Disorienting the Subject in Djebar's *L'Amour, la fantasia*" (151–57).

6. The fact that Djebar reveals the given name of her relative, Zohra, exemplifies the double act of unveiling/veiling, which is for her the necessary condition of writing an autobiography. The unveiling of her relative's name functions at the same time as an unveiling and veiling of her own. "Assia Djebar" is a pseudonym; her real first name is Fatima-Zohra, which is never revealed in her novels. The double first name links her, not only to her ancestor, but also, symbolically, to one of the two nineteenth-century women mentioned in *Fantasia*, Fatma, whose fate was transmitted by a French text, as well as to the Prophet's daughter, "[c]elle qui dit non à Médine" [the woman who says no to Medina] (*Loin* 68). Autobiography as a "mise à nu" [stripping naked] and "mise à sac" [plunder] (178/157) can only be expressed through the mediation of other women's stories and voices as a reveiling that constitutes itself as protection. According to Derrida, in the logic of the palimpsest, it is the mediation of writing that constitutes itself as a protection against the risk it implies (331). This link reinforces the parallels between writing and oral transmission developed by Brahimi in her article on *Fantasia*.

7. For a structural study of *La Nouba* as a "*topography of feminine places*" and an exploration of dislocated "feminine time(s)," see Réda Bensmaïa's essay, "*La nouba des Femmes du Mont Chenoua*: Introduction to the Cinematic Fragment" (878).

8. In Djebar's short story, "La femme qui pleure" [The woman who weeps], another female protagonist stands up and repeatedly utters the same words (*Femmes d'Alger* 72, 75).

9. The alternation and similarity between dream and memory were already a feature of Djebar's work in her early novel *Les Alouettes naïves* (1967).

10. Djebar's work on sound is particularly remarkable in her second film, *La Zerda ou les chants de l'oubli*, in which she reedited strips of film discarded from newsreels taken by "[des] caméramen parisiens" [Parisian cameramen] who accompanied "les ministres français en voyage officiel [et] filmaient . . . ce qui attirait leur regard" [French ministers in their official travels (and) filmed whatever attracted their gaze] (Djebar, Comments made at the roundtable). The subversion of these images operates, not only at the level of the choice of images themselves among miles of archival film, but especially at the level of the film's sound, with the addition of the "chants de l'oubli" [songs of forgetting] that "correspondent à ce qu'il n'y avait pas dans l'image" [correspond to what was not filmed] (Comments made at the roundtable). The film is divided into four parts, in the form of four songs that retrace a

history erased by French camerawork but preserved in the oral memory: insubordination (Emir Abd el-Kader's time), intransigence (the guerrilla war period), sunstroke (colonial times), and emigration between 1912 and 1942. A fifth part had been planned but could not be shot because of technical difficulties. It was to have been called "Le Chant des morts les yeux ouverts" [Song of the dead with open eyes] and was intended to display the ways in which both communities, Algerian and French, bury their dead (Djebar, Comments made on *La Zerda*).

11. Similarly, in Djebar's *Les Alouettes naïves*, the memories that are foregrounded are those that continue to have an emotional impact on the characters. Memory is an active process, which is rekindled by strong emotions. When Rachid evokes with great pain his sister's death in childbirth long ago, his friend Omar thinks, "Par ce gémissement, la morte revint en moi" [with this moan, the dead woman was revived within me] (82).

12. The asphyxiation of the Ouled Riah was perpetrated in order to subdue Bou Maza. Like Abd el-Kader, he surrendered at the end of 1847.

13. For an analysis of Djebar's subversive rewriting of official French and Algerian history, see Maïr Verthuy.

14. Djebar made a similar link in *Le Blanc de l'Algérie* (1996) by associating the deaths of intellectuals, such as Mouloud Feraoun, during the war of liberation with the more recent deaths of writers, such as her brother-in-law Abdelkader Alloula and journalist Tahar Djaout, at the hands of fundamentalist Islamic forces. This audacious association implies a parallelism between French colonial and fundamentalist Islamic violence, on the one hand, and evinces a sharp critique of the internal politics of the FLN and subsequent Algerian governments, on the other. See Accad, "Assia Djebar" 811, and Gafaiti, "Blood" 819–20.

15. As early as 1967, she had the narrator of *Les Alouettes naïves* suggest, at the end of the novel, "que la guerre qui finit entre les peuples renaît entre les couples" [that the war ending between two peoples is reborn within the couple] (423).

16. For a study of *Femmes d'Alger* as a response to Fanon's "Algeria Unveiled," see Rita A. Faulkner.

Chapter 4
▼▼▼▼▼▼▼▼▼

Inter/Textual Subversions

Djebar's oeuvre spans four decades and is usually divided into two periods separated by an approximately ten-year-long publishing hiatus (during the 1970s). Works from the second period show a maturity in style best exemplified in her 1985 *L'Amour, la fantasia*. *Fantasia*, *Ombre sultane* (1987), and *Vaste est la prison* (1995) are the first three volumes of a projected quartet, although *Ombre* and *Vaste* are in no way sequels to the first volume. In *Fantasia*, an unnamed female narrator returns to a double past, individual and collective. The personal story is constructed in counterpoint to the history of the Algerian people, a history erased under French colonization. *Ombre sultane* (*A Sister to Scheherazade*) explores the complex issue of women's situations in contemporary Algeria by centering on the characters of two cowives, the "liberated" Isma (cast as narrator) and the more "traditional" Hajila (addressed by Isma). *Vaste est la prison*, the most directly autobiographical volume ever written by Djebar, opens with the narration of a platonic passion and then focuses on the theme of retrieving the lost Berber alphabet. Djebar also interweaves a rewriting of the lives of women in her family with a reflection on her experiences as a filmmaker. The unity between the three novels is not to be found at the level of the plot, but rather at the structural and thematic levels, as exemplified in Djebar's use of epigraphs. In her novelistic quartet, Djebar uses a complex system of epigraphs that can be seen as a cartography, a type of road map providing guideposts by which to read and interpret the texts. All three novels follow a tripartite structure and are framed by a complex system of epigraphs and short, lyrical passages in italics.[1] Each novel opens with a general epigraph. The parallels are most striking between the first two novels, which were written around the same time, whereas the third came eight years later, after the writing of *Loin de Médine*. The following discussion focuses, therefore, on the first two novels. In both works, each of the three parts is preceded by one or two epigraphs: in Parts 1 and 3, Djebar uses Western authors; in Part 2, she uses Arabic sources (the famous historian Ibn Khaldun in the first book of the quartet, and a classic text of the Middle Eastern literary tradition, *The Arabian Nights*, in the second one).[2]

By moving from Western (French) to Arabic and, seemingly, back to Western sources, Djebar is establishing a dichotomy that is immediately subverted at several levels. For instance, in the first parts of both novels, she alternates chapters in counterpoint: in *Fantasia*, historical and personal chapters; in *Ombre sultane*, chapters on Hajila and on Isma, the former written in the dialogic "tu," and the latter in the personal "je." However, this strict compartmentalization is subverted in both novels through the recurring use of similar vocabulary in the paired chapters, and in *Ombre sultane*, by the meeting of second and first persons at the end of Chapter 6, repeated in Chapter 13. In this way the lives of the seemingly radically different women come to mingle.

Similarly, the opposition established between Western and North African or Middle Eastern quotations is destabilized in the third parts of both books. In *Fantasia*, one of the two epigraphs opening Part 3 is by Saint Augustine, who can be said to belong to both traditions: he was a Father of the (Catholic) Church, and he founded the tradition of Western autobiography. As Djebar herself points out in *Fantasia*, he was also an Algerian who wrote his autobiography in a language other than his own, the language of the dominant power of the time (241–42/215–16). In the third part of *Ombre sultane*, the excerpt from Victor Hugo's *Les Orientales* reminds the reader of the main protagonist of *The Arabian Nights*: "La sultane regarde" [the Sultana looks on] (*Ombre* 151/141). Scheherazade, the sultana who speaks only in the anonymity of the night, before dawn, is thus also endowed with sight. The organization of epigraphs reflects the internal structuring of the novels. In *Ombre*, Djebar uses the sexual division of space in traditional Algeria as a structuring principle, showing how Hajila and Isma move from inside to outside and vice-versa. The dichotomy imposed at the beginning of each novel is then methodically deconstructed.

One of Djebar's main purposes in her novels is both to expose and to subvert the loss of sight associated with gaining a voice, or the loss of voice associated with gaining vision/visibility, for women in Algerian society. In *Ombre*, Hajila discovers that when outside, unveiled, she loses her voice: "tu découvres ton aphasie" [you realize you have lost the power of speech] (50/42). As soon as she re-veils herself, her voice reappears: "Anonyme de nouveau, tu retrouves la voix" [Now that you are anonymous once more, you find your voice] (43/34). This may explain in part why Isma, the narrator, wishes to "disparaître, se dissoudre là, renaître ailleurs . . . se voiler, ou se dissimuler" [vanish from the scene, fading away to be reborn elsewhere . . . put on the veil, or go into hiding], in order to recapture the fullness of her voice (169/159).

Significantly, the main epigraphs to the first two volumes of the quartet, both from French painters, deal with voice and sight. A quotation from Fromentin (from his Algerian travelogue *Une Année dans le Sahel*) provides the opening, as well as the conclusion, of *Fantasia*: "Il y eut un cri déchirant—je l'entends encore au moment où je t'écris—, puis des clameurs, puis un tumulte" [There was a heart-rending cry— I can hear it still as I write to you—followed by screams, then an uproar] (*Fantasia* 7/n.p.). The problematic of the prohibition of women's "cri," of their outspoken voice, outside traditional or ritual situations, is explored throughout the novel. In *Ombre sultane*, Pierre Bonnard's words, spoken a few months before his death, center around light and sight, thus providing a contrast with the "shadow" of the title (a title whose dichotomy Djebar deconstructs throughout the text).[3] The novel itself foregrounds Hajila's move to the outside, into the light, unveiled, and Isma's parallel disappearance into the dark. *Ombre sultane* ends with the narrator's fear of seeing women relegated once again to the dark of Arabian nights without ever being able to see the light of day. A postscript brings the reader back to the problematic of the voice: it identifies a quotation used in italics in the text a few pages earlier: the same quotation by Fromentin that was used to open *Fantasia* now closes *Ombre sultane*. However, the quotation (as well as the title of Fromentin's book) is slightly altered. Through the repeated use of Fromentin's words, Djebar creates a common thread, a reverberation, between the two novels, using in *Ombre sultane* echoes of the main intertext of *Fantasia*.

Theoretical Parameters

Having established the structural links between the novels of the quartet, I now turn to an analysis of the significance of the epigraphs in Djebar's texts. The epigraphs are part of what Gérard Genette called the paratext, meaning everything around the text per se, which presents and accompanies it (*Seuils* 7). He defined the epigraph as "une citation placée en exergue, généralement en tête d'oeuvre ou de partie d'oeuvre; 'en exergue' signifie littéralement *hors* d'oeuvre, ce qui est un peu trop dire: l'exergue est ici plutôt un *bord* d'oeuvre, généralement au plus près du texte" [a quotation in *exergue*, usually heading a work or part of a work; "in exergue" literally means *outside* the work, which might be saying too much: the exergue is rather a *border* or edge of the work, generally placed as close to the text as possible] (*Seuils* 134). The following analysis illuminates the ways in which this definition, with its insistence on the border, is relevant to Djebar's text. Genette classified four functions of the epigraph (145–49): commentary on the title (as in the play between the words "ombre" [shadow] and "lumière" [light], or the revelation that "vaste est la prison" are words taken from a Berber song); commentary on the text itself (the most obvious function); legitimating one's text thanks to the presence of a famous author's name; and finally, linking one's text to a particular intellectual and cultural tradition (in Djebar's case, a multiple Arabic and European tradition).

My analysis centers on the two functions Djebar's works engage most fully, those of legitimization and insertion in a preexisting tradition. Simone Rezzoug's argument in her article "Ecritures féminines algériennes" relates to the category of legitimization. Rezzoug insists on the difficulty for Maghrebian women writers of speaking outside what Djebar would call "l'anonymat des aïeules" [my foremothers' anonymity] (*Fantasia* 243/217). For Rezzoug, the use of quotations, polyphony, and doubling in the works of writers such as Djebar, together with Djebar's use of a pseudonym, are ways of hiding behind a mask, of remaining anonymous, of forming "un système de défense dans le procès de la parole féminine . . . et de légitimer son dire en lui donnant des garants" [a defense system in the trial of female speech . . . and of legitimating her account by safeguarding it] (88). This interpretation is amply supported by Djebar's insistence on the difficulty and danger for an Algerian woman of speaking out individually— one of the major themes of *Fantasia*. In this novel, which she has identified as being "une préparation à une autobiographie" [a preparation for an autobiography] (quoted in Mortimer, "Entretien" 203), Djebar repeatedly emphasizes the transgression of a woman who speaks (and dares to write) outside the anonymous collectivity in a society in which individual women like Scheherazade, the sultana of the *Arabian Nights*, may only be heard speaking softly in the darkness of the night as part of a chain of oral transmission.

In grounding her text in the works of others before her, Djebar inscribes herself in a long Arabic, even Koranic, tradition in which one must quote someone else in order to support an assertion, to legitimate one's report. Within religious, literary, and historical Arabic tradition, authors must name their sources so as to inscribe themselves as intermediaries in a long chain of transmission of knowledge in order to validate their intervention (Cheddadi 21). In *Le Harem politique* (in English, *The Veil and the Male Elite*), Moroccan sociologist Fatima Mernissi explains that because "[l]e Prophète recevait le message d'Allah oralement et le transmettait oralement" [the Prophet received Allah's message orally and transmitted it orally] (40/29), after the Prophet's death it became necessary to record the *Hadith*, or "tout ce qu'il est supposé avoir dit ou fait" [everything that he is supposed to have said or done] (47/34), in writing. The *Hadith* transcribers collected direct and indirect testimonies of a *Hadith*, established "la chaîne de transmetteurs qui se le sont transmis depuis la source" [the chain of people who transmitted it from its source], and documented the reliability of the informant (48/35). In light of their oral origin, the *Hadith* are "extrêmement variées parce qu'on a droit à plusieurs versions du même événement" [extremely varied because there are various versions of the same event] (48/35).

Applying this knowledge to a secular context, it is possible to suggest that Djebar's slight alteration of Fromentin's words may be interpreted as a desire to remain true to the (oral) spirit of the quotation while going beyond the constraints of its (written) letter. She grounds her written texts in the oral tradition by incorporating into them testimonies told to her by Algerian women and by creating variations on the written quotations she employs. Thus, when using Fromentin's sentence as an epigraph, she quotes it word for word; but when incorporating his words into her own text, she appropriates them by altering them: "Un grand cri s'éleva (je l'entends encore au moment où je t'écris), puis une clameur, puis un tumulte" [A great cry arose (I can hear it still as I write to you), followed by a scream, then an uproar] (*Ombre* 168/158). The marginal changes, together with the variation in the title which she quotes as being *Une Année au Sahel* (*Ombre* 172/158), seem to point to the workings of memory and oral transmission. Djebar inscribes orality within her very choice of citations, from Fromentin's "cri" to Scheherazade's telling of stories. Djebar's engagement with the tradition of the *Hadith* is most complex in her treatment of Ibn Khaldun's epigraph, as I demonstrate later in this chapter.

In considering Djebar's epigraphs, it becomes necessary to expand on Genette's fourth definition of the use of the epigraph (to insert one's text into a particular intellectual and cultural tradition). The epigraph may also be highlighted only to underscore its manipulation by the text it frames, thus subverting the tradition it represents. The text enters into a dialogical relation with its epigraphs as it rewrites them. The epigraph loses its function as commentary on the text. The roles are reversed, as Djebar's text becomes a subversive commentary on its epigraph. The division between text and paratext becomes blurred, as the text takes over its epigraph. In what follows, I analyze three theoretical paradigms that can be useful in understanding Djebar's subversive strategy.

Djebar's strategy is very close to Luce Irigaray's theory of mimicry in "Pouvoir du discours" ["The Power of Discourse"]. Irigaray posited that it is first through their deliberate repetition of a male discourse of female representation that women will be able to reappropriate language. This repetition will be subversive because of its difference: spoken from a different position, it might extend into the realm of parody; female mimicry will "faire 'apparaître,' par un effet de répétition ludique, ce qui devait rester occulté: le recouvrement d'une possible opération du féminin dans le langage. C'est aussi 'dévoiler' le fait que, si les femmes miment si bien, c'est qu'elles ne se résorbent pas simplement dans cette fonction. *Elles restent aussi ailleurs*: autre insistance de 'matière,' mais aussi de 'jouissance'" [make "visible," by an effect of playful repetition, what was supposed to remain invisible: the cover-up/recovering of a possible operation of the feminine in language. It also means "to unveil" the fact that, if women are such good mimics, it is because they are not simply resorbed in this function. *They also remain elsewhere*: another case of the persistence of "matter," but also of "*jouissance*"] ("Pouvoir" 74/76). Djebar makes use of this strategy in both *Fantasia* and *Ombre sultane*, reappropriating and subverting, not only the discourse of (Western and Arab) patriarchy about women, but also the discourse of colonialist imperialism about Algerians—thereby creating an original form of female Algerian mimicry.

Irigaray's concept of mimicry differs from that of postcolonial studies theorist Homi Bhabha (as developed in his article, "Of Mimicry and Man"). Bhabha applied mimicry to the colonizer's discourse and to the discourse of so-called mimic men, whose minds have been colonized (88). The mimic men are local elites chosen to be educated in the colonialist tradition to serve as mediators between the colonizer and the local population. In this context, "mimicry emerges as one of the most elusive and effective strategies of colonial power and knowledge" (85). Bhabha argued that the British attempted to construct an Other "*as a subject of a difference that is almost the same, but not quite*. Which is to say, that the discourse of mimicry is constructed around an *ambivalence . . . Almost the same but not white*" (86, 89). Bhabha compared mimicry's effects to those of the Freudian concept of the fetish, which "mimes the forms of authority at the point at which it deauthorizes them" (91).

Both Bhabha's and Irigaray's concepts of mimicry are indebted to Freud's central concept of the repetition compulsion, in which repetition always entails difference. However, Bhabha, like Freud, used the concept at the level of the unconscious, suggesting that it is in the "native's" earnest effort to imitate the colonizing Other that difference appears and unsettles the colonial project. For Irigaray, mimicry is a conscious strategy of opposition to hegemonic discourse, one that must be taken up "deliberately" and that points to a feminine elsewhere ("Power" 76).

Because he analyzed unconscious phenomena, Bhabha did not consider what Benita Parry called the anticolonialist "counter-discourses which every liberation movement records" ("Problems" 43), and instead tended to remain within the arena of the colonial master text. As Robert Young analyzed it in *White Mythologies,* for Bhabha, mimicry "describes a process . . . which works instead more like the unconscious in Lacan, and could . . . be described, after Jameson, as 'the colonial unconscious'" (148). Irigaray's definition of mimicry as an oppositional strategy—which Young rightly links to Derrida's deconstructive project rather than to Lacanian theory (209)—applies to narratives such as Djebar's, especially since it reintroduces the presence of women into the analysis, an aspect Bhabha's exploration leaves uncharted. However, Djebar's strategy, as opposed to Irigaray's, does not focus solely on gender mimicry but rather, like Bhabha's, underscores mimicry in the colonial context. Anne McClintock, who discussed the parallels and differences between Irigaray and Bhabha in *Imperial Leather,* criticized them both for their blind spots: whereas Irigaray viewed mimicry solely through an appeal to gender difference and thereby erased other issues, Bhabha bypassed "Irigaray's gendered intervention" to take "the idea of mimicry into the colonial arena" (62). Djebar's strategy goes beyond those of both theorists by attending to the workings of gender in the colonial context.[4]

Djebar's use of mimicry is also close to what Barbara Harlow, using Elias Khouri's formulation, called *mu'aradah* (resistance or confrontation). *Mu'aradah* "is also the designation given to a classical Arabic literary form, according to which one person will write a poem and another will retaliate by writing along the same lines, but reversing the meaning" (24). Like Djebar's texts, mu'aradah is essentially dialogical (with the verb retaliate indicating that violence is part of the dialogue) and is expressed by a writing inscribed through orality (poems are written but also meant to be recited or read aloud).

However, Djebar's work does not purport to *reverse* the meaning of previous (colonial) texts. As Irigaray, Bhabha, and others such as Jacques Derrida have suggested, inversion would entail remaining within the logic of the master('s) text. Djebar goes further, playing with that master('s) text in order to make it collapse. Her purpose, like Derrida's, is "to subvert it [the master's text] by repeating it, dislocating it fractionally through . . . a mimicry that mocks the binary structure" (Young 209). While Bhabha's mimicry set out to deconstruct the hegemonic colonial text from within and Harlow's concept of mu'aradah functions mostly as a counterhegemonic strategy, Irigaray's concept of mimicry, although it has too narrow a focus on gender, applies to a text (such as Djebar's) that moves away from Manichean dualism to subversive reappropriation, exploding hegemonic structure by circulating both inside and outside it. In other words, Bhabha's perspective centers on the colonizer's master text undoing itself from the inside, whereas Harlow's view privileges the countertext of the colonized as it attempts to undo the master text from the outside. Irigaray's perspective, once modified to take the colonial context into account, applies well to a postcolonial, subversive text such as Djebar's, which undoes the dichotomy between inside and outside.

I have shown in the previous chapter how Djebar reappropriates the French archives on Algeria by using them as the palimpsest on which she deciphers the trace of her people, especially the women, and rewrites Algerian history over that palimpsest, thus subverting and decentering the texts of the colonizers and endowing them with new meanings. I will now conduct a detailed analysis of Djebar's rewriting of her intertexts through the study of her treatment of three exemplary epigraphs: from Ibn Khaldun, *The Arabian Nights*, and Fromentin.

Writing Autobiography and History: Ibn Khaldun

Although the first volume of the quartet, *L'Amour, la fantasia*, covers the period from 1830 to the early 1980s, some of Djebar's epigraphs tie that history to a much more ancient one, going back to the fourteenth century, with Ibn Khaldun, and to the fourth century, with Augustine's *Confessions*. Her reference to Ibn Khaldun's autobiography (*Ta'arif*), in particular, helps us better grasp the links between autobiography and history in *Fantasia*.

Djebar is not the first Maghrebian author to have conjured up Ibn Khaldun's presence in a novel. Both Algerian novelist Rachid Boudjedra (in *Les Mille et une années de la nostalgie*) and Tunisian writer Albert Memmi (in *Le Désert*) used the figure of Ibn Khaldun as ancestor.[5] In *Fantasia*, there is a double reference to Ibn Khaldun: first, the epigraph that opens the second part of the text, "Les cris de la Fantasia" ["The Cries of the *Fantasia*"] is taken from Ibn Khaldun's *Ta'arif* (*Fantasia* 59/47). Ibn Khaldun is also mentioned toward the end of the novel, in the crucial chapter "La Tunique de Nessus," in which the narrator explains in very moving terms that the French language has turned into a kind of tunic of Nessus for her, as her father's gift of love has become a destructive poison. At the point in which writing her autobiography is revealed to be a doubly dangerous undertaking—because it is written both in "la langue adverse" [the enemy's language] and by a woman (*Fantasia* 241/215)—the narrator inscribes herself in a long-standing tradition of Maghrebian autobiography, going back to Augustine and Ibn Khaldun to justify her project (241–42/215–16). The allusion to Augustine's *Confessions* is easily understood in the context of Djebar's autobiographical narrative. The reference to Ibn Khaldun is more enigmatic for a French or U.S. reader, which is one of the reasons I choose to focus on it. Moreover, I take to heart Hafid Gafaiti's warning about the dangers of interpreting Djebar's work mostly in terms of the orality of Algerian female culture while sidestepping the importance of the Maghrebian literary intertexts in her works ("Blood" 822).

Ibn Khaldun was a writer and statesman who was born in Tunis in 732 (by the Muslim calendar) or 1332 (by the Christian calendar) and died in Cairo in 808/1406. His monumental universal history, the *Kitab al-'Ibar*, is generally recognized as the first to have established a science of history, some five centuries before Western historiography. A historian by training, Djebar is well aware of the importance of his universal history, assessments and interpretations of which vary greatly.[6] The *Kitab* is divided into several books: the *Muqaddimah* (the most translated and analyzed part, in which Ibn Khaldun develops his theory of history), the *History of the Arabs*, and the *History of the Berbers*. At the very end of the *Kitab*, Ibn Khaldun included his autobiography, the *Ta'arif* (Enan 100). Djebar uses a quotation from the *Ta'arif* rather than from the *Muqaddimah*, thus drawing attention to a generally marginalized aspect of his work. Such a refocalization is a typical move in Djebar's works. For example, in *Fantasia*, she focuses on Fromentin's lesser-known travelogues rather than on his famous paintings. Laurence Huughe called this literary strategy the "writing of detail" and rightfully linked it to the obstructed view of the veiled woman, who has fragmented vision but also a more acute perception of details (Huughe 872). Just as Fromentin's travelogue gave Djebar a literary model for a palimpsestic, hybrid text (as I argue in the last part of the chapter), Ibn Khaldun's *Ta'arif* provided her with a model of historical autobiography that allowed her to justify her own writing project.

Ibn Khaldun is not the first Muslim writer to have written his autobiography. In the Islamic tradition, the writer transcribing the *Hadith*, the record of everything the Prophet said and did, was not only supposed to faithfully record the *Hadith*, but also to "établir son *Isnad*, c'est-à-dire la chaîne de transmetteurs qui se le sont transmis depuis la source. . . . La règle de l'*Isnad* (chaîne de transmission) impose donc la nécessité de donner la biographie du transmetteur" [establish its *isnad*, that is, the chain of people who transmitted it from its source. . . . The principle of the *isnad* (transmission chain) thus makes it necessary to give the biography of the person transmitting] (Mernissi, *Harem* 48–49/35). Ibn Khaldun himself was a *Hadith* professor. At the beginning of the *Ta'arif*, he lists all of his educators with a short biography of each, following the rules of Isnad (177–85, 45–71). According to Abdesselam Cheddadi, in contrast to a European, confessional autobiographical tradition, Islamic culture only allows one to speak about the self in the context of validating the chain of transmission of knowledge (20–21). Many chroniclers before Ibn Khaldun included a short biography at the end of their works (Merad 54). This biography was not supposed to include allusions to one's intimate life or psychology. In general, Ibn Khaldun follows this rule, which has led some critics to call his autobiography selective and partial (Fischel 162). Ibn Khaldun mentions his private life only in indirect ways. For instance, he includes a letter of congratulations sent to him by a vizir, which allows him to inform his readers that a son was born to him (131).

A more revealing example involves one of the crucial events of his life, the death of his wife and children in a 786/1384 shipwreck as they were traveling to join him in Cairo. This event is only briefly mentioned, without any details, but it is repeated four times in the *Ta'arif*, thus giving a poignant indication of the author's deep sorrow. In the concise sentence, "[m]on malheur et mon affliction furent extrêmes" [my pain and affliction were extreme], one can detect the restrained expression of unspeakable grief (158). The first manuscript version of the *Ta'arif* ends a chapter later. Many years afterwards, when Ibn Khaldun took up his autobiographical narrative again, he began by repeating the story of his family's death. This strange stutter in the text provides the reader with a slightly more detailed version, as if the temporal distance together with the fact of having already written about it had made a chink in his armor. His comment, "[m]a peine fut si grande que j'en eus l'esprit altéré" [my sorrow was so great that it affected my mind] (174), is also more revealing. The third mention of his family's death and his extreme sorrow is followed by the ritual phrase, "Dieu a le pouvoir d'accomplir Sa volonté" [God has the power to have His will be done] (186), which seems to indicate a distancing and acceptance of fate that are reinforced in the fourth repetition, "[i]l y a un destin pour chaque chose" [to each its fate] (209). Following the *Hadith* tradition, Ibn Khaldun provides several versions of this crucial event (Mernissi, *Harem* 48/35).

Both Ibn Khaldun and Djebar provide second-degree autobiographies, or in other words, the autobiography of the historical character or writer rather than the person (Merad 63). Djebar's autobiography also reveals very little about her personal life. In it, she mixes the story of her relation to the French language with the story of the French language in Algeria. For both Ibn Khaldun and Djebar, the autobiographical paradox rests on the fact that their reticence to speak about the self never prevents them from presenting themselves with strict honesty. Ibn Khaldun mentions that he switched allegiance from one ruler to another several times, choosing the winning side. Toward the end of his life, he managed to have Tamerlane spare him during the siege of Damascus, but was unable to prevent the looting and destruction of the city. Mohammad Enan called him an opportunist (15). Critics Fuad Baali and Ali Wardi appear surprised by Ibn Khaldun's unusual frankness as, in the autobiographies of the time, members of the ruling class were allowed to unabashedly relate their religious exploits but not their secular activities (20). Ibn Khaldun was the only one of these to transgress this rule, perhaps wishing to justify his desire to retire from political life.

As for Djebar, her works break several taboos, especially the description of female sexual pleasure in *Les Alouettes naïves* as early as 1967 and, in the second installment of the quartet, *Ombre sultane*, twenty years later: "Ecrire *devant* l'amour. Eclairer le corps, pour aider à lever l'interdit, pour dévoiler" [To write *confronting* love. Shedding light on the body to help lift the taboo, to lift the veil] (*Fantasia* 75/62). In *Ombre sultane*, the narrator depicts female sensuality in the first person with unequaled depth and nuances. For example, in the second chapter of Part 1, the senses of hearing, touch, sight, and taste converge in a maelstrom of memory that is closely related to the motions of the body (19/11). In the chapter titled "La Chambre" ("The Bedroom"), the narrator describes the pleasure of love-making in lyrical and suggestive terms that are never directly graphic. The beauty of the passage, with its half-tones and its richness of observation, reminds one of a painting (31–32/22).

According to critics, Ibn Khaldun's autobiography is extremely original, not only because it is the longest and frankest in Islamic history, but especially because it mixes autobiography and history (Enan 106–7). Ibn Khaldun includes historical chapters in his autobiography, and incorporates autobiographical elements into the rest of the *Kitab* (Fischel 162). For instance, in the *Ta'arif*, he reiterates his theories about the cycles of dynasties, geography, and climate and provides a historical survey from the

beginnings of humankind to Tamerlane (189–90, 216–27). He thus positions himself in his times, considering that his experiences as a statesman
are part and parcel of the history of the states about which he writes
(Rosenthal 19, Enan 107). Borrowing Ibn Khaldun's separation of theoretical, historical, and autobiographical books as well as his combination
of the various elements within each book, *Fantasia* alternates between historical and autobiographical chapters. The narrator's first-person voice is
present in the historical chapters as she rereads and rewrites colonial archives; similarly, she blends the life stories of other women with her own
in the autobiographical chapters.

In both cases, the autobiography is placed within the context of a history that begins much earlier than the authors' birth dates. Ibn Khaldun
begins the *Ta'arif* with providing his genealogy, the historical events preceding his birth, and his family's history from their arrival in Andalusia to
their emigration to North Africa. He then sketches his childhood, education, and public life (Enan 107–8). Djebar opens her autobiography with
the image of a little girl going to school for the first time, but the following chapter focuses on the instant before the capture of Algiers in 1830.
The historical chapters underscore Algerian resistance to French colonization in the nineteenth and twentieth centuries. Djebar mixes autobiography with the history of the country as seen through Algerian women's
eyes.

Both authors undertake a subversion of historiographical tradition. Ibn
Khaldun was the first thinker to develop a science of history in the
Muqaddimah. Ferial Ghazoul explained that "[t]he chain of reliable transmitters or *isnad* was the major criterion for establishment of authenticity
in Arab historiography. Ibn Khaldun added a reflective criterion by which
to judge the reliability of such reports. His work . . . opened the door for
a new method" (52). The *Muqaddimah* established parameters allowing
historians to judge more scientifically how authentic and credible their
sources were. History became a science of narrative. Ibn Khaldun first
outlined the characteristics and general principles of a given culture; then
he gauged the plausibility of historical narratives according to whether or
not they corresponded to that culture's organizational principles. He did
not reject Islamic historiographical tradition, since he valued Islamic narratives over non-Islamic ones, and biblical narratives over nonbiblical ones
(Al-Azmeh, *Ibn Khaldun: An Essay* 126–31). However, he subverted tradition by refusing to authenticate a narrative based on its transmitter's piety
or morality (Lahbabi 104). This may help explain why he insisted on his
own political fickleness (contrasting with his unbending integrity as a judge
in Egypt) in the *Ta'arif*: instead of only focusing on his moral qualities, he

presented both his positive and negative aspects. Thus, his own historical work must be evaluated only for its scholarly value and not on its author's moral worth.

As I showed in the previous chapter, Djebar also inscribes herself both *within* and *against* historiographical tradition. In contrast to this tradition, she underscores the fictional aspect of historical narrative. In *Fantasia*, she exposes the ideology underpinning French colonial archives and uses fiction to fill in the blanks of history. As David Kelley rightly noted, these archival documents themselves are also autobiographical texts (diaries and letters) (845). In *Loin de Médine*, Djebar uses fiction to add to the slim commentaries on women's presence in ancient Islamic history, remaining faithful to the spirit if not the letter of the religious Tradition (Zimra, "Not So Far" 825–28). Djebar follows *Isnad* and considers herself a *rawiyat*, a link in the chain of transmission. She rewrites parts of Al-Tabari's monumental history in *Loin de Médine*, using his writings and criticizing them for their tendency to place women's presence and agency under erasure: "elles [les femmes] trouent, par brefs instants, mais dans des circonstances ineffaçables, le texte des chroniqueurs. . . . Transmetteurs certes scrupuleux, mais naturellement portés, par habitude déjà, à occulter toute présence féminine" [In brief instants but in unforgettable circumstances, women pierce through the Chroniclers' texts. . . . Although they are scrupulous transmitters, these men are already, by force of habit, naturally inclined to occult all female presence] (*Loin* 5). In *Fantasia*, Djebar cites her sources as well as the chain of transmission of knowledge. For example, when the narrator tells Lla Zohra, her relative, the story of the two nineteenth-century Algerian prostitutes immortalized in Fromentin's travelogue, Zohra demands to know the source of the story: "—Où as-tu entendu raconter cela? reprend-elle avec impatience. —Je l'ai lu! rétorqué-je. Un témoin le raconta à un ami qui l'écrivit" ["Where did you hear this story?" she went on, impatiently. "I read it!" I replied. "An eye-witness told it to a friend who wrote it down"] (188/166).

Like Ibn Khaldun but for different reasons, she is ambivalent about Isnad: "Chaîne de souvenirs: n'est-elle pas justement 'chaîne' qui entrave autant qu'elle enracine? Pour chaque passant, la parleuse stationne debout, dissimulée derrière le seuil. Il n'est pas séant de soulever le rideau et de s'exposer au soleil" [Chain of memories: is it not indeed a "chain," for do not memories fetter us as well as forming our roots? For every passer-by, the storyteller stands hidden behind the threshold. It is not seemly to raise the curtain and stand exposed in the sunlight] (*Fantasia* 201/178). Djebar operates a double transgression: she places Algerian women (herself included), not only within, but at the center of, history. Whenever possible, she follows a female Isnad. She focuses on female figures, which is one of the main differences between her work, on the one hand, and Ibn Khaldun's (and Islamic historiography in general), on the other. Whereas women are almost entirely absent from Ibn Khaldun's historical autobiography, *Fantasia* and *Loin de Médine* foreground women's presence and resistance in Algerian history. Ibn Khaldun only mentions women briefly, in his discussion of marriages linking two dynasties. The only woman who merits a paragraph is Shajar ad-Durr, who led her Turkish troops to victory against the French in Egypt and took Saint Louis as a prisoner (*Ta'arif* 192). Shajar ad-Durr recalls the legendary figure of Messaouda leading her brothers into battle in Djebar's *Femmes d'Alger* (179–81/143–44).[7]

Both Ibn Khaldun's and Djebar's texts mix genres and are crafted in very sophisticated ways. The *Ta'arif* contains, not only historical passages, but other literary forms as well (poems, letters, rhymed prose, speeches, quotations, etc.) (Fischel 162). Maya Shatzmiller indicated that "on peut retrouver dans le *Ta'rif* tous les éléments littéraires de l'époque" [in the *Ta'arif*, all the literary elements of the time are present] (52).[8] Djebar included archival documents, letters, official reports, and lyrical chapters in *Fantasia*. For both Djebar and Ibn Khaldun (but for different reasons), language, especially the written word, is both a bridge and a veil. Ibn Khaldun viewed writing as inferior to direct communication through speaking, and therefore as a double veil; for Djebar, the difficulty of writing rests on the fact that the "langue adverse" [enemy's language], French, is used to translate and transcribe Algerian women's voices (*Fantasia* 241/215; see also Mahdi 114).

Mushin Mahdi brilliantly demonstrated that Ibn Khaldun had two different intended audiences, the general public and the initiated reader. Consequently, there are two levels of reading in the *Kitab al 'Ibar*, to ensure that the general public will not be able to understand the book's concealed, subversive aspects. Ibn Khaldun thus made use of an indirect style, alluding to other authors or works that use a similar style in order to attract the initiated reader's attention toward this technique (Mahdi 118). The language used reminds the initiated reader "of other contexts in which he had met that particular word or phrase . . . and it may dawn upon him that the text may mean something different from, or contradictory to, the first impression it made upon him" (Mahdi 119).

Djebar uses a similar strategy. For example, she chooses the same words to depict sex and sleep, as well as torture and death. In *Ombre sultane*, the description of Isma's body after sex takes on a pessimistic connotation: the vocabulary used calls to mind the earlier description of Sarah's tortured body in the dream sequence opening the 1980 short story, "Femmes d'Alger:" "Gisante, tête renversée, chevelure en corolle de palmier, cou étiré en ligne convexe. . . . Corps labouré . . . un profil aux traits de cire apparaît, la sueur perle au front" [Lying with head thrown backward, hair spread out like the corolla of a palm tree, neck arched towards the bed. . . . A plowed body . . . a profile with waxen features appears, droplets of sweat on the brow] (*Ombre* 34/25). This description of Isma recalls that of Sarah: "Tête de jeune femme aux yeux bandés, cou renversé, cheveux tirés . . . une perle de sueur sur une tempe. . . . Et le profil tangue soudain" [A young woman's head, blindfolded, neck thrown backward, hair pulled back . . . a droplet of sweat on one temple. . . . And the profile pitches sharply] (*Femmes* 13/5). The pessimism is reinforced in this story through the repeated use of the same words to describe a dead patient: "Dans la salle de chirurgie, tête aux yeux bandés, profil de pierre renversé. Le malade est mort sur la table" [In the operating room, a blindfolded head, a profile of stone thrown backward. The patient has died on the operating table] (30/20).[9] In Djebar's work, each attempt at describing love implies danger and death. Conversely, each description of violence and war carries within itself the inscription of desire. This ambivalence is at the heart of the quartet's project, as the title, *L'Amour, la fantasia*, indicates: "L'amour, si je parvenais à l'écrire, s'approcherait d'un point nodal: là gît le risque d'exhumer des cris, ceux d'hier comme ceux du siècle dernier" [Love, if I managed to write it down, would approach a nodal point: there where lies the risk of exhuming buried cries, those of yesterday and those of a hundred years ago] (*Fantasia* 76/63). Djebar's novels render the female body present and give voice to its cries, in love as in rape and war.

Another way of attracting the initiated reader's attention is to insert a quotation or a cryptic commentary in the text. Ibn Khaldun often used other authors' words to convey his own ideas, sometimes altering citations to give them a slightly different meaning (Mahdi 121–23), a tactic Djebar uses as well. When incorporating Fromentin's sentence within *Ombre sultane*, she makes more than simple editorial changes; she repeats his words with a difference not only in the text, but also in the context. Although the meaning of his quotation is in no way changed, its context, which remains one of death, is diametrically altered, as I argue in the last part of this chapter. In the *Ta'arif*, Ibn Khaldun justified the repetition of historical narratives he had already detailed in the rest of the *'Ibar* by explaining that he wanted to provide "un éclairage d'un autre point de vue, susceptible d'intéresser le lecteur attentif" [another perspective that may be of interest to an attentive reader] (*Ta'arif* 166). In turn, Djebar, in addressing a double audience, Algerian/Maghrebian and French/Western (Gafaiti, *Femmes* 226), used a similar technique to destabilize her intertexts, turning Ibn Khaldun's literary strategies against his own text.

The quotation by Ibn Khaldun used by Djebar as an epigraph to the second part of *Fantasia* reads as follows: "Je dus moi-même diriger une expédition chez les tribus berbères des régions montagneuses de Béjaia, qui refusaient depuis plusieurs années de payer l'impôt. . . . Après avoir pénétré dans leur pays et vaincu leur résistance, je pris des otages en gage d'obéissance" [I myself had to lead an expedition into the mountainous region of Béjaia, where the Berber tribes had been refusing to pay taxes for some years. . . . After I had penetrated into their country and overcome their resistance, I took hostages to ensure their obedience] (*Fantasia* 59/47). This event took place in 766–67/1365–66, when Ibn Khaldun was governor of Bejaia. The taking of hostages had been common for a long time, and Ibn Khaldun reports having suffered from this practice himself several times (*Ta'arif* 106, 150, 174). For instance, he explains that his family did not immediately join him in Cairo in 784/1382 because the sultan of Tunis was keeping them hostage to ensure his return (174). In the context of the *Ta'arif*, the fact that he would mention his actions against the Berbers can be interpreted as part of his brutal honesty concerning his political and military activities and goes a long way toward explaining why he spent so much of his time trying to retire from political life. In the context of *Fantasia*, the meaning of the quotation is destabilized because it echoes a part of the novel in which the narrator rewrites the story of her tribe, the Beni-Menacer, in 1843. Because the family was one of the leaders of the resistance to French invaders in the region, a French officer named Saint-Arnaud took hostages from the family of Caliph Berkani (199–201). Djebar uses her quotation from Ibn Khaldun's autobiography in a subversive way by placing it in a context that leads the reader to draw parallels between Ibn Khaldun's actions and those of the French colonizers centuries later. The sexualized vocabulary used by Ibn Khaldun (the metaphor of penetration) strangely echoes that of the French colonizers and military officers. Because she is putting these two situations in parallel, Djebar could be criticized for perpetuating a colonial, Orientalist ideology that highlighted the dissentions between Arabs and Berbers according to the "divide and conquer" strategy, in order to facilitate French colonization.[10] However, such is not her goal. Djebar is highly critical of all forms of subjugation, including but not restricted to French colonization. As a woman of partly Berber descent,

she is equally critical of both the French and the Maghrebian subjugation of women, and she includes muted critiques of Arab treatment of
Berbers in several of her works, particularly in *La Zerda* and here,
through her use of Ibn Khaldun's epigraph.

Djebar's position vis-à-vis her intertext is thus an ambivalent one: the
Ta'arif is used as a reference point for *Fantasia*, just as *Fantasia* serves to
critique the *Ta'arif*. Using a quotation from the *Ta'arif* allows Djebar to
inscribe her text in a historical, autobiographical, and literary tradition
from the Maghreb. She can thus justify her project by modeling her book
on Ibn Khaldun's, but she is also critical of the latter. This ambivalent
attitude is characteristic of Djebar's relation to her epigraphs and intertexts
in general. The same movement of attraction-repulsion is present in the
original title of the novel. The title *L'Amour, la fantasia* [literally, *Love,
fantasia*, or *Love and war*] reflects Djebar's complex relation to her intertexts
and to her history through her interweaving of the multiple traditions
(Arabic and French, female and male, oral and written) in which she
inscribes her works.

The Arabian Nights as Narrative of the Frame

In *Ombre sultane*, Djebar rewrote a classic text of the Middle Eastern
literary tradition, *The Arabian Nights*. The only non-Western epigraph used
by Djebar in *Ombre sultane* comes from the passage in *The Arabian Nights*
where Scheherazade, having decided to put an end to the sultan's daily
killing of his wives, marries him and enlists the help of her sister,
Dinarzade.[11] The success of Scheherazade's plan depends upon her sister's
presence in the nuptial chamber (*Ombre* 101). The choice of the passage is
in itself illuminating, since Djebar's rewriting of the famous tale shifts the
focus from the power of words in deferring death to the lifesaving solidarity between the sultana and her hidden sister (Hannouche 1). In *Ombre*,
this theme is woven through the parallels and doublings created between
Scheherazade, Dinarzade, Isma, and Hajila.

Djebar gives her interpretation of *The Arabian Nights* in the passage
following her epigraph. There, she rewrites the tale, and thus makes her
own focus even more explicit: "Et la sultane sera sauvée pour un jour
encore, pour un deuxième, parce qu'elle invente certes, mais d'abord parce
que sa soeur a veillé et l'a réveillée. . . . Et notre peur à toutes aujourd'hui
se dissipe, puisque la sultane est double" [And the Sultana will be re-
prieved for one more day, then for another; indeed it is because she is
inventing tales, but first and foremost because her sister has stayed awake
and woken her in time. . . . And the fear of all of us women is dispelled

today, because of the two faces of the Sultana] (*Ombre* 103–4/95). Not only, then, do epigraphs place a text in a particular frame, but, more importantly, the text decenters the quotation by placing it on the margin, as a frame, recontextualizing it.

In her juxtaposition of two versions of the same event (the epigraph followed by her own rewriting), Djebar is foregrounding a process of repetition, which is already the founding gesture of her intertext itself (and is actually a central characteristic of Arabic literature). *The Arabian Nights* begins with an excess of female death: the sultan's brother finds that his wife was unfaithful to him, so he beheads her and her lover. When he witnesses his brother's wife and her maids having sex with slaves, he warns the sultan. The latter wishing to witness these illicit affairs for himself, the voyeuristic scene is repeated, this time with two spectators. A third independent example of female infidelity is provided before the sultan has his wife and servants killed. He then resolves to marry a new maiden each night and then to have her strangled in the morning in order to prevent any possible infidelity. Cheating and death increase with each repetition, from one occurrence to ten, then one hundred, to a final determination to destroy all young women. Repetition becomes woven into the fabric of the text as each day a new woman is wedded, bedded, and then put to death.

In order to defer and eventually stop the deathly repetition, Scheherazade's plan involves its substitution by a linguistic repetition. This linguistic repetition then becomes the central structural element of the book: every morning before dawn, after Dinarzade wakes her up, Scheherazade begins to tell a story to the sultan. At dawn, he allows her to live one more day in order to hear the end of the story. *The Arabian Nights* is a tale structured by repetition and *différance* [deferral/difference], in which the repetition itself makes a difference.

The first story told is that of the Genie and the Merchant. Like several other tales, it functions as a *mise en abyme* of Scheherazade's strategy. It is a tale of death deferred and eventually pardoned through the exchange of stories. Not only does the tale mimic Scheherazade's strategy, it also is clearly meant to be a message to her husband, the sultan, since she interrupts herself three times in the story—at precisely the point when a character is about to kill another whose death (like hers) is thus postponed by daybreak. In this tale, three old men tell a story to a genie in exchange for another merchant's life. It is through their solidarity with the merchant that the latter is saved. "The Genie and the Merchant" thus foregrounds the central themes of the framing story, including solidarity. It also repeats its structural premise of endless mirrorings through the presence of embedded narratives.

The repetition of tales and the daily deferral of death begin to slowly effect change, as the sultan decides first to give his wife a one-month reprieve, then a second one, without, however, letting her know of his decision. Sensing his wavering, Scheherazade takes the risk of ending one of her tales one morning, promising to begin a new one on the next day, and is spared. Later, the sultan will take it upon himself not to wait for Dinarzade's call, waking his wife up himself. After one thousand and one nights, he finally lifts her death sentence, telling Scheherazade: "[J]e veux que vous soyez regardée comme la libératrice de toutes les filles qui devaient être immolées à mon juste ressentiment" [I want you to be considered as the liberator of all the young girls who were to be sacrificed to my just resentment] (*Mille et une nuits* 3:496). Womankind is thus saved from male repression thanks to female solidarity and to the seizing of language by a woman, two themes that are at the heart of Djebar's work.

As Dalila Hannouche remarked, "[C]ontrairement à son intertexte, le roman de Djebar fera des personnages féminins de son prologue, l'objet de la narration" [As opposed to its intertext, Djebar's novel makes the female protagonists of its Prologue the object of the narrative] (3). For her, the second part of *Ombre sultane* corresponds to the methodical female destruction on which the sultan embarks, prompting Scheherazade's action. Although Hannouche did acknowledge that the various stories told in Part 2 of *Ombre sultane* are "une série de récits enchâssés au sein du récit principal" [a series of narratives embedded within the main narrative] (5), she did not make the link between these and the stories told by Scheherazade. Rather than seeing them as emblematic of female destruction, I view the six tales embedded in Isma and Hajila's story as a short version of Scheherazade's tales, foregrounding the oral transmission of female knowledge. They are introduced by a commentary on Scheherazade and Dinarzade. The irruption of "je" [I] in the first story indicates that Isma is taking up the role of the narrator (*Ombre* 110/101). In *Ombre sultane*, as in *The Arabian Nights*, the content of the tales, even though they introduce new characters, is directly relevant to the main story. Isma insists on the importance of the events she recounts in her process of coming to consciousness as an Algerian woman. The tales foreground what the silence of women usually covers up. They also represent steps toward progressive enlightenment—culminating in personal memory. In the last story, Isma's father, the one who saved her from the harem, is revealed to be a man who still subscribes to traditional sexual politics, which shows her the limits of alliances with seemingly open-minded men. (This theme will be repeated in her relationship with her husband.) The tales represent both a reflection of Isma's and Hajila's predicaments and a will to weave other women's stories with those of the novel's protagonists.

In *Ombre sultane*, repetition is inscribed in the tales, at the thematic level (the sexual oppression of women in Algerian society as it is perpetuated both by men and by women themselves) as well as at the textual level. For instance, in the first story, one of the women, who significantly remains anonymous, voices her distress at having to be sexually available to her husband at night and having to cook and keep house for him all day. The complaint that should not have been voiced is hushed by the other women, but it is loudly repeated by little Isma, prompting a second silencing from the group of women. Instead of agreeing to hide what was not to be said, Isma the narrator repeats it once more, transcribing it in writing and in another language (112/103); as it had begun to open her consciousness, she hopes that it will have a similar effect on other women reading it.

Repetition is also inscribed in *Ombre sultane* through the mirrorings and doublings between Scheherazade, Dinarzade, Isma, and Hajila, as the sultana and her sister begin to exchange roles. Hajila, watching herself in the mirror, recurrently experiences a feeling of alienation. At the beginning of the novel, as she contemplates her face in "le petit miroir, près de la fenêtre" [the little mirror near the window], the narrator asks: "ton visage serait-il celui d'une autre?" [could your face be that of another woman?] (15/7). She thus establishes an early parallel between the two cowives. The mixing of their fates was already announced in the first pages of the book: "Isma, Hajila: arabesque des noms entrelacés. . . . Avons-nous interverti nos rôles? Je ne sais" [Isma, Hajila: an arabesque of intertwining names. . . . Have we reversed our roles? I cannot tell] (9, 11/1–2). This theme culminates at the end of Part 1, when the drunken husband, seeing Hajila, mistakes her for Isma, his first wife (93/84).

The similarity between the situations of the two women is reinforced by the repetition of "Comme moi" [like me], "Comme toi" [like you], at the beginning of several paragraphs in Chapter 13 (93–94). The repetition of the abusive situation in which the only difference is the woman present indicates that Hajila and Isma have become almost interchangeable (Hannouche 6). It is in this chapter that Isma, thoroughly blending "I" and "you," clearly states her purpose: "je mélange. Je mêle nos deux vies" [I mix our two lives, I make them merge] (91). The difference, however, is that Isma has arranged the marriage between Hajila and her own husband through Hajila's mother Touma. As Katherine Gracki noted, Isma herself is guilty of participating in the structure of the seraglio (839). The movement toward solidarity is hampered by the participation of women in their own—and other women's—oppression.

The fact that the two women should be seen as mirror images of each other, rather than as rivals per se, is exemplified in the many references to mirrorings and doublings throughout the novel. Isma's words to Hajila, "toi qui me remplaces cette nuit" [you who stand in for me tonight] (94/85), create parallels between Isma and Hajila's destinies and the fates of the two sisters from *The Arabian Nights*. Cowives who wound each other (the term *derra*, used to refer to the second wife, means "wound" in Arabic), the two women must become sisters grappling for lifesaving solidarity (*Ombre* 13, 100/5, 91). In the second part of the novel, this theme becomes central. From the start, Djebar introduces the possibility that the women may switch places. At the beginning of *Ombre sultane*, Isma seems to be playing the part of Scheherazade, since she is the narrator of the story. Like Dinarzade under the bed, Hajila is described as "une ombre-soeur" [a shadow-sister] (91) whose voice is covered (or at least mediated) by Isma's "tu." In the title, "ombre" would refer to Dinarzade and Hajila, and the word "sultane" to Scheherazade and Isma.

The doubles intersect, however, in an inversion of *The Arabian Nights*, as the storyteller (Isma as narrator) becomes the sister under the bed who awakes the sultana (*Ombre* 113/103), the sister who, in the darkness of the hammam, gives the sultana (Hajila) the apartment key that will allow her to escape her predicament (163–64/153). The two women, like Scheherazade and Dinarzade in Djebar's rewriting of the tale, become doubles of one another: "[T]our à tour, toi et moi, fantômes et reflets pour chacune, nous devenons la sultane et sa suivante, la suivante et sa sultane!" [(Y)ou and I, ghost and mirror-image of each other, we become in turn the sultana and her attendant, the attendant and her sultana!] (*Ombre* 168/158).

In spite of this doubling, their trajectories remain distinct: as Hajila escapes, Isma chooses to reenter the shadow (169/159). She first attempts to free herself by going away alone, sacrificing two other women in the process (she abandons her daughter and victimizes Hajila). She chooses Hajila as mother for her daughter (155/145), even though Isma knows her husband's abusive streak (93–94/84–85). However, she realizes that she must come back "par un sursaut de solidarité avec la petite" [in an impulse of solidarity with my little girl] (165/155). She eventually extends solidarity to Hajila by giving her the apartment key. Isma thus discovers the impossibility of separating herself from other women's fates.

Isma's actions may be interpreted as a criticism of a certain form of Western emancipation based on individualism, and may explain her desire to reenter the shadow. Because breaking free from the harem necessarily entails separation from the women who live there, rejoining that community requires a return to that space, which can also be a space of sisterhood. Moreover, Westerners (and specifically, French colonizers) have used a strong critique of the veil (as a symbol for women's lower status in Algerian society) as a way to strengthen their own power over the colonized by disturbing part of the existing social structure (Fanon, "L'Algérie" 18/37). Isma's desire to re-veil herself can be viewed as a rejection of Western (neo)colonialism's monolithic equation of the veil to female subordination (Ahmed, "Western Ethnocentrism" 523; Mohanty, "Under Western Eyes" 66–67). This (Western) equation serves to reinforce stereotypes about the general barbarism and inferiority of peoples whom the colonial powers sought to dominate, and, thereby, justifies colonization (Lowe 39–44). Isma's decision to reenter the shadows is thus a choice that navigates between the influences of patriarchal impositions and of Western traditions. The presence of Hajila's opposite trajectory shows that liberation can and must follow paths as diverse as those of women themselves. Sisterhood is the challenge women must embrace in order to free themselves from the death sentence pronounced against them, overcoming institutionalized female rivalry to protect each other like Scheherazade and Dinarzade.

It is possible to interpret the Isma-Hajila dyad as two sides of the same woman and to attribute autobiographical valences to each of them. The back cover of *Ombre sultane* displays a picture of Djebar, standing inside looking out through a window, perhaps representing both Hajila yearning to go out and Isma losing herself in the desired "shadow" of the novel's title. This picture could be interpreted as a staging of the Victor Hugo epigraph in the third part of the book: "La fenêtre enfin libre est ouverte à la brise / La sultane regarde" [Finally free, the window is open to the breeze / The sultana looks on] (151). Such an interpretation suggests the possibility that the novel's protagonists could be seen as the outside representation of an inner struggle; as in *Fantasia*, the autobiographical revealing is hidden behind the veil of fiction.

In this respect, it becomes interesting to consider the parallels between the character of Isma and the unnamed narrator of *Fantasia*. Djebar explicitly identified herself with the latter in an interview (quoted in Mortimer, "Entretien" 203). Critics such as Mildred Mortimer seem to have taken for granted that the two women are one and the same (Mortimer, *Journeys* 159). The passage in which Hajila's accident is described provides clues to verify this hypothesis. The passage is uncannily reminiscent of an accident that befell the narrator of *Fantasia* when, after a fight with her boyfriend, she ran out and threw herself under a street-car. Both accidents take place in a similar location, near the harbor; the verb "se précipiter" [to rush forward] is used to describe both actions; and death's touch is in both cases described as a wing: "l'aile de la mort vous caresse" [death caresses you with its wing] (*Ombre* 168/158) recalls the "parure de la mort dont l'aile traîne, un instant, sur le sol" [death's finery briefly trails a wing along the ground] (*Fantasia* 130/114). More importantly, it is Isma herself who provides the link: "Je me suis revue, dix, onze ans auparavant. . . . Moi, j'ai regardé ton visage pâle. J'ai vu le mien, que je n'avais jamais pu voir, à ce même instant où l'aile de la mort vous caresse, où son sourire imperceptible semble vous dire 'pas maintenant, ce n'est point l'heure!' Mon visage que je n'ai pas trouvé" [I saw myself, as I had been ten, eleven years before. . . . I gazed at your pale face. I saw my own face, as I had been, as I had never seen myself, at that same instant when death caresses you with its wing and its imperceptible smile seems to say to you, "Not yet, the time is not yet right!" My own face, the face that I never discovered] (*Ombre* 168–69/158–59). This would seem to indicate that Isma is in fact the same woman as the narrator of *Fantasia*. If this is true, then it appears that one of the narrator's aims in *Ombre sultane* is to overcome the "aphasie amoureuse" [aphasia of love] that she self-diagnoses when using the French language in *Fantasia* (142/125).[12]

This desire to overcome her aphasia of love brings Djebar to center on an aspect of *The Arabian Nights* that had been repressed (at least in the nineteenth-century French edition)—namely, the sexual relation between the sultan and his wife. (It is mentioned in passing that during the thousand nights, Scheherazade managed to do more than tell stories, since she gave the sultan several children.) Isma as narrator of her own story "choisi[t] de ne réveiller que les nuits . . . mille peut-être" [choose(s) only to awaken the nights . . . a thousand of them perhaps] (*Ombre* 20/12). The nights she describes, especially in Chapters 4 and 6, are an attempt to speak of the unspeakable—the sexual pleasure experienced by an Algerian woman in love.[13]

Once again, Djebar creates an opposition between the pleasure and harmony existing in Isma's sexual relation to a man in these chapters, and the rape experienced by Hajila with the same man in Chapter 9. Then, Djebar blurs this opposition in Chapter 10, when Isma recalls the violence and lack of communication that was sometimes present in a generally satisfying sexual relation. Djebar thus breaks another taboo, exposing not only what Irigaray would call the persistence of *jouissance*, but also its darker side, the power struggle involved in the sexual relation. Indeed, the night of love and *jouissance* can turn into the violence of rape: the first wedding night is recurrently described as a rape in most of Djebar's works (*Alouettes* 177–78; *Femmes d'Alger* 178; *Fantasia* 122–24; *Ombre* 66–67). The violence of the sexual relation is exemplified by the vocabulary of war in Chapters 9 and 10 of *Ombre sultane*: "lutte" [battle], "résistance" [resistance], "le phallus . . . épée" [the penis . . . sword], "Tu te bats, il te fouaille" [You struggle against him, he lashes at you] (66–67/57–58) are words used to describe Hajila's first sexual encounter with her husband. In parallel, Isma remembers the occasional nights of violent "affrontement" [confrontation] when she would reject her husband and he would pursue her: "me barricader" [put up barricades], "l'intrusion" [the intrusion], "je défie. Me débats" [I am defiant. I struggle] (75/66). Once again, the opposition between the two women is deconstructed when it is revealed that both experienced violence at the hands of the same man. Rather than being polar opposites, they become doubles of each other, two different sides of one woman.

If we consider Isma's character to be autobiographical, Hajila would be an autobiographical figure as well—Djebar's hidden side perhaps. This puts Djebar in the impossible position of wishing to both unveil herself on the outside and reenter the shadows, a position that is precisely that of the bicultural writer circulating between two worlds. Both Mildred Mortimer ("Assia Djebar's *Algerian Quartet*" 107, 110) and Christiane Achour (cited in Gafaiti, *Femmes* 184) view Hajila as a fictional character and Isma as an autobiographical character. Since both women are shown to be doubles of each other, however, it follows that they must both encompass fictional and autobiographical aspects. The parallels between the scenes of domestic violence against Hajila in *Ombre* and against the narrator in *Vaste*, a novel in which narrator and author are closer than ever in Djebar's fiction, bear witness to the autobiographical nature of at least some of Hajila's experiences.[14]

In his book *Les Femmes dans le roman algérien*, Hafid Gafaiti proposed a reading of *Ombre sultane* as a *roman à thèse* [didactic novel]. He claimed that Djebar uses the *Arabian Nights* intertext and a monolithic narrative voice (Isma's) to create a reductionist feminist novel that refuses a plural reading (181–83). While the novel is clearly about "une dénonciation de l'oppression des femmes dans le cadre de la société patriarcale" [a denunciation of women's oppression in a patriarchal society] (185), I hope to have shown that *Ombre sultane*, like Djebar's entire novelistic production, only sets up binary categories such as emancipated versus traditional women in order to undermine and deconstruct them. Therefore, Isma, the "emancipated woman," wants to re-veil herself; women as well as men are shown to have a responsibility in perpetuating patriarchal structures; Isma and Hajila turn out to be two facets of the same woman.

One of the main problems Gafaiti seems to have with the novel is its presentation of the husband as the Other, and the shift Djebar makes most clearly in this novel and in her rewriting of her *Arabian Nights* intertext from a focus on the couple to a focus on relationships between women. The husband, as well as all the male characters in *Ombre*, only play a secondary role (like that played by female characters in much fiction, including Maghrebian literature written by men). Rather than interpret this shift in focus as ideologically reductionist (*Femmes* 214), it may be argued that Djebar is transgressing a well-established literary and cultural code. Djebar's feminist perspective, both in the manipulation of her intertext and in the body of the novel, is much more subtle than Gafaiti gave her credit for. He preferred the ambiguities, ambivalences and "zones d'ombre" [shadowy zones] (215) of *Fantasia* to the outspoken feminist problematic that subtends *Ombre*. He does not take into account the transgressive nature of Djebar's articulation of the *non-dit* (the unspoken of her culture), the subversion enacted in her refusal to speak from the shadows and the margins when it comes to taboo subjects such as women's sexuality and women's status in patriarchal societies. Through her recourse to the intertext of *The Arabian Nights*, Djebar beautifully rises to the challenge of breaking the taboo around writing sexuality from a female perspective and doing so with *pudeur*, a feat that, to my mind, only she, among all writers from Algeria, has achieved.

Eugène Fromentin and Djebar's Algerian Mimicry

Djebar's Algerian mimicry is most complex in her use of Eugène Fromentin's travel narratives. In *Fantasia*, as in *Une Année dans le Sahel*, Fromentin's words announce the death of the mysterious Haoûa, an Algerian woman living alone, who had befriended the painter and his companion. She is purposely trampled to death by one of the horse riders of the fantasia, a man she had left earlier. Since Haoûa's veil and robe hide her face and body, her voice is what first strikes Fromentin. She is revealed by Djebar to be a woman, not only on the margins of her society, but also on the margins of French literature: "Première Algérienne d'une fiction en

langue française à aller et venir, oiseusement, première à respirer en marge
et à feindre d'ignorer la transgression" [The first Algerian woman to circulate within a narrative written in French, the first to breathe in its margins, pretending not to realize she is trespassing] (*Fantasia* 253/225). While
her story provides the common thread in Fromentin's travel narrative, the
painter himself insists (possibly in order to elicit a contradictory response
on the part of the readers, or in an unconscious denial of his own emotional involvement) on the fact that Haoûa's story is only on the margins
of his text. He writes of their first meeting: "Je note entre parenthèses cet
incident, de peu de valeur du reste" [I am merely recording this incident
(which has little value in itself) between parentheses] (*Une Année* 67). The
"parentheses" slowly come to absorb a large portion of Fromentin's text,
and Haoûa's death, occurring at the height of the fantasia, serves as the
climax of the book.

Haoûa's story becomes the pre-text giving impetus to *Fantasia*, and the
postscript to *Ombre sultane*. However, in the shift from the first novel to
the second, Djebar endows her intertext with a more liberating meaning
for Algerian women by insisting on the active "transgression" in which
Hajila engages. *Fantasia* closes with these pessimistic words: "j'attends, je
pressens l'instant immanquable où le coup de sabot à la face renversera
toute femme dressée libre, . . . j'entends le cri de la mort dans la fantasia"
[I wait, foreseeing the inevitable moment when the mare's hoof will strike
down in the face any woman who dares to stand up freely, . . . I hear the
death cry in the fantasia] (256/227). In contrast, in *Ombre sultane*,
Fromentin's sentence is inserted in a key passage in which Hajila aggres-
sively takes her fate in her own hands and crosses the point of no return
by committing one of the most taboo acts in a society depicted as valuing
women mostly for their childbearing capacity: she throws herself under a
car in order to abort her fetus. She loses her abusive husband's baby, and
survives. Like Haoûa before her, Hajila will leave her husband to attempt
life as a free woman. While her survival remains framed by death (the final
words of the novel prophesy a dark future for Maghrebian women, 171–
72/160), the Algerian woman in a narrative written in French nevertheless
gains agency and survives.[15]

Djebar's use of mimicry with respect to Fromentin's narrative extends even further. Fromentin himself had introduced intertextuality
into *Une Année dans le Sahel*, not only by his art criticism—he discusses the merits of several Orientalist painters—but also in a small
passage less than two pages long in which he brought one of his sources
into his own text in order to comment on it. This passage provided
Djebar with a model on how to incorporate archival materials in *Fan-*

tasia. Like Fromentin before her, she makes herself both reporter of other texts and commentator on them. She recurrently applies the technique Fromentin once used: she reports from archival texts in order to reconstruct Algerian history and she transcribes oral testimonies of Algerian women—commenting on both of these sources in order to weave her own text through them.

In the presentation of his source, *L'Esquisse de l'Etat d'Alger* by U.S. diplomat W. Shaler, Fromentin seems to reproduce, whether consciously or not, the pattern of Arabic religious texts that Fatima Mernissi depicts in *Le Harem politique*. In the gathering of the Prophet's *Hadith*, the transcriber(s) documented the reliability of the informants so that the reader can "juge[r] à tout moment s'ils sont dignes ou non de foi" [continually judge whether they are worthy of credence or not] (49/35). In a striking parallel, Fromentin begins by providing us with a summary of Shaler's life, insisting on his link to various sources of information (personal observation, knowledge of intelligence reports), his neutrality as outside observer in a pending Anglo-Algerian conflict, and his precision in taking notes "jour par jour, heure par heure" [day after day, hour after hour] (*Une Année* 166).

Djebar follows a similar pattern, providing her reader with as much information as is available on her sources. However, her purpose is different. While Fromentin was legitimating his intertext, Djebar's comments on the French officers' documents (which she uses to recreate Algeria's history) question the reliability of the French archives on Algerian history, in order to make manifest the authors' presuppositions and political goals. For instance, she notes that the publication of some of the French officers' correspondence from Algeria "entretient le prestige de ces auteurs" [ensures the continuing prestige of these authors] (*Fantasia* 63/51), one of whom later went on to become "hero" and "martyr" (63). In order to question the reliability of their reports, Djebar begins by writing (in a very vivid style interspersed with dialogue) her own account of a battle in which Algerian teenage boys and women were massacred by the French army. She then concludes by quoting from the correspondence of two French captains: "Notre petite armée est dans la joie et les festins"; "la poésie . . . de la razzia" and "Ce petit combat offrait un coup d'oeil charmant . . . tout cela présentait un panorama délicieux et une scène enivrante" [Our little army is celebrating with feasts . . . the poetry . . . in the *razzia*. . . . This little fray offered a charming spectacle . . . all this combined to present a delightful panorama and an exhilarating scene] (*Fantasia* 67/54). In the abyss created between the fictionalized account and the cover-up in the letters, the latter is destabilized: the historical documents (which dull the violence of combat by describing it in aesthetic terms as one would a Delacroix painting) fall into the realm of fiction, while Djebar's own reconstruction gains legitimacy as historical narrative.

The use of this technique makes Djebar's peculiar style in *Fantasia* reminiscent of the passage in *Une Année dans le Sahel* in which Fromentin initiated the strategy. But Fromentin himself was already mimetically reproducing Shaler's writing, a mixture—as he informs the reader—of personal testimony, reports of intelligence leaks, and an accumulation of precise details. The final product, according to Fromentin, could be called a hybrid text: "un journal fort original, une sorte d'histoire panoramique qui devient vivante à force de précision, et pittoresque à cause du point de vue" [quite an original journal offering some kind of panoramic history enlivened by details, and whose point of view makes it picturesque] (*Une Année* 166). Fromentin's narrative, in turn, defies categorization: partly travelogue, partly philosophical diary, Orientalist commentary, art criticism, and autobiographical novel, the terms "text" or "narrative" are the only ones broad enough to encompass it. Similarly, *Fantasia*, although billed as a "roman" [novel], participates in the same hybrid nature: it is at once an autobiography, a historical narrative, a rewriting of archives, a transcription of oral testimonies, and a socio-political commentary. Intertextuality, which was marginally present in Fromentin's text, becomes a central structural element of *Fantasia*. As a model for her novel, Djebar chose a hybrid text that already contained another hybrid text embedded within it, thus creating a mise en abyme of the palimpsestic process of writing.

The mise en abyme reappears at another level. Fromentin introduces Shaler's book in order to center on "un détail . . . insignifiant" [an insignificant detail] within it (*Une Année* 166): a description of a blooming cactus whose beautiful flower died within a day. These words bring to mind the way in which Fromentin downplayed his first meeting with Haoûa: "cet incident, de peu de valeur du reste" [this incident (which has little value in itself)] (67). The similar vocabulary that he used could imply the self-referential nature of Fromentin's text: Haoûa's story could well correspond to the detail that illuminated Shaler's book and pleased Fromentin so much that he confessed to wanting to write in such a way, telling his implied reader: "Si jamais il m'arrivait d'être l'historiographe d'un événement politique ou militaire, sois bien assuré qu'à mon insu je trouverais moyen de faire épanouir à un moment donné . . . quelque chose comme le *cactus grandiflora* de l'Américain Shaler" [If I ever became the historiographer of a political or military event, be assured that, unbeknownst to me, I would find a way to make something like Shaler's *cactus grandiflora* bloom at some point] (167). In the middle of the military event of the fantasia, Fromentin, consciously or not ("à mon insu" [unbeknownst to me]), created his own *cactus grandiflora*, the story of the Algerian woman who was, to him, "comme une fleur odorante" [like a sweet-smelling flower] (143), doomed to an early death. This interpretation is supported by Fromentin's insistence on the fact that Shaler's detail "encadre l'histoire" [frames the story] (167). This is exactly the structural function that Haoûa's story has in *Une Année dans le Sahel*. Djebar, in turn, reproduces the same pattern by using Haoûa's story as a central framing and structural device in *Fantasia*: she appropriates it to open and close her text, and rewrites it in one of her final chapters. The "insignificant detail" of an Algerian woman's life and death becomes an emblematic story framing Algerian history in Djebar's rewriting.

Djebar also found another *cactus grandiflora* in Fromentin's other Algerian travelogue, *Un Eté dans le Sahara*: in the last chapter, near the corpses of three Algerian women, the painter finds the severed hand of one of them. Djebar repeats this gruesome detail in the last chapter of *Fantasia*, but with a difference. She picks up the hand that Fromentin had literally thrown out in fear, in order to attempt to give it—and herself—new life through writing: "[J]e me saisis de cette main vivante, main de la mutilation et du souvenir et je tente de lui faire porter le 'qalam'" [I seize this living hand, hand of mutilation and of memory, and I attempt to bring it the *qalam*] (*Fantasia* 255/226). Just as Fromentin had remarked about Shaler's *cactus grandiflora*, then, for Djebar, the small paragraph about the severed hand functions as "[c]e mince détail observé par hasard [qui] illumine à mon avis tout le cours du volume" [this slight detail observed by chance [that] to my mind casts a new light on the course of the entire book] (*Une Année* 167). The endings of both of Djebar's novels, however, are prophetically pessimistic: to the fear of the destruction of the woman standing in *Fantasia* corresponds the fear that the dawn of women's liberation in the Maghreb is already turning into dusk in *Ombre* (171–72/160). Shaler's *cactus grandiflora*, whose beautiful flower blooms and dies within a day, can serve as a metaphor for Djebar's ultimately pessimistic view of the future of Algerian women. Eight years after the publication of *Ombre sultane*, after the repression of a popular uprising in October 1988 and the beginning of the downward spiral of violence in which Algeria is still embroiled, the third volume of the quartet also ends on the death of another woman, a journalist and teacher who was killed in 1994 for holding the *kalam* [pen] (*Vaste* 344).[16] The term marks the juncture between *Fantasia* and *Vaste*, connecting the death of the nine-teenth-century woman to that of her contemporary compatriot. It casts the shadow of death not only over the woman who dares stand up in the light, but on the woman who tells stories and writes in the darkness of the night as well.

Djebar treats her diverse epigraphs in similar ways. She inscribes her-self in a Maghrebian literary tradition in which intertextuality plays a fundamental role (Gafaiti, *Femmes* 331). She uses Ibn Khaldun's autobiog-raphy as a model for her project at the same time as she criticizes some of his historical and political practices. She reduces the importance of the many tales that are the focus of *The Arabian Nights* and centers on the book's exemplary frame, its pretext for the telling of stories. She chooses to foreground Scheherazade and Dinarzade's story as both frame (epigraph) and center (the focus of her own text). Finally, she reframes her nine-teenth-century intertext, Fromentin's *Une Année dans le Sahel*, by incorpo-rating it into *Ombre sultane*. In Julia Kristeva's terms, Djebar transformed the "univers" [universe] imposed on her text by "la juridiction des autres discours" [the jurisdiction of other discourses] (*Révolution* 339). By appro-priating other discourses through mimicry, Djebar transforms their con-text of production, underscoring both the tensions inherent in her writing project and her desire to bring out women's voices, even at the risk of death.

Notes

1. Although the table of contents in *Vaste* indicates that the text is divided into four parts, the last part is extremely short and functions structurally exactly like the finale in *Fantasia*.

2. In *Vaste*, the alternation is less obvious. In the last part, Djebar brings together two epigraphs that both focus on suffering, one from the contempo-rary French feminist writer Jeanne Hyvrard and the other from the four-teenth-century Persian Sufi poet Hafiz.

3. I analyze the parallels between Djebar's and Bonnard's works in Chapter 5 (on painting).

4. Diana Fuss also compares Irigaray's and Bhabha's concepts of mimicry in "Interior Colonies" (24–25).

5. Boudjedra's protagonist, Mohamed SNP (sans nom patronymique [no last name]), searches during the entire novel for traces of Ibn Khaldun's sup-posed presence in his village centuries earlier, only to realize in the end that the famous historian must have been his own ancestor. However, this lineage will never be officially recognized. SNP will not be allowed to name himself Ibn Khaldun. This highlights the irony of the postcolonial situation, which

cannot erase the gaps between past and present caused by colonization. On *Le Désert*, see Judith Roumani. I have used the same version of Ibn Khaldun's *Ta'arif* as did Djebar: a French translation by Abdesselam Cheddadi titled *Le Voyage d'Occident et d'Orient*.

6. Academic research on Ibn Khaldun has a long history of being self-interested: each scholar seems bent on proving that Ibn Khaldun was the father of a discipline or body of thought. He variously becomes the father of the science of history (Lacoste; Al-Azmeh, *Ibn Khaldun: An Essay*), sociology (Enan, Lahbabi), and even Marxism (Lacoste). As Aziz Al-Azmeh demonstrated, Ibn Khaldun's work was reappropriated by nineteenth- and twentieth-century Orientalist scholars who wanted to prove the following presuppositions: Ibn Khaldun was an exception in his time and culture; moreover, he used modern concepts that were later developed more fully by Western social science; therefore, he was closer to a Western, as opposed to a Maghrebian, Arab, or Islamic, intellectual tradition. One of the reasons why Orientalist scholars were so interested in Ibn Khaldun, according to Al-Azmeh, is that "[s]cholarship follows the flag" (*Ibn Khaldun in Modern Scholarship* 209). In other words, a selective reading of Ibn Khaldun was used by the Orientalists to justify the French colonial venture in the Maghreb (219–22). Yves Lacoste (65–68, 75–76) and Abdesselam Cheddadi (14–22) make similar arguments.

7. Rachid Boudjedra plays on the same intertextual register in *Les 1001 années de la nostalgie*, giving these two names to his protagonist's wife, who, like her historical counterpart, is hailed as "symbole de la résistance et libératrice des hommes" [the symbol of resistance and liberator of men] (343).

8. On the style and literary aspect of Ibn Khaldun's work, see Mahdi 113–25; see also Al-Azmeh, *Ibn Khaldun in Modern Scholarship* 48, and Cooke, "Ibn Khaldun" 27–36.

9. The female body asleep is often connected to death in Djebar's works. In *Les Alouettes naïves*, Nfissa's body is compared to "un corps fusillé, cadavre" [a body shot, a corpse] (164). In the film *La Nouba*, Lila dreams of men being shot dead by a firing squad. In the short story "La Femme qui pleure" (*Femmes d'Alger*), the description of the spouses' bodies in bed is one of death, including the words "squelette" [skeleton] and "gisants" [tombstone statuary] (71/53). In *Les Nuits de Strasbourg*, the fragmented syntax of the sentence following the description of Thelja's orgasm is modeled after her uncomfortable position: "Peu après, Thelja, cou ployé, face en arrière" [Not long afterward, Thelja, neck bent, face thrown back] (272).

10. See Lacoste 65–68, 75–76, and Cheddadi 14–22.

11. As Hafid Gafaiti correctly noted, however, *The Arabian Nights* is a liminal text, "[un] texte oriental . . . que l'Occident a intégré depuis fort longtemps" [an Oriental text, which the West integrated long ago] (*Femmes* 226).

12. In *Les Nuits de Strasbourg*, Djebar's narrator, Thelja, tells the same story of her own attempted suicide (314–18).

13. Djebar refers to this intertext again in *Les Nuits de Strasbourg*, in which she describes nine nights of pleasure experienced by an Algerian woman and a Frenchman.

14. See Katherine Gracki's analysis of the parallels between the two scenes (especially pp. 840–41); see also Mildred Mortimer, "Assia Djebar's *Algerian Quartet*" 107–10. A similar scene of domestic violence had already been quickly sketched in Djebar's short story "La femme qui pleure" (*Femmes d'Alger* 71–72, 76/53, 56). I contend that in *Vaste est la prison*, Djebar engages in fully autobiographical writing for the first time and no longer feels the need to hide behind a screen narrator. At the very end of the book, she wonders whether to bring Isma, the narrator, back into her text, a question she leaves unanswered (331). By the time Djebar wrote *Vaste*, she was clearly moving away from a conception of writing as veiling to one of writing as revelation.

15. Beïda Chikhi noted that "la quasi-totalité des romans d'Assia Djebar, aboutissait à un final dysphorique" [almost all of Djebar's novels have dysphoric endings] ("Histoire" 28).

16. The word is spelled differently from one novel to the other.

Chapter 5

▼▼▼▼▼▼▼▼▼

Refiguring French/Orientalist Painting

Ces guerriers qui paradent me deviennent, au milieu des cris que leur style élégant ne peut atténuer, les amants funèbres de mon Algérie. Le viol ou la souffrance des anonymes ainsi rallumés devraient m'émouvoir en premier; mais je suis étrangement hantée par l'émoi même des tueurs, par leur trouble obsessionnel [These parading warriors become for me the deathly lovers of my Algeria, in the middle of cries that cannot be subdued by the elegance of their style. I should first and foremost be moved by the rape or suffering of the anonymous victims, which their writings rekindle; but I am strangely haunted by the very agitation of the killers, by their obsessional inner turmoil].

—Assia Djebar, *Fantasia* 69/57

Dans l'album de photographies de la guerre d'Algérie, des hommes, des parachutistes ressemblent à celui-là [un milicien libanais]. Elle n'a pas le droit de le trouver beau, comme elle s'empêchait d'être troublée par ces jeunes guerriers des colonies, lorsqu'elle feuilletait le livre dans la librairie des deux soeurs [In the book of photographs on the Algerian war, the men, the paratroopers look just like him (a Lebanese guerrilla). She does not have the right to think that he is handsome, just as, when she leafed through the book in the two sisters' bookstore, she would repress within herself the inner trouble caused by the sight of the young colonial warriors].

—Leïla Sebbar, *Le Fou de Shérazade* 101

[Julien] se dit qu'il fallait en finir avec ce trouble étrange qui lui faisait battre le coeur, chaque fois qu'il voyait dans un tableau

orientaliste ces deux figures, si présentes dans la peinture occidentale
du XIXe siècle, la Noire et la Blanche [Julien told himself he must
get rid of this strange trouble which made his heart beat faster
every time he saw these two female figures in an Orientalist picture, so ubiquitous in Western nineteenth-century painting, the
one Black, the other White].

—Leïla Sebbar, *Shérazade* 75/78–79

European painting (and film and photography to a lesser extent) plays a
pivotal role in Djebar's and Sebbar's works. Djebar has gone as far as to
claim that "I could not have done it [inscribed my innermost self in my
work] without the mediation of painting and the 'intercession' of painters"
(quoted in Zimra, "Afterword" 171–72). Both writers sometimes refer to
the same paintings; their protagonists take on the Orientalist tradition and
lucidly assess both their fascination with and their distance from it. The
main characters insist on the essentially ambiguous nature of their fascination. They feel a deep ambivalence toward these representations of Algerian women. Interestingly, Djebar, as opposed to Sebbar, does not engage
only the Orientalist tradition in painting. She holds a special place in her
fiction for postimpressionist painter Pierre Bonnard. In this chapter, I begin by analyzing her interest in this non-Orientalist painter, before focusing on Djebar's and Sebbar's engagements with Orientalist paintings.

Pierre Bonnard and the Aesthetics of the Margins

A French painter who haunts Djebar's fictional universe, Bonnard has
so far remained in the shadows in terms of critical attention. *Ombre sultane*
opens with an epigraph by him. Bonnard is never once referred to in the
text, and the unexpected choice of the turn-of-the-century postimpressionist painter and member of the "Nabi" group intrigued me. When I asked
Djebar specifically about the choice of Bonnard, she told me that he was
one of her favorite painters, and that she was so touched by his art that
she had even thought of calling the novel *L'Avant midi*, after one of
Bonnard's paintings (Montreal 1994).[1] The eighty-year-old painter once
told an admirer on the French Riviera at sunset one evening, "[J]amais la
lumière n'a été aussi belle" [Never has the light been so beautiful] (Leymarie
22). These words are decontextualized in Djebar's *Ombre sultane* to take
on a different dimension in the face of Hajila's experience. For a traditional Algerian woman daring for the first time to go outside "nue" [na-
ked] (the word for "unveiled" in the Algerian dialect), the luminosity of
daylight becomes a promise of freedom through the reappropriation of a

space in which traditionally, only men may circulate "dans l'étincellement de la lumière" [into the dazzling light] (*Ombre* 17/9).[2] The light fully seen for the first time from outside the frame of the veil or the window truly appears glorious to Hajila.

Djebar insists on the perceived nudity of the unveiled woman outside; significantly, Pierre Bonnard is most famous for his *intimiste* paintings of the female nude. His work is dominated by certain thematic and structural characteristics that also recur in Djebar's novels, such as the move to the margins, and the inside/outside dichotomy created and subverted through the use of framing devices like the window and the mirror. The parallels between Djebar's and Bonnard's art are striking. Although Bonnard had an early "Oriental" period, he was almost exclusively influenced by Japanese composition and, unlike his friend Matisse, never depicted North African motifs such as the Odalisque.

Just as Djebar is the writer of the palimpsest, Bonnard could be called a palimpsestic painter: critics recount that he took years to finish some of his paintings and used to retouch them even years after having sold them (Cogniat 45). Under the influence of Japanese art, Bonnard decentered his compositions, believing that "pour commencer un tableau, . . . il faut qu'il y ait un vide au milieu" [in order to begin a painting, . . . the center must be empty] (Leymarie 21). He often made the "marginalized" figure, the woman on the margin, "the central character of the painting" (Clair, "Adventures" 44).

In 1908, Bonnard traveled to Tunisia and Algeria, where his brother worked as a chemist in the vineyards (Vaillant 31). Very little else is known about the trip. This experience could have been one of the reasons why his painting shifted from more somber to shimmering colors, as exemplified in *Nu à contre-jour* (*Nude against the Light*). While this shift is remarked upon by most critics (Nash 20), to my knowledge no commentator has suggested that the change may have been triggered by the influence of the North African light. I have not been able so far to pinpoint any paintings of specifically North African scenes in Bonnard's work, with the possible exception of *Woman with Parrot* (1916), although he was very influenced by the luminosity of the landscapes of southern France.[3]

A strong connection between Djebar and Bonnard can be established because of the importance both attach to composition as architectural structuring. For both, the concepts of inside/outside zones and threshold are central. Gérard Genette argues in *Seuils* that the paratext, rather than being a true border, can be seen as "un *seuil*, ou . . . un 'vestibule.' . . . 'Zone indécise' entre le dedans et le dehors," "frange" "entre le texte et le

hors-texte" [a threshold, or . . . a "vestibule." . . . "An undefined zone"
between inside and outside, . . . on the fringe . . . between text and *hors-
texte*] (8). Djebar situates herself in this space (as a reader/listener and
writer/teller) at the border between past and present: "je m'insinue, visiteuse
importune, dans le vestibule de ce proche passé" [I steal into the vestibule
of this recent past, like an importunate visitor] (*Fantasia* 16/8).

Djebar's art is structured by the staging of borders that at first seem
impassable, such as the division in chapters referring to Isma or Hajila
in *Ombre sultane*, or referring to the personal or the historical in *Fantasia*. These borders are then methodically deconstructed; the frontier
between inside and outside, past and present, personal story and collective history, emancipated and traditional women, is purposefully
blurred. In *Ombre sultane*, she subverts the opposition between inside
and outside by insisting on the threshold, a word that recurs at least
nine times. Not only does the threshold mark the boundary between
inside and outside, but at the same time, it deconstructs the opposition between the two terms by allowing the passage from one to the
other. For instance, as Winifred Woodhull argued, the husband whom
Isma and Hajila share "forms an 'ambiguous border' (160) between
them, . . . a 'common wall' (91) linking inside and outside" (85). The
threshold is also a central characteristic of Djebar's film *La Nouba*, in
which several scenes show the husband, Ali, on the threshold of the
bedroom, without being able to enter, or a little neighbor girl, standing outside the window, looking at the family inside the house. Similarly, several of Bonnard's paintings show a landscape seen through a
French window or a door. In *Salle à manger à la campagne* (*Dining
Room in the Country*) (1913), for example, "the contrast between the
outdoors and the interior" (marked by the difference in color and ar-
chitecture) is offset by the use of "transitional devices." These include
color reflections, curtains stirred by the outside wind, and especially
the presence of the woman, outside but leaning on the window-sill,
looking in (Fermigier 88), as well as the lively figures of the little girl
picking flowers outside and the cat sitting on the chair inside.

La fenêtre ouverte (*The Open Window*) (1921) also exemplifies the central characteristics of Bonnard's art. The opposition between inside and
outside immediately strikes the spectator: slightly to the upper left, a window opens onto a curvaceous landscape of springtime mountains in
bloom, in which the colors green and purple dominate. The spectator is
looking at the mountain from within the space of an orange room structured by horizontal and vertical lines (wallpaper, chair, shutters, window-

panes). However, the dichotomy established between inside and outside is subverted by the mountain colors reverberating on the shutters and the purple color of the wallpaper, the chairs, and the floor. Finally, a closer look reveals the presence of a red-haired woman lying on a deck chair inside, her back to the window, looking at a cat she is petting. Only the upper part of her body (and of the cat's) is visible, the rest being cut off by the frame. Once the woman on the margin has been spotted, she becomes the focus of the painting for the spectator, and can never again blend with the backdrop. (James Elliott noted this regarding the presence of the young girl outside in *Salle à manger à la campagne* [Elliott, "Bonnard and His Environment" 26].) Just as Hajila moves outside the traditional frame of the house and veil into public space, Bonnard's women, because of their marginal position, seem to be moving outside the frames of the paintings.

Djebar also uses the French window as a way to subvert the inside/outside dichotomy she has established. In her apartment, Hajila leaves the windows open, with the result that the outside (noise, dust, and sun) is allowed in (*Ombre* 48/40). According to Arnold Rothe, light is used in the novel as another element breaking up the inside/outside dichotomy (49–50). Even more strikingly, as Dalila Hannouche remarks, on the first day that Hajila and her mother, Touma, enter the apartment, Touma is attracted by the kitchen, while Hajila goes through the French window to the balcony, outside (6): "Le panorama te laissa émerveillée, par ses contrastes de lumière, surtout par l'exubérance des couleurs, comme sur le point pourtant de s'évaporer sous le ciel immuable: sur le côté, un lambeau de mer presque violette, puis une étendue zébrée de taches de verdure sombre séparant les terrasses des maisonnettes blanchies de neuf; au fond, un minaret aux briques roses rutilait d'ampoules multicolores" [The view that stretched out before you had taken your breath away, with the contrasting light, the extravagant colours which seemed about to dissolve under the steady glare of the sky: on the side lay a shred of sea verging on purple, then stripes of dark green between the terraces of the newly whitewashed houses; in the distance a pink brick minaret glowed with multicoloured lights] (*Ombre* 23/14). Roland Barthes might call this description of the landscape "painterly"; the insistence on colors and structural divisions into zones of light and darkness is reminiscent of a Bonnard Mediterranean painting (with the difference of the minaret). Similarly, in *Fantasia*, one can note the influence of Delacroix's North African scenes and of Fromentin's vivid descriptions in the painterly tableaux Djebar crafts for her readers. Critics such as Martine Guyot-

Bender, for example, have noted the parallels between the description of Algiers as seen for the first time from the French ships in 1830 and Orientalist paintings (Guyot-Bender 178–79).[4] In *Ombre sultane*, several descriptions of Hajila recall Bonnard's interiors and his focus on light: "Dame assise: nature morte. La chaise rustique en bois sur laquelle tu te figes est vert pâle. Tant de lumière ruisselle déjà; elle te vêt d'une cape d'or" [Still life with seated woman. You are frozen on a pale green rustic chair. Already, the room is flooded by so much light that streams in, wrapping you in a cloak of gold] (17/9).

Another very important element used by both Djebar and Bonnard to structure and subvert the opposition between inside and outside is the mirror. As a framing device, it "makes it possible both to break up perspective continuity and to link together two incompatible spaces . . . dislocating space" (Clair, "Adventures" 37). Bonnard favored scenes in which only the woman's reflection can be seen, framed through a mirror, the source of the reflection itself remaining outside the painting, in a mise en abyme of the process of representation. The boldest example of this is undoubtedly the 1909 *Effet de glace (Le Tub)* (*The Tub*), in which the framing mirror comes to take up most of the painting's space and the vision of the woman bending over is inverted and removed. When both the woman and her reflection in the mirror are visible, as in *La toilette ou Nu au miroir* (*Washing up or Nude at the Mirror*) (c. 1933), the two images of her are different, since each is seen from a distinct point of view. The woman (like Isma/Hajila) is split—not quite the same from the front as from the back. It is interesting to note that these two paintings have a double title in French, playing on the two different perspectives that coexist in the paintings themselves. The spectator's attention is thus drawn at the same time to both the theme of the painting and the medium of its representation.

Djebar uses the mirror effect extensively in her bathroom scenes. For instance, early in the novel, Hajila takes a bath at home: "Tu contemples ton corps dans la glace, l'esprit inondé des images du dehors, de la lumière du dehors, du jardin-comme-à-la-télévision. Les autres continuent à défiler là-bas; tu les ressuscites dans l'eau du miroir pour qu'ils fassent cortège à la femme vraiment nue, à Hajila nouvelle qui froidement te dévisage" [You study your body in the mirror, your mind filled with images from outdoors, the light from outdoors, the garden-like-on-the-television. The others go on walking about there; you conjure them up in the water reflected in the mirror, so that they can accompany this woman who is truly naked, this new Hajila who stares back at you coldly] (*Ombre* 43/

35). Hajila brings the outside in through the use of memory, recreating the presence of others in the mirror. The theme of rebirth ("ressuscites" [conjure up], "Hajila nouvelle" [new Hajila]) intersects with that of the split subject, as the rebelling Hajila distances herself from a history of obedience by associating with the outside world.

Significantly, Pierre Bonnard liked to depict his female nudes in the space of the bathroom. In *Ombre sultane*, Isma describes Hajila's "pose de baigneuse" [pose of woman bathing], as if she were in a Bonnard painting (163). As Jean Clair explained, "Bonnard's favorite motif will be the place which provides him with both mirror and window: the bathroom" ("Adventures" 39). The bathroom also provides other reflecting surfaces such as the water and the tiles. Of particular interest are a series of paintings of Marthe, Bonnard's wife, lying in the bathtub, with the sun reflecting off the wall and floor tiles. He worked on this motif for many years, creating numerous studies which he confessed did not satisfy him (Clair, *Bonnard* n.p.). This repetition of an identical subject is, however, marked by difference. An early version (1925) centers on the woman in the tub, eyes closed, lying motionless, lifeless. The division of the painting into zones of color is very marked: the floor and wall tiles are yellow, the tub white, the water (and most of the body) blue. In the 1935 version, the tub is seen from further away; the color of the wall tiles varies by panels (yellow, blue, off-white, yellow, mauve), and is reflected in the tub's water and on the woman's body. Her motionless body is still framed by the tub, giving an impression of entrapment (Nelson 15). In the last painting of the series, *Nu dans le bain au petit chien* (*Nude in the Bath with a Small Dog*) (1941–46), an even larger portion of the bathroom is visible; the play of light on the tiles follows a random pattern, illuminating single tiles all through the room with a wider variety of colors (including green and reddish-brown) also reflected on the floor tiles. The play of light in Bonnard's painting calls to mind a passage in *Ombre sultane* in which the sun pours through the window without curtains into Isma and her husband's bedroom, reflecting off the brass curtain rod onto their intertwined bodies (31/22). In both pieces, the outside becomes present within the most intimate spaces of the house and is reflected on the nude bodies. In *Nu dans le bain au petit chien*, the woman's leg has risen, giving an impression of relaxation rather than death. The water around her neck ripples, suggesting motion and life, and a small brown dog lies on the bath mat. In this series, Bonnard moved from an orderly and more rigid representation of the nude to a celebration of life, light, and color.

In turn, Djebar's text repeats Bonnard's obsession with the woman in the bathroom, but it displaces this scene, thus endowing it with a more liberating meaning. With Djebar's shift from France to Algeria, Bonnard's scene of the painter's wife in her bathroom is replaced by the scene of women meeting in a public bath, or *hammam*, as seen through the eyes of a female narrator. The dark and moist hammam is described as "un harem inversé" [a harem in reverse] (*Ombre* 158/148) that allows rebirth through a symbolic return to the womb. Both the French bathroom and Algerian hammam are metaphors for a feminine space, since the female element is usually associated with water. After the consummation of her marriage, Hajila goes to the hammam, the only place in which she can open up and reach down to her deepest self, "parler enfin à soi-même, l'inconnue" [commune with oneself at last, that real self whom no one knows] (73/64). The hammam thus functions as a sacred place where women can regain wholeness. Hajila's desire to purify herself by going to the hammam also recalls what art critics consider Bonnard's wife Marthe's obsession with cleanliness.

The hammam is the place in which unrelated women may meet and extend networks of solidarity outside the male gaze. Djebar moves away from the totally private space of the French bathroom to a center where women are no longer isolated. In *Ombre sultane*, the hammam becomes the antithesis of the kitchen. While the latter, according to Dalila Hannouche, is "espace métonymique de l'aliénation et du drame dans le texte" [the metonymic space of alienation and tragedy in the text] (6), the hammam comes to represent the space of escape, reconciliation, and *sororité* [sisterhood].

In both Djebar's and Sebbar's fiction, nineteenth- and twentieth-century European painting is foregrounded and reassessed, especially that in the Orientalist tradition. Writing becomes a way of facing one's ambivalence toward Western representation by probing the question of reciprocal fascination, that is, by dealing with one's response (as a woman from Algeria) to what Edward Said has called Orientalism.

Reassessing Orientalism

In Said's definition, Orientalism is a complex discourse by which the West produced the "Orient." It is a system of knowledge based on the difference between the Orient and the West in which the Orient must be defined as inferior and backward and the West superior and civilized (*Orientalism* 2–3, 7). While distinct from "political power in the raw" (12), this authoritative discourse based on Western domination did participate in enabling and facilitating colonial rule (39). Said believes that Orientalism was neither a web of lies, myths, and fantasies about the Orient nor a truthful discourse about it; he prefers to view Orientalism as a set of representations that acts as "a sign of European-Atlantic power over the Orient" (6). The economic, political, and cultural hegemonic power of the West allowed Orientalist discourse to gain unchallenged intellectual authority. It is this question of the power signified by Orientalist discourse that fascinates Djebar and Sebbar, especially when this power is further signified for them by male representations of female bodies.

Said claims that although Orientalist discourse purported to tell the truth about the Orient, "what is commonly circulated by it is not 'truth' but representations" (*Orientalism* 21). It is not surprising, then, that women writers from Algeria would engage in the study of these representations, thus becoming critics of Orientalism. However, one may wonder to what extent an examination of the fascination Orientalism exerts on contemporary writers from Algeria may in itself be a furthering of Orientalism. It could be argued that I am only reproducing Orientalist parameters and doing a disservice to these texts. Yet, any postcolonial subject who has been educated in the Western tradition (like Said, Sebbar, and Djebar) functions both *in and out* of these same parameters. Djebar is particularly, and painfully, aware of a cultural predicament that consists of "the material reality of a Westernized subjectivity that is indelibly present [within] the non-Western intellectual" (Chow, "Violence" 97). Consequently, mimicry becomes a critical strategy for her, as she repeats a Western Orientalist discourse with a difference. I chart this process of creating repetition and difference in Sebbar's and Djebar's works in the rest of this chapter.

Both writers insist on their characters' fascination with Orientalist representations. They grapple with issues of colonial representation in very complex ways. They trespass, transgressing borders, not only by seizing the qalam, but also by exploring taboo themes such as the colonized's attraction/repulsion toward the colonizer's own feelings of attraction/repulsion. Therefore, it is important for critics to foreground these very issues. After all, it is a central tenet of Orientalism that "the Oriental generally acts, speaks, and thinks in a manner exactly opposite to the European" (quoted in Said, *Orientalism* 39). Sebbar and Djebar complicate such polarized discourse by deconstructing dichotomies such as the "East" and the "West." They show that there is no such easy distinction and that the boundaries between the two are much more flexible, especially since the Maghreb has been a zone of contact, migration, and commerce for so many centuries.

Said's *Orientalism* is a landmark of cultural theory and arguably the book that initiated the field of postcolonial studies. Since its publication in 1978, however, it has sustained much criticism, most notably by Homi Bhabha, in "The Other Question," and by Robert Young, both from a Foucaldian, postmodern framework.[5] They take issue with what they perceive to be Said's monolithic view of colonial discourse as a closed and fixed hegemonic system. They argue that Said discounts the inherent ambivalence of colonial discourse. In Bhabha's formulation, it is the very ambivalence at the heart of colonial and Orientalist discourse that makes such discourse "productive" by opening the possibility for an "'otherness' which is at once an object of desire and derision, an articulation of difference contained within the fantasy of origin and identity. What such a reading reveals are the boundaries of colonial discourse and *it enables a transgression of these limits from the space of that otherness*" ("The Other Question" 67, italics added). It is this work of subversion and transgression that renders Sebbar's and Djebar's novels so intricate. Both writers foreground the presence of desire and the articulation of power and fantasy within Orientalist discourse. They scrutinize the colonial gaze and explore its fetishistic undercurrents by making it the object of their own gaze. As H. Adlai Murdoch suggested, "Djebar writes woman as object of desire into woman as desiring subject" (75).

In contrast to Bhabha and most of Said's critics, Said himself insists throughout his book on the links between Orientalism and sexuality, between colonial and libidinal economies in Orientalist discourse. Said noted that Orientalists created "an almost uniform association between the Orient and sex" (*Orientalism* 188). Representations of the Orient marked it as female: female gender stereotypes such as passive, penetrable, silent, fertile, and supine were used to describe it (137–38, 206). If the Orient is female, then Oriental women become doubly female, inscribed as enigmatic, sensual and mysterious objects of the male, Western gaze. Representations of "Oriental" women in painting (such as Delacroix's *Femmes d'Alger dans leur appartement*) illustrate the repetition of an encounter forced on the Orient by the West, and portray the site of an impossible desire. In much Orientalist literature, the conquest of the land is expressed in sexual terms, as Western desire for the Orient mixes with the violence and death inflicted on its people.

In *Fantasia*, Djebar shows the Frenchmen's perspective on Algeria to be a very Orientalist one. She depicts the sexualization of the country enacted in the archival materials and the Orientalist paintings from which she draws. In an extremely painterly description of the minutes preceding the French invasion, Algiers is seen as the mysterious Other, represented as

man's ultimate "other," woman; moreover, she is a woman to be conquered and seduced, or in other terms, plundered and raped: "Premier
face à face. La ville . . . surgit dans un rôle d'Orientale immobilisée en son
mystère . . . ces lettres parlent, dans le fond, d'une Algérie-femme impossible à apprivoiser. Fantasme d'une Algérie domptée. . . . Y pénètrent
comme en une défloration. L'Afrique est prise malgré le refus qu'elle ne
peut étouffer" [Face to face for the first time. The city . . . looms up in the
role of "Oriental Woman," rendered motionless by her mystery. . . . between the lines these letters speak of Algeria as a woman whom it is
impossible to tame. A tamed Algeria is a fantasy. . . . Penetrated and
deflowered; Africa is taken in spite of the protesting cries that she cannot
stifle] (*Fantasia* 14, 69–70/6, 57). The sexual aspect of the war of conquest is foregrounded in this passage. Rape is one of the sites where desire
and death intersect in the colonial context.

Said used sexual metaphors to insist on the link between sexuality
and the power signified by the colonial conquest: "A certain freedom
of intercourse was always the Westerner's privilege; because his was the
stronger culture, he could penetrate" the Orient (*Orientalism* 44). Therefore, if the Orient is like a passive and willing woman, this justifies
viewing it as "something inviting French interest, penetration, insemi-
nation—in short, colonization" (*Orientalism* 219). The sexual metaphor for the colonial conquest thus comes full circle. Taking the land
and taking the women become two parallel activities intimately connected in the male colonizer's psyche.[6] In much masculinist discourse,
colonialist and anticolonialist, the subjectivity and suffering of the
women raped are erased by the allegory of Woman as the plundered
land. Djebar takes up this discourse in order to force it to acknowledge
both its erasure of women and to reaffirm their presence. To use Emily
Apter's formulation, the works of Djebar and Sebbar, rather than
reinscribing colonialist tropes equating women and the land, highlight
"the sexual dimension of colonial mastery while at the same time pointing to the colonial paradigm within the politics of sexual possession"
(213).

In his analysis of Orientalism, Said tried unsuccessfully to bring out
this articulation but instead fell back on referring to women in metaphori-
cal terms. However, by insisting that the West always has the upper hand,
he showed that power and domination are essential to an understanding of
how desire can bring about violence. The link between war, death, sexuality, and the female body resides in the unequal struggle for power between
"man" and "woman," "the West" and "the Orient." These connections
recur throughout Sebbar's and Djebar's works and are highlighted by the

very title, *L'Amour, la fantasia*: "Love and War." As Murdoch remarks, the title inscribes "the very paradox of love as forcible appropriation whose intricacy the text will seek to explore" (76).

For the colonized or postcolonial subject, it is perhaps easier to explore the violent legacy of colonization, an endeavor which is the most likely to create a spirit of resistance, than to delve into the intricate connections between desire and violence. Both Sebbar and Djebar enact strategies of resistance, as examined in the previous chapters, but their texts do not solely remain in an oppositional framework. The complexity of the sexual metaphor for colonial conquest resides in the central ambiguity of a desire which, because it had the power to express itself violently, was able to find fulfillment by forcing itself on its object of desire. In Orientalist representations, Djebar's and Sebbar's characters perceive, enmeshed in the omnipresent violence, a desire that unsettles them. Djebar and Sebbar represent Orientalism as a site of (mostly male) desire to which their characters respond.

In the passages I cite at the beginning of the chapter, Shérazade's inner turmoil echoes that of the narrator of *Fantasia*. Their reaction to the presence of European men (real or represented) mirrors the equally ambiguous fascination exerted by the "Orient" (and especially "Oriental" women) on Western warriors, travelers, and artists alike (e.g., Julien's strange trouble in front of nineteenth-century Orientalist paintings). Djebar's passage is the most explicit: her narrator wonders why she is drawn less forcefully to what these representations bring to light (the rape and suffering of Algerian victims) than to what they cover up (the sexualized attraction of Frenchmen for her country). All three passages use similar vocabulary to describe the protagonists' feelings of transgressing a deep-seated prohibition by responding to that attraction: "devraient," "pas le droit," "elle s'empêchait," "il fallait en finir" [should, not have the right, she would repress within herself, he must get rid of]. Many other examples could be chosen to point to the fine line between rape and seduction, love and war, sex and death, in both writers' literary production.[7] Sebbar herself has explained, in very postcolonial terms, that she is drawn to "la violence et l'ambiguïté des rapports entre fascination et répulsion, oppression et résistance, domination et séduction" [the violence and ambiguity of the relationship between fascination and repulsion, oppression and resistance, domination and seduction] (quoted in Bekri 56).

In "Rape or Obscene Copulation?" Andrea Page took Djebar to task precisely for this postcolonial ambivalence toward the relationship between domination and seduction. She countered earlier readings (such as my own) of Djebar's texts as feminist and liberatory by criticizing

Djebar for "replicat[ing] at key moments in the text the Western patriarchal economy of desire linking violence and sexuality" (53). She
claimed to be disturbed by Djebar's highlighting of ambivalence and
complicity and to yearn for a more directly oppositional stance that
would refuse to admit of any "sort of reciprocal desire, even if admit-
tedly 'perverse'" (48). Yet this is precisely what makes Djebar's and
Sebbar's texts *post*colonial rather than anticolonial. With brutal honesty, they expose all the layers of the colonial encounter and its aftermath to underscore the impossibility of complete oppositionality in
the postcolonial context. Gender issues, unrecognized by the Algerian
anticolonial movement and most subsequent Algerian governments, are
what allow such ambivalence. While Page's argument is perfectly valid,
it ignores the postcolonial context in which Djebar is writing, and
which Murdoch highlighted when he wrote: "Djebar undoes centuries
of overdetermination, while at the same time putting into place a self
which draws on the complicitous dialectic of the colonial encounter in
order to express the multivalency of its subjective codes" (72). Djebar
does not simply replicate a Western patriarchal libidinal economy, she
repeats it with a difference that makes all the difference. She foregrounds what such an economy could only place under erasure, Algerian women's agency and subjectivity. Through the mediation of writing and rewriting, she seeks to unearth and recreate Algerian women's
responses to an oppressive situation. At the end of her essay, Page falls
back on metaphors of rape when she ends up making the highly problematic claim that Djebar "is forced to rape her own culture" (53).
Djebar's subversive strategy of repetition with a difference is missed by
Page.

Said's remarks on Orientalism as a closed system of citations whose
referent is other Orientalist writers' works, rather than actual places and
peoples, are helpful to understanding the importance of intertextuality in
Djebar's and Sebbar's works (23). Both writers take on this system of
citations, displacing it by responding to it in ways that highlight the presence and agency of Algerian people. The best example of the two writers'
complex responses to Orientalist material is to be found in their treatment
of Delacroix's painting *Femmes d'Alger dans leur appartement*, a painting
each interpreted somewhat differently.

Femmes d'Alger: Delacroix, Djebar, Sebbar

Both Djebar and Sebbar have made Delacroix's *Femmes d'Alger* a central
intertext of their works. To an extent, their protagonists accept Delacroix's

representation—which they feel has something to teach them about their own identity—at the same time as they subvert and modify it. As Winifred Woodhull commented, "[L]ike Julien, Shérazade is fascinated by the figure of the odalisque; however, rather than fixing her within an oppressive frame, the seductive power of the odalisque moves her to re-invent her ties to both Algeria and France" (115). For many of the female protagonists, the painting becomes the obligatory referent against which identities are negotiated.

Early on in the Shérazade trilogy, Julien and Shérazade note that one of the women in the painting has green eyes like Shérazade (*Shérazade* 13/9). Sebbar thus foregrounds the long history of *métissage* in the Maghreb between Berbers, Arabs, and Europeans. Like Shérazade, the women of Algiers are also métisses. Because of the centrality of cultural mix in Sebbar's project, it is not surprising that she would emphasize the presence of the black servant. Shérazade, examining the painting, wonders "qui elles attendent? Elles s'ennuient . . . un peu. La belle négresse, l'esclave du harem, leur parle. Elles l'écoutent?" [who are they waiting for? They are getting bored . . . a little bored. The beautiful Negro woman, the harem's slave, is talking to them. Are they listening to her?] (*Fou* 27). This passage introduces the possibility of communication between Arab and black women, between mistress and slave, between oppressor and oppressed. Sebbar's reading of the servant is much more positive than Djebar's, who wonders if she is a spy or an accomplice (*Femmes d'Alger* 181/145), and finally decides in favor of the former (187/149). It is regrettable that, in a text such as *Femmes d'Alger*, with its emphasis on female solidarity that is extended to the pied-noir Frenchwoman Anne, the black woman in Delacroix's painting—who, Djebar remarks, has disappeared in Picasso's version (187/149)—is explicitly excluded from these networks of solidarity, and her subjugated position as a servant to the women of Algiers is never once broached. She is seen only as an instrument of patriarchal oppression, and her own class and race positions are erased in the process. This is all the more problematic as a sizable number of Algerians are of mixed sub-Saharan African descent, especially in the south of the country. Very few Algerian writers, with the exception of Malika Mokeddem, represent this group in their fiction (Mokeddem herself has black ancestors).

Both Djebar and Sebbar rewrite the painting in their novels. In the Afterword, "Regard interdit, son coupé" ("Forbidden Gaze, Severed Sound"), to her collection of short stories, *Femmes d'Alger dans leur appartement* (a book whose cover boasts a reproduction of Delacroix's painting), Djebar reconstructs the genesis of the painting in order to insist that the women are perceived through "un regard volé" [a stolen glance] (172/137), not only by Orientalist painters and viewers, but also by Arab men, because of the sexual segregation of space (173/138). Djebar hails Pablo Picasso's "rewriting" of Delacroix's painting for liberating the women from the enclosure and portraying them in motion, dancing rather than sitting, free from the constraints of their clothing. Woodhull criticized Djebar for holding too positive a perspective on Picasso's painting: "the genius of the masters holds sway over women's *gaze* and directs their future efforts to free themselves" (116). Woodhull may be too critical of Djebar's project. Since Djebar always uses intertextuality, it makes perfect sense for her to put both sets of paintings in relation. Picasso's series of paintings, composed at the beginning of the Algerian War of National Liberation, do indeed prefigure a time of emancipation from the shackles of colonialism, although the full liberation of Algerian women, like that of women the world over, is still to occur.

Moreover, Djebar is not content with using Picasso's vision as the alternative to Delacroix's. She also creates her own rewriting of the painting throughout the book, especially in the opening short story, whose title repeats that of the painting and of the collection as a whole. The title, *Femmes d'Alger dans leur appartement*, thus becomes a floating signifier referencing Delacroix's two paintings (one of which is present on the cover of Djebar's book), Picasso's series, as well as Djebar's book and one of her short stories. In this way, Djebar deconstructs the masters' sway by superimposing onto their representations her own portrayal of women of Algeria going inside and outside their apartments. In the initial short story, Djebar weaves the stories of three modern-day women of Algiers, Sarah, Anne, and Leïla. Leïla and Sarah are two former mujahidat who participated in the liberation of their country in the Battle of Algiers, giving new meaning to the concept of going outside one's apartment. The third woman, Anne, is a pied-noir woman who returns to her native land to commit suicide but, because of her friendship with Sarah, ends up deciding to remain in Algeria out of solidarity, to witness Algerian women's final liberation. Rather than being frozen on a painting, these women are in motion, actively and outspokenly involved in political and cultural pursuits. Just as in the painting, the short story also features a fourth woman, whose status parallels that of the servant: Fatma, the water carrier and hammam masseuse, is included in the network of female solidarity.

Like Djebar, Sebbar also rewrites the painting in her novels. It is interesting to note that Djebar's *Femmes d'Alger* is one of the books Shérazade carries around in her bag (*Shérazade* 234/252). In *Les Carnets de Shérazade*,

during a Moroccan wedding, a young woman's gracefulness and attire are
compared to one of Delacroix's women by Shérazade.[8] This time, as in
Picasso's painting, the woman is dancing (253). In *Le Fou de Shérazade*,
directly after Shérazade's comment about the women listening to the servant, Sebbar drastically alters the scene of the painting, moving it from
inside (the dark apartment in Algeria) to outside (a McDonald's restaurant in Paris). Shérazade plays the part of the green-eyed woman, accompanied, not by cowives, but by her lover, Julien. Both are listening to
Shérazade's friend Zouzou, a young Beur woman who works at
McDonald's and thus plays the part of the servant: "Tu vois, c'est moi la
servante" [See, I am the servant] (28). In Sebbar's rewriting, Shérazade's
question, "Elles l'écoutent?" [Are they listening to her?] is answered affir-
matively. Shérazade's network of solidarity is very broad, encompassing
many people who find themselves on the margins of French society. One
of her best friends is a young Caribbean woman named France, an ironic
comment on the continued colonization of the islands of Martinique and
Guadeloupe.

It is in *Le Fou* that the painting is rewritten most fully. In Beirut, three
women, Shérazade, an old Lebanese lady, and her Egyptian servant, "sont
assises sur le plus beau des tapis persans elles parlent et elles fument comme
les femmes de la peinture orientaliste, l'Egyptienne fume le narguilé" [are
sitting on the most beautiful Persian rug they are speaking and smoking
like the women in the Orientalist painting, the Egyptian woman is smoking the hookah] (164). The women are not prisoners of any harem, although the villa provides them with a refuge from the war. Whereas Djebar
marginalizes the servant by making her a "personnage presque accessoire"
[an almost incidental character] (*Femmes d'Alger* 170/135), thus repeating
Delacroix's gesture of placing that woman on the margin, on the fringe of
the painting, in Sebbar's rewriting the servant becomes one of the three
central figures, the one holding the hookah and on whom most of the
painting's light is focused.

This scene is repeated a third time at the end of *Le Fou* as part of
Julien's film (202). This time, a fourth woman is present: Yaël, a Moroccan Jew who, according to Julien, looks like Shérazade because both remind him of the green-eyed woman of Delacroix's painting (62–63). The
four women "s'allongent à demi—comme des odalisques" [are half reclining, Odalisque-like], but they only comply with this representation up to
a point (202). The old Lebanese lady tells them: "vous êtes aussi belles que
les odalisques de harem, mais des *odalisques évadées*" [you are as beautiful
as Odalisques in a harem, but you are *escaped Odalisques*] (202, italics
added). If characters such as Shérazade are irrevocably marked by Western

representations of themselves as Odalisques, they are also able to subvert these representations by giving new meanings to the word, breaking free from jail and traveling wherever they wish. Sebbar and Djebar effect parallel moves: Sebbar's female characters are proclaimed "odalisques évadées" at the end of the Shérazade trilogy, just as at the end of *Ombre sultane*, Djebar comments that "l'odalisque est en fuite" [the odalisque is in flight] (169/159).

Sebbar and Djebar continually disrupt Orientalist clichés of the passive, silent, and supine Oriental at the same time as they confess their own fascination for Orientalist material. Shérazade is a runaway, always in movement, always outside; she is, therefore, the opposite of the Odalisque, yet she ironically finds her momentum and impulse for the journey by examining Matisse's *Odalisque à la culotte rouge*, a painting of a sensually languid woman reclining on a bed (*Shérazade* 244–45/ 263–64). Like Matisse's Odalisque, Shérazade too wears a red "culotte" (*Shérazade* 130, 233/139, 251). A first displacement is evident at the linguistic level, in the slippage of meaning of the word "culotte" from pants (archaic usage) to panties (contemporary usage). Moreover, her red underwear has been shoplifted, a gesture typical of her subversive spirit. Rather than being a complacent Odalisque lavished with gifts, Shérazade is a runaway who steals what she needs to function. Her fascination with the figure of the Odalisque, then, does not prevent her from measuring the distance between herself and Matisse's and Delacroix's painted women, a distance to which her Orientalist, pied-noir boyfriend Julien is oblivious, and which prompts her to leave him with the note "Je ne suis pas une Odalisque" [I am no Odalisque] (*Shérazade* 206/222). This message, which remains unsigned and is written on a scrap of paper, indicates a refusal to be defined by fixed Orientalist parameters of representation. Shérazade, the runaway, not only engages in petty theft, but participates in a hold-up in a fancy restaurant (*Shérazade* 64–68/65–70) and a break-in (105–9/112–17) with her gang. She thus literally steals/flies, not only through language, but also through French society, disrupting both its representations and its material organization.[9] Because both the hold-up and the break-in are depicted humorously, from the point of view of Shérazade and her friends (who refer to the need to eradicate class- and race-based social injustices in French society) and because Sebbar presents her protagonists' parodic activities as subversive of the dominant order, these scenes both engage and distort French colonial stereotypes of Arabs and Beurs as thieves. As Danielle Marx-Scouras noted, "[A]s immigrant children at the periphery of French culture and society, whose parents were colonized by France, they are merely demanding what France stole from them" ("Mother Tongue" 54).

While Djebar identifies herself as an Algerian woman who writes in French only because she went to French school and never mastered written Arabic the way she has mastered the French language, Sebbar prefers to be considered a French writer on the margins, exiled at the crossroads between two cultures. Unlike Djebar, she claims not even to speak dialectal oral Arabic: "Ce que je connais de la civilisation et de la culture arabo-islamiques, je le sais par les livres écrits en français ou traduits de l'arabe, de l'anglais, de l'espagnol" [What I know of Arab and Islamic civilization and culture I got from books written in French or translated from Arabic, English, Spanish] (Sebbar and Huston, *Lettres parisiennes* 149). The Orientalist tradition, then, is absolutely necessary to her, since she has no other way of learning about her origins.

Even though she lives outside Algeria, Djebar positions her fiction within Algeria and centers her concerns on the situation of Algerian women in history as well as today. Sebbar foregrounds the difficult situation of Beur youngsters within France. Whereas Djebar identifies with her main protagonists (as shown in the previous chapter), Sebbar rejects any such identification with Shérazade or Mohamed: "Je ne suis pas Shérazade, je ne suis pas 'Le Chinois'" [I am not Shérazade, I am not "Le Chinois"] (quoted in Hugon 35–36). She claims not to write about her own identity in her novels, even though she adds in the same interview: "je me sens plutôt proche d'un personnage comme Julien Desrozier [sic]" [rather, I feel closer to the character of Julien Desrozier] (36). This comment is critical to an understanding of Sebbar's positionality, and explains why she identifies as a French writer rather than an Algerian writer writing in French.[10] Although Sebbar's novels are not autobiographical, she does weave autobiographical components into her texts. These elements recur especially in the case of Julien. In *Shérazade*, the reader learns that Julien's father, like Sebbar's, was an elementary school teacher in Algeria (12/8–9). Sebbar uses her father as the model for the character of an Arab colleague of Julien's father: like her father, that man came from Ténès, attended teachers' training college with Algerian writer Mouloud Feraoun, married "une Française de France" [a Frenchwoman from France], and settled in Aflou (Sebbar's own birthplace) (23/19).

In identifying with Julien rather than any other character, Sebbar is creating a sexual cross-over between Julien and herself. The inversion is linguistic as well: "La mère de Julien savait l'arabe, Julien un peu, mais le père n'avait pas réussi à l'apprendre" [Julien's mother could speak Arabic, Julien only a little, but his father had never managed to learn it] (21/17). Sebbar, like Julien, only speaks "a little" Arabic; Julien's parents' situation is an inverted reproduction of Sebbar's, since it is her father, an Algerian, who speaks Arabic and her mother who was never able to learn it.[11]

A passage in *Le Fou de Shérazade* brings to mind one of Sebbar's early autobiographical short stories, "Si je parle la langue de ma mère." Sebbar's identification with Julien's situation is exemplified when she endows him with one of her own childhood memories: her mother commented about her hair curling on humid days. In both narratives, the setting is the same: the child is coming back from the seashore with her/his mother and the mother's friends, "le soir après le dernier bain" [in the evening, after one last swim] (*Fou* 58, "Si je parle," 1180). The sea spray ["les embruns" (*Fou* 58)/"l'embrun" ("Si je parle" 1180)] causes the child's hair to curl and the mother to remark: "Il a de beaux cheveux tout frisés, comme si je l'avais fait avec un Arabe" [He has beautiful, very curly hair, as if I had had him with an Arab]; "ses cheveux frisent, ils sont presque crépus. Elle a de beaux cheveux" [her hair curls so much, it's almost kinky. She has beautiful hair] (*Fou* 58, "Si je parle" 1180). This memory marks both children because it teaches them something about their identity in the colonial context: both are métis, living between Algeria and France. Whereas Julien's own feelings toward that revelation are not disclosed, young Leïla's reaction is negative: "J'aurais voulu des cheveux plats. Pas frisés comme ceux des petites Arabes" [I wanted straight hair, not curly hair like that of the little Arab girls] (1180). In young Leïla's remark, as in Julien's mother's comment, *métissage* is experienced as an embarrassing transgression.

The short story's central theme is the search for one's métis identity. As a child, Leïla wishes she could identify herself as totally French, but her name will not allow this. Her inner journey toward accepting her frag-mented identity is mediated by books, war, and other women (1181). It is no wonder, then, that Sebbar would feel close to Julien, a character whose identity was also formed by the Algerian war, books written on the Maghreb, and paintings of Maghrebian women. That this childhood memory is cen-tral to Sebbar is made evident by the fact that she repeats it once more in *Le Fou* and that in all three cases, the scene is staged as a memory. This time, it is the old Lebanese woman who remembers how her mother would say that her hair was too curly ["trop frisés"] (165). If Julien embodies Sebbar's position, it is, above all, because of their shared obsession with representation, especially in painting and photography. As a pied-noir, Julien is a cultural métis like Sebbar. Both are in exile from their native land, a fact that helps explain Sebbar's tenderness for his character in spite of his Orientalist tendencies.[12]

By presenting, not only masculinist representations of desire for colonized women and lands, but also these women's ambivalent responses, Djebar's and Sebbar's narratives underscore the complexities of the colonial encounter in its violence as well as in its expressions of desire and open the possibility that not all sexual encounters were sites of violence. The references to many mixed unions in Sebbar's texts and to Pierre Leulliette's and Eugène Fromentin's books in *Fantasia* serve this function. Because such references occur in a textual context in which the violence of the colonial encounter takes center stage, I do not interpret them as totally complicit with Western patriarchy, but as a desire to account honestly for the complexities that do not fit in a clean, binary framework. I further trace Sebbar's manipulations of written intertexts in the next chapter.

Notes

1. She also uses the term at the beginning of *Fantasia* (16).

2. Djebar describes the experience of feeling exposed in detail in *Femmes d'Alger dans leur appartement*: "L'arabe dialectal transcrit l'expérience d'une façon significative: 'je ne sors plus *protégée* (c'est-à-dire voilée, recouverte)' . . . 'je sors *déshabillée*, ou même *dénudée*'" [Colloquial Arabic transcribes the experience in a significant way: "I no longer go out *protected* (that is to say, veiled, covered up)" . . . "I go out *undressed*, or even *denuded*"] (175/139). That the experience is lived as a transgressive one for both women and men is attested to by the fact that it is precisely at the moment when Hajila confesses to her husband that she had gone out "nue" [naked] that he begins to hit her (95/86).

3. Bonnard and his wife, Marthe, lived for many years in a small town on the outskirts of Cannes called Le Cannet, which is also where I grew up. Delacroix had earlier created a painting with the same title, *Femme au perroquet* (Brahimi, "Orientalisme" 33).

4. See also Beïda Chikhi, *Les Romans d'Assia Djebar* 32–33, and Jean-Jacques Hamm 38, 45–47.

5. For a sustained Marxist critique of Said, see Aijaz Ahmad 159–219.

6. The equation between the land and the women also influences colonized men who see any Western attempt at bettering women's status in the colony as an imperialistic move against indigenous societal structures. This reaction against Western involvement in any aspect of an indigenous cultural tradition is not necessarily paranoid or opportunistic; it often is a painful lesson drawn from history. In "L'Algérie se dévoile" [Algeria unveiled], Fanon showed how the French used the "plight" of Algerian women as pawns to further their colonial enterprise. What remains problematic, however, is the equation of women with cultural traditions and the selective appeal to a congealed view of tradition to avoid implementing any positive change in women's situations (see Kandiyoti).

7. This is especially evident in *Fantasia* 14–17, 25–29, 68–70, 88–93, 236–37. In her autobiographical short story, "Si je parle la langue de ma mère" [If I speak my mother's language], Sebbar described feeling guilty about being attracted to French paratroopers in the same terms as she described Shérazade's and Julien's emotions in the passages cited at the beginning of the chapter: "Je ne devais pas aimer les parachutistes français. Ils étaient les ennemis de mon père, nos ennemis. Quand ils passaient le long du grillage de l'autre côté de la cour, je les regardais. Malgré moi. J'étais troublée. Coupable. Ils sont venus un jour, ils ont pris mon père, ils l'ont mis en prison. C'était la guerre" [I was not supposed to like the French paratroopers. They were my father's enemies, our enemies. When they passed by the wire fence on the other side of the schoolyard, I would watch them. In spite of myself. I felt troubled. Guilty. They came one day, they took my father, they put him in prison. It was war] (1181). The sentence fragments referring to the young protagonist's muddled emotions contrast with the long sentences surrounding them. They stylistically render the sense of trespassing and shame experienced by the little girl and her difficulty in acknowledging her inappropriate feelings of ambivalence in a colonial world structured by Manichean dichotomy. Shérazade's feelings toward pictures of the same paratroopers are modeled on those of the young Leïla.

8. See Madeleine Van Strien-Chardonneau 35–37.

9. The two words (*steal* and *fly*) are the translation of *voler*, which serves as a play on words used by Hélène Cixous in "Le Rire de la Méduse" (The Laugh of the Medusa).

10. For a different analysis of this phenomenon, see the chapter "Exile" in Woodhull.

11. For a study of linguistic role reversal in the works of Beur writers, see Alec Hargreaves.

12. Sebbar's treatment of Michel Salomon, another Orientalist image hunter, is much less sympathetic (*Fou* 128–32; 142–44).

Chapter 6

▼▼▼▼▼▼▼▼▼

Métissage *and Representation*

Assia Djebar and Leïla Sebbar base large parts of their novels on Western representations of Arab people, both pictorial and written. As analyzed in the previous chapters, they use a variety of materials: colonial archives, travelogues, letters, novels, and essays, as well as nineteenth- and twenti-eth-century paintings and photography. Since, in Sebbar's fiction espe-cially, more space is devoted to Western representation than to works origi-nating from the Arab world, an obvious question arises for the reader: how are we to interpret the influence of Western representation on her works? Why is it given such importance? Are we to view Sebbar's texts either as having fallen into the trap of Orientalist repetition or as engaging in op-positional dialogue with the Orientalist tradition so as to expose its impe-rialistic and colonialist presuppositions? Or is it impossible in her case to use such dualistic frameworks?

To all groups that have been subjected to a dominant group's hege-mony and whose history has been wrenched away from them, two main types of psychological and ideological resistance are open. One is to cre-ate a framework negating the presence and power of the hegemonic domi-nant, centering instead on an enabling vision of one's group as strong, free, and empowered. This strategy involves *mythologizing* and is often built around a nostalgic, imaginary return to a prehegemonic world. The *Négritude* movement participated in that strategy, as do separatist cultural feminism and feminist theology of the Goddess. They look back to a world without the Other's hegemony, without the "epistemic violence" of colonization and/or patriarchal power (Spivak, "Three Women's Texts" 804). However, this desire to mythologize an elsewhere originates in the historical presence of a crippling force acting on the dominated group; this desire often upholds stereotypical characteristics imposed by the hegemonic dominant over subordinate groups (e.g., blacks as essentially emotional and irrational, women as inherently nurturing and peace making). This radical strategy that would eradicate hegemony is resorted to because of that very hegemony. Thus, it is a form of oppositional discourse.

The other strategy of resistance involves the realization that the hegemonic dominant uses its power to enforce what gets transmitted and what gets forgotten. This hegemonic discourse can be subverted, but not ignored. Therefore, this strategy, which is more historical than mythological, involves *reappropriation*. Instead of creating new myths, it exposes the old ones for what they are: ideological constructs and not objective truths. As a historian, Djebar must work with whatever documents are left, including the enemy's archives, in order to reconstruct the past. She reappropriates French discourse and its representations of Algerian women and men, transforming the context and meaning of these representations in her novels. Sebbar's protagonists are too young to have direct knowledge of recent historical events such as the Algerian war, and they are exiled from their land of origin by their families' immigration. Therefore, their search for origins must be mediated by historical and artistic representations of their ancestors' presence.[1]

Since Djebar and Sebbar use the strategy of reappropriation rather than mythologizing, they must engage Western representation rather than circumvent it. Because French (neo)colonial discourse attempted to erase Algerian culture and history, Western sources are necessarily omnipresent in their texts. Sebbar and Djebar's strategy is double: it is not only a strategy of reappropriation—characters using aspects of Orientalist representation to fashion their own multiple identities— but also a strategy of subversion. By unearthing the traces of the repressed in Western documents, traces that point to the presence and resistance of her people under the attempted erasure, Djebar brings them to light. Sebbar's protagonists gather as many traces of their historical presence as possible, so as to create a new, mosaic-like memory out of the fragments of history: Shérazade, for instance, spends hours reading books that "racontaient une vieille histoire, l'histoire de sa mémoire en miettes, et une histoire nouvelle, moderne où se croisent les continents et les civilisations, une histoire qui serait la sienne" [told an old story, the history of her tattered memory, and a new, modern story where continents and civilizations intersect, a history that would be her own] (*Carnets* 129). These tattered bits of memory are gathered

from wherever they can be found, throughout books, in various encounters, in paintings, stories, photographs, and so on.

Sebbar's Pedagogy: "East Meets West"

As described in previous chapters, Sebbar's and Djebar's sources are
both Western and Arabic. Because the colonial hegemony could not control everything, Arabic and Berber sources remain, whether written (the
literary tradition, historical texts) or oral (stories, the oral tradition). In
particular, the figures of Ibn Khaldun and of Abd el-Kader (who unified
the tribes to fight against French colonization in the nineteenth century),
as well as the tale of the *Arabian Nights*, are prominent in the two writers' fiction.[2] The history of resistance to the colonizer that both writers
foreground is also enacted by their use of Arabic sources. The influence
of the oral tradition is central, especially because of the role of the
foremothers in passing down family history for Djebar. In Sebbar's works,
the oral tradition comes not only from the women of the family when
they gather together to sew (*Shérazade* 200–203/215–19) but also, and
perhaps more important, from the grandparents who remain in Algeria
and become the grandchildren's main affective ties to their parents' land.
Throughout the Shérazade trilogy, Shérazade remembers her grandfather's
ritual purifications (*Shérazade* 136–37/145–46, for example). The memories of the summers spent in Algeria with her sister Mériem revolve around
the figure of the grandfather as transmitter of Algerian culture. For
Mohamed, the protagonist of *Le Chinois vert d'Afrique*, both grandparents play a central role because they are his strongest links to the land
and to his multicultural roots. He is very close to his Vietnamese grandmother, Minh, who used to tell him stories, who taught him how to
make amulets (70), and with whom he enters into an elaborate correspondence. His grandfather is equally important, since he initiates
Mohamed into specific aspects of Algerian culture, teaching him, for example, how to eat cactus pears (29).

This episode is very telling in many respects, including linguistically.
The cactus pear, Sebbar tells us, has two names in Arabic: *handiia* and
karmous nsara, which she translates as "la figue des Français, la figue des
Infidèles" [French people's fig, the Infidels' fig] (29). It is significant that
Mohamed chokes at first on the "French people's fig," but learns from his
grandfather, a man who lived through colonization and the war of liberation, how to eat the fruit, which is subsequently stripped of its colonial
connotation by only being referred to as *handiia*. This is a perfect metaphor for reappropriation and mimicry: by learning to "swallow" their past

in a particular way, the colonized can find nourishment and strength; the legacy of colonization is a heavy burden which can choke to death an unprepared youth; the role of the elders is to teach the young how to come to terms with that legacy and to make it their own in a way that will give them strength by rooting their sense of identity in the history of their people. That the colonial legacy is still present in postcolonial times is evidenced by the fact that the figs' color is problematically compared to the stereotype of Native American skin color, "rouges comme les Indiens" [red like Indians] (28).

The French language only has one word for the fruit, one which Sebbar uses as well, in an ironic parallel: "figues de Barbarie" [figs of Barbary] (29). Barbary, as the 1988 Petit Larousse dictionary informs us, is the Western name that was given to North Africa west of Egypt in the past. The preceding entry, on *Barbares*, explains that this name was given by the Greeks to all non-Greek civilizations. The etymology of the term means "foreigner, alien," and has come to mean incorrect, or inhuman and cruel. Of course, the adjective corresponding to Barbary is not *barbare* [barbaric] but *barbaresque* [from the Barbary Coast], but this does not prevent the two concepts from being connected at least at the connotative level. The linguistic parallel between the "French people's fig" and the "Barbary's fig" points to an ancient encounter between the two cultures, an encounter that interestingly created linguistic métissage on both sides of the Mediterranean, showing that if the colonized is forever changed by the contact with the colonizer, the reverse is true as well.

While in Djebar's work the maternal lineage provides the link with the ancestors, both maternal and paternal lineages are important for Sebbar's characters. The presence of the grandfather in Sebbar's fiction has no parallel in Djebar's because the latter bases her novelistic geography on the separation between men's and women's space in Algeria whereas the former places her characters outside that segregation: as visitors, the grandchildren are not aware of any such division. In the case of Mohamed (as in the case of Sebbar herself), it is only the father's lineage that provides the link with Arabic Algeria, since Mohamed's mother is Turkish.

As her young protagonists' travels allow them to gather heterogeneous bits and pieces of their history, Sebbar mixes all these sources into a cultural mosaic that maps their interior landscape. By juxtaposing historical and contemporary sources, Arabic and Western, she brings together "high" and "low" cultures. The French cultural "patrimony" (literature, nineteenth- and twentieth-century painting) mingles with photojournalism and film. Like Djebar, who brings the same concerns and themes to novels and films, Sebbar insists upon the importance of visual culture and on the power of the image.

Just as a film shot in Arabic is a better way of reaching Algerian women than a book written in French, Sebbar's insistence on pictorial representation and popular culture is a way of attracting a young readership whose eclectic learning is often done outside school, so that allusions to Marilyn Monroe will help them "digest" references to Richard Wagner. Such a pedagogical strategy (perhaps culled from Sebbar's many years of experience as a high-school teacher) is meant to ease the learning process, to make learning painless and even unnoticed, and thus to use entertainment for pedagogical purposes. There is no hierarchy of disparate elements, only a juxtaposition in which the reader is free to pick what s/he chooses to remember. This pedagogical process is mirrored in the ways in which the protagonists themselves learn about their cultural environment. The lack of hierarchy between high and popular culture is obvious in the following passage: "Jean-Luc aimait l'opéra. Dans sa boutique, Momo entendait une musique qui le faisait penser à de la musique de film, surtout les films américains en cinémascope. Jean-Luc lui dit que c'était Wagner" [Jean-Luc loved the opera. In his shop, Momo heard music that reminded him of the movies, especially American films in Cinemascope. Jean-Luc told him it was Wagner] (*Chinois* 53). Sebbar attempts to clear opera of its inaccessible status as highbrow and bourgeois by revealing its link to popular culture. In this case, the allusion is to *Apocalypse Now*, the 1979 American blockbuster about the Vietnam War that introduced younger generations to Wagner's music. Linking opera to something more familiar such as its manifestations in popular culture creates the possibility that readers, like Mohamed, may become more directly interested in opera.[3] In the case of Mohamed, the possibility is reinforced by his interest in wars in general, and his own historical and personal connection to the Vietnam War in particular.

Sebbar's pedagogical strategy is designed not only for readers who may directly identify with the novels' young protagonists, but also for a more mainstream French readership that might profit from learning about sociological, linguistic, artistic, and historical aspects of both Beur and Arabic cultures. In a library scene in *Shérazade*, Sebbar alludes by implication to her multiple intended audience. The librarian mentions the names of a dozen contemporary Maghrebian writers (including one woman, Assia Djebar), whose works she has included in the library because of (female) Beur readers. She adds that "de plus en plus de . . . Français, prennent [c]es livres qu'ils n'auraient pas eu l'idée de demander avant" [more and

more . . . French people borrow these books, which they wouldn't have
thought of asking for before] (133/142).

Part of the learning process includes gaining an awareness of the centuries of interlocked histories of the countries on both sides of the Mediterranean. In *Les Carnets de Shérazade*, the heroine, a modern-day Scheherazade,
hitches a ride on Gilles Rivière's truck, telling him stories in exchange for
the free trip. As they pass through different regions in France, she super-
imposes the historical Arab and Turkish presence in France over the current presence of immigrants. For instance, she sets in parallel the writings
of two early eighteenth-century travelers, Turkish ambassador and historian Mehmed Efendi, writing on France, and British aristocrat Lady
Montagu, on Turkey (*Carnets* 181–83). It is interesting that both writers
comment on the freedom of the "other" women, French in the first case,
Turkish in the second.[4] These writers even met once: "L'Orient croisant
l'Occident, chacun de retour dans son pays natal, le bagage alourdi de
notes, des anecdotes piquantes et pittoresques, des deux côtés de la mer"
[The Orient meeting the West, each going back to their native countries,
their luggage heavy with notes, with titillating and picturesque anecdotes
from both sides of the sea] (183). This quotation illustrates how the impulse to objectify the other can exist on both sides. For example, blond
hair functions as a sign of complete otherness that fascinates, not only
Efendi, but also the Turks who come in contact with Montagu, as well as
contemporary Turkish immigrants whom Shérazade meets in France. The
fascination for blond hair prevents them from seeing the person behind it
(183). Blond hair, for them, could be said to function in the way the veil
does for Westerners visiting Arab countries. The attraction exerted by the
sign of absolute difference impedes the recognition of the other as subject.
I am not arguing for a reading that would posit a (false) symmetry between Orientalist and "Occidentalist" impulses in Sebbar's works. Obvi-
ously, the (economic and ideological) power to other a group was, and
remains, mostly on the side of the West. As Said has shown, Orientalism
contributed to creating an overdetermined discourse that facilitated the
process of European colonization (*Orientalism*). The similarities in objectification take place at the individual level, whereas the structural and institutional power to implement this objectification remain on the side of
Orientalism.[5]

One of the characteristics of objectification is to focus on the least
representative but most strikingly different aspects of the Other world:
both Efendi and Montagu neglect to describe rural areas, centering
instead on the eccentricities of court life. Sebbar insists on this class
clash, compensating for Efendi's and Montagu's narrow perspectives

by bringing contemporary Turkish immigrants into her novel. The exotic eighteenth-century travel narratives are put in parallel with the situation of poor Turks in France to shock her readers into an awareness of the distance between Orientalist fantasy and the material conditions of people's existence.

The juxtaposition of knowledge, literary and personal (Shérazade visited the village where these Turks now live), creates a subtler, more complex picture of the reality of Turkish-French involvement, a context with which most readers may not be familiar since there is rarely a focus on Turkish immigration in France. This juxtaposition occurs in an exchange between Shérazade and Gilles, the truck driver giving her a ride, pointing to the pedagogical purpose of such dialogue. Shérazade, the cultural métisse, teaches the Frenchman that he is also part of the same mixed heritage, whether he likes it or not. She also reminds him of the fact—often easily forgotten by the French—that the Arabs occupied the south of France for almost three hundred years, from the eighth to the eleventh centuries, that is, longer than the French presence in Algeria. She foregrounds the parallels between the two occupations by comparing two similar incidents, one in France before the Arabs left and one in Algeria during the last war of independence. The history of conquest, loss, and cross-cultural mixing between the Mediterranean world and Europe is a long-lasting one that repeats itself (*Carnets* 264). This history lesson is not offered to justify French colonization and neocolonialism, but to unsettle French assumptions of superiority over Arab cultures as well as to work against the myth that French identity is based on racial purity. The pedagogical imperative takes on a particular urgency in the intertextual context that marks the Shérazade trilogy. At the end of their journey, Gilles asks Shérazade if she has been telling him stories "comme Schéhérazade, pour m'empêcher de te tuer, de te violer?" [like Scheherazade, to prevent me from killing or raping you?] (*Carnets* 280). For the sultana of *The Arabian Nights,* as for the young métisse, telling stories becomes a matter of life and death.

Throughout the novel, Sebbar insists on many instances of cross-fertilization and cultural encounters between Arab and French worlds. Toward the end of the book, Nasser, a Tunisian historian, puts in relation two texts on the Other, the twelfth-century *Chroniques arabes des croisades* and François de Chateaubriand's nineteenth-century *Itinéraire de Paris à Jérusalem.* Nasser turns the tables on contemporary French anti-Islamic discourse by critiquing Chateaubriand's bias against Islam, calling him a Christian "fanatique, un intégriste" [fanatic, a fundamentalist] (*Carnets* 270). He uses words the French usually reserve for religious Muslims.

Sitting at the terrace of a café, Nasser then reads out loud (for all to hear) a quasi-ethnographic description of the European women who participated in the Crusades. The author of the *Chroniques* placed these women in two categories, the prostitute and the warrior. The text, whose tone is similar to many French books on "The Arab Woman," infuriates the bar patrons, who start a brawl. On both sides, the cultural clash plays itself out on the bodies of women.

Juxtaposing Arab texts on the French and French ones on the Arabs is a very important part of Sebbar's strategy, one that has no equivalent in Djebar's fiction. Since Djebar's purpose is to bring out the presence, gaze, and voice of Algerian women throughout history, the sources she uses are Arab and French texts dealing with women. She is less interested in Arab sources on the French. For Sebbar, on the other hand, it is crucial to stage an encounter between Western Orientalist representations and Arab representations of the West to show that the impulse to render the Other exotic is present on both sides and to destabilize both kinds of objectification. As Michel Laronde argues in his book, *Autour du roman beur*, dismantling binary oppositions is the privileged tactic of those who belong to neither side *and* to both sides, especially Beur writers (44). This destabilization also allows Sebbar to remind the French of a history in which they too were conquered, dominated, and represented as Other. Gilles's impatient reaction to Shérazade's historical teachings and the riot in the café created by Nasser's reading bear witness to the fact that such history is not welcomed by many French people, some of whom, rather than discussing the Crusades, "s'emportent à propos des immigrés en France" [rail about immigrants in France] (Sebbar, *Carnets* 272). The power of Sebbar's juxtapositions lies in the fact that they force mainstream French people to confront the reductive objectifications they have engaged in by placing them in the position of objects of another's discourse.

The long history of military conquest and cultural interaction between the two regions has resulted in métissage, a cross-cultural connection embodied, not only by the characters of Shérazade and her boyfriend, Julien, but also by their relationship itself. As a pied-noir (member of a family of French settlers in the Maghreb), Julien is also a cultural métis. His profession of faith about his work in *Shérazade* is very close to Sebbar's own project:

> Il travaillait à la fois sur des archives coloniales et des archives de
> la civilisation et de la littérature arabes. On s'étonnait toujours,

lorsqu'il en parlait qu'il prît le même intérêt à des productions aussi différentes—antagonistes—lui disait-on. Mais ces contradictions, s'il y en avait, ne le gênaient pas. Il était curieux de tout ce qui constituait du plus loin de l'histoire, sa propre histoire et celle de deux peuples, deux cultures qui se fréquentaient depuis les croisades. (113)

> [He was working simultaneously with the colonial archives and those of Arabic literature and Arab civilization. When he talked about this, people were always surprised that he took the same interest in such different works—so antagonistic—as they said. But these contradictions, if they existed, didn't worry him. He was curious about everything that constituted the most distant history, that of his own people, and that of two peoples, two civilizations who have been in close contact from the time of the Crusades.] (121–22)

Sebbar, like Julien, thrives on these contradictions and antagonisms, refusing to reduce the richness and complexity of the Arab/French connection and foregrounding its ambiguities.[6] As Madeleine Van Strien-Chardonneau noted, Shérazade, as well, "cherche les vestiges d'une histoire qui serait conjointement celle de son peuple et celle de cette France où elle est née" [is looking for the traces of a history that would be both that of her people and of the France where she was born] (41).

This ambivalent connection is symbolized by Julien and Shérazade's relationship. They come from "different," "antagonistic" backgrounds. The son of French colonists, Julien grew up in Algeria. After the war—in which his parents participated on the side of the Algerian National Liberation Front—he and his family were forced to seek exile in France. For Shérazade, born in France to Algerian immigrants, Algeria is the place of distant origins and summer vacations. Both characters are in between, neither completely exiled nor totally at home.

For Sebbar, this contradiction, however painful to live through, is also a source of richness. Shérazade and Julien's relationship is a love story marked by mediation and absence. It is punctuated by Shérazade's repeated disappearing acts. Both characters are absent from Algeria, the country of origins. This exile is expressed linguistically: both speak Arabic with an accent (*Fou* 37; *Shérazade* 113/121). Their relationship is also marked by an important pedagogical element. As Mildred Mortimer remarked in *Journeys through the French African Novel*, Shérazade and Julien teach each other their own fragmented knowledges of the Algerian/French historical and linguistic juncture (185). For example, Shérazade teaches Julien sentences in the Algerian dialect, while he teaches her literary Arabic vocabulary (*Shérazade* 146/157–58). The exchange is also cultural: Shérazade tells Julien popular, oral Algerian stories (147/158); he reads to her famous Arabic poems (*Fou* 116) and introduces her to Orientalist paintings (*Shérazade* 13/9–10). Just as Djebar creates an unlikely encounter by bringing Lla Zohra's story together with Fromentin's, Shérazade, the modern-day descendant of Algerian women, is made to meet Delacroix's representation of the nineteenth-century women of Algiers.

Because of its colonial and neocolonial context, the exchange between Shérazade and Julien is fraught with danger and must be constantly renegotiated. This explains why Shérazade leaves Julien each time he is about to incorporate her into one of his colonial fantasies. Their relationship is not to be read as an apology of colonization as fruitful encounter or as the site of an unproblematic multiculturalism but rather as the realization that the colonial encounter, in its violence, created a hybridization that can never be erased. Such a métis history must be dealt with, and the search for one's roots and identity must, of necessity, pass through this crossroads.

Orientalism as Masquerade

Sebbar focuses on Shérazade's responses (as a young woman between Algeria and France) to Orientalism. In the trilogy, she foregrounds the elements of an Orientalist discourse of representation that can be of use to her character's process of identity formation, while also addressing the violence inherent in these representations. Shérazade goes through the process of identity formation in part by grappling with Western representations, in turn subverting, overthrowing, or reappropriating these representations for her own purposes in a playful, parodic, and sometimes violent exchange. Masquerade is one of the means by which, to paraphrase Judith Butler, identity and the contests over its "authenticity" are produced (159). In other words, it is through donning the trappings of the Odalisque, through performing the role of the "Oriental Woman," *and at the same time distancing herself from these representations*, that Shérazade constructs her own identity. In this repetition of Orientalist representation, a difference emerges. Whereas such representations were meant to stand in for the absent "Algerian woman," the fact that Shérazade is partially present under the Orientalist layers creates a surplus, an excess of meaning that displaces the fixed, overdetermined category of "Oriental Woman." Sebbar's texts provide a way to go beyond the current binary oppositions between essentialism and postmodernism in postcolonial and feminist theories. She neither subscribes to the position that there is such a thing as a core identity formed before entry into sociocultural structures, nor that identity is only a performance, a mask underneath which only absence can be found. The assumption that the hegemonic dominant has always already completely overdetermined all representations is a highly problematic theory defusing the possibility of what Chandra Talpade Mohanty called "dynamic oppositional agency": "The relations of power I am referring to are not reducible to binary oppositions or oppressor/oppressed relations. I want to suggest that it is possible to retain the idea of multiple, fluid structures of domination which intersect to locate women differently at particular historical conjonctures, while at the same time insisting on the dynamic oppositional agency of individuals and collectives and their engagement in 'daily life'" ("Cartographies" 13). The Shérazade trilogy exemplifies such postcolonial, dynamic oppositional agency. Shérazade's identity is not solely constructed out of her encounters with Orientalist scholars and representations but also out of her relationships to the Maghrebian immigrant community, family ties to Algeria, and contact with marginal figures. It is through the power relations existing between these different cultural sites that she negotiates her identity and establishes her agency.

Homi Bhabha makes a related point in "DissemiNation," arguing that narratives of the nation are always already split at the moment of enunciation. On the one hand, "the People" are presented as a pre-given, unified essence; on the other, they are continually being interpellated into entering this group.[7] This split provides room for minority discourses to arise within the nation. Cultural difference can then intervene through "a logic of supplementary subversion . . . to rearticulate the sum of knowledge from the perspective of the signifying position of the minority that resists totalization—the repetition that will not return as the same" (162). The words used by Bhabha to describe the position of the protagonist in Salman Rushdie's *Satanic Verses* apply perfectly to Shérazade: "[T]he migrant hybrid in masquerade . . . mimics the collaborative colonial ideologies of patriotism and patriarchy, depriving those narratives of their imperial authority" (167–68). For Shérazade, disguise is experienced as a subversive gesture of identity formation.[8] During her travels through France, she and her French friend Marie visit nineteenth-century Orientalist writer Pierre Loti's house in Rochefort. They manage to stay after hours, putting on some of Loti's outfits from his Orientalist collection: "[E]lles s'étaient déguisées en guerriers ottomans, en princesses de harem, en odalisques, en esclaves noires. . . . Rien ne manquait dans le bazar de Loti" [They dressed up

as Ottoman warriors, harem princesses, Odalisques, black slaves. . . .
Not one thing was missing from Loti's bazaar] (*Carnets* 161).

As she repeats Loti's masquerading gesture, Shérazade recognizes how
reductive his construction of the Orient is for her, whereas her friend
Marie does not see the difference. The stereotypes perpetuated by Loti
anger Shérazade: "elle avait eu envie de tout casser. . . . Ces orientaleries
accumulées l'avaient exaspérée, pas Marie. —Un Orient de Prisunic . . .
Il l'a trouvé dans Bonux . . . avait dit Shérazade en riant, avant de
s'envelopper dans la soie, pour sa nuit exotique" [she had felt like breaking it all. . . . This accumulation of Orientalish stuff had exasperated her,
not Marie. "This Orient is straight out of K-Mart . . . He must have
found it in a cereal box . . ." Shérazade said, laughing, before she wrapped
herself in silk for her exotic night] (*Carnets* 161–62). The use of words
like "bazaar" and "Orientalish" and the references to the discount store
and household product put Loti's collection in parallel with cheap, mass-
produced, normalizing artifacts.[9] Shérazade resents the epistemic violence
of this exotic collection, which encapsulates the Orientalist impulse to
appropriate, collect, possess, classify, and accumulate in an effort to conquer through stereotyping the other. She channels her anger through derision. She mocks Loti's pathetic collection, laughing at it, wearing it
tongue in cheek, as a disguise. Shérazade's gesture is all the more subversive because it is forbidden, since Loti's house, now turned into a museum to his glory, is closed at night. The two women clandestinely stay
in the museum overnight and play with items that are not supposed to
be touched or tampered with. Shérazade is even tempted to steal a few
things, although Marie convinces her that they would be too heavy for
the two runaways to carry.

After her anger and her desire to destroy Loti's exotic bazaar, her
laughter at his colonial fantasy as she dons some of its trappings frees
her from its hold. Like the Medusa's laugh in Cixous's rewriting,
Shérazade's laughter allows her to distance herself from the dominant
representative order. In contrast, it is much harder for mainstream French
people to shake the Orientalist hold over them because they lack other
frames of reference. Part of Sebbar's project can thus be understood as
an attempt to provide French readers with another frame of reference
through her fiction. Shérazade's friend Marie, for instance, does not
understand Shérazade's anger at what the French girl considers to be
Loti's "innocent" whims. As for Julien, who may identify with the
Orientalist writer at some level, Loti's imaginary world peoples his own:
immediately attracted by Shérazade when he meets her for the first

time, he compares her to Loti's Oriental lover, Aziyadé (*Shérazade* 7–8/ 1–2).

The context in which the scene of Shérazade's masquerade takes place reinforces the reductive and naturalizing character of Loti's collection. The scene occurs directly after a passage in which Shérazade explains to Gilles that the young Beur singers they just met are *not* dressed up, *not* masquerading: "[L]es habits traditionnels de leurs grands-pères turcs, arabes, berbères, africains sont à eux et les habits européens sont à tout le monde et eux, leur look, c'est de tout mélanger, mais pas n'importe comment, c'est très étudié" [Their Turkish, Arab, Berber or African grandfathers' traditional clothing belongs to them, and European clothes belong to everyone, so their own look is about mixing it all up, but not any which way, it's very calculated] (*Carnets* 159). As opposed to Loti's, this way of dressing, which to an extent is also Shérazade's, is not a disguise, although Gilles believes it to be so because it appears exotic to him. Rather than being the expression of a colonial fantasy, the Beurs' mixed clothing is a sign of what Françoise Lionnet called métissage, a cultural and/or racial mixing that, turned into an aesthetic and artistic creation, highlights the element of masquerade in Loti's cheap bazaar (*Autobiographical Voices*).

Resisting Representation

Just as she wraps herself in Loti's silk, consciously playing along with his taste for the "exotic," Shérazade often *appears* to be complying with men's representations of the "Oriental" woman. She lets herself be photographed and filmed over and over by several different men, including Julien and Michel Salomon, a Jewish, pied-noir photographer. Yet she remains highly conscious at all times that the men are creating their own fantasy of her, and she keeps on destabilizing these representations. For instance, while she lets Julien take endless rolls of pictures of her, she always chooses her own poses: "Elle . . . n'obéissait jamais à ses injonctions" [She . . . never obeyed his injunctions] (*Shérazade* 148/160). She uses disobedience, escape, and laughter as strategies of refusal that allow her to subvert the men's representations of her. In *Le Fou*, she makes the entire film unit wait for her for the duration of the book while she travels through the Middle East. When the men begin to take their representations as reality, she laughs in their face (*Fou* 131). For example, free from stereotypical macho representations of male sexuality, she can only laugh out loud at the fantastical proportions of the "phallus géant" [giant phallus] in the pornographic film that Gilles and other truckers are watching (*Carnets* 121).

In contrast to the men's seriousness about their "work" of representation, Shérazade envisions it as game-playing: "Elle joue la scène" [She performs the scene] (*Fou* 131). She makes herself elusive, proving that none of these representations can ever define her completely. However, she also resists being reinscribed as the enigmatic, mysterious, and silent Oriental woman. For instance, she teaches Julien how to change his perception of her. Throughout *Shérazade* and *Le Fou de Shérazade*, Julien alters "le scénario qu'il a écrit pour elle" [the (film) script that he had written for her] because Shérazade's agency forces him to confront the inadequacy of his representation of her (*Fou* 180). Communication and dialogue are possible between them: "Shérazade fit des remarques que Julien écoutait. . . . Il . . . modifia le scénario en tenant compte de ce qu'elle avait dit" [Shérazade made some observations which Julien listened to. . . . He . . . modified the script taking into account what she'd said] (*Shérazade* 160/171). Although Julien pursues his inner vision of Shérazade, he proves himself open to the young woman's challenges of that vision. The space of their dialogue is thus one of constant negotiation.

Communication does, however, break down sometimes, even with Julien. In such cases, Shérazade does not hesitate to resort to violence. She tears up the pictures of herself that Julien had posted all over his apartment when she realizes that these representations may mean more to him than she herself does: "[T]u as pas besoin de moi vivante, finalement" [(Y)ou don't need me in the flesh after all] (*Shérazade* 158/169–70). A parallel can be drawn between Julien and Pierre Loti, for in both cases, their colonial fantasies rely on the absence of the object of desire. The Other's actual presence is in excess in the economy of colonial desire. Shérazade's violent act allows her to break through Julien's colonial unconscious: "[I]l sentit que Shérazade avait raison" [(H)e felt that Shérazade was right] (*Shérazade* 159/170).

In her book, *Transfigurations of the Maghreb*, Winifred Woodhull analyzed other instances in which Shérazade uses violence as a response to the violence exerted upon her by men's representations of her (118–20). Woodhull noted the sexualized vocabulary used to describe a photographer's camera that Shérazade breaks after he surreptitiously tries to take a picture of her at a party: "son appareil gravement mutilé" [his equipment severely mutilated] (*Shérazade* 125/translated in Woodhull 118). The camera explicitly symbolizes the phallus. Sebbar thus exposes the libidinal investment attached to the use of photography to appropriate women's images.

By attacking the camera, Shérazade hits where it hurts the most—literally below the belt. Her violence, as a response to violence of a sexual nature exerted against her, is experienced as sexually castrating. By breaking the camera, she effectively neutralizes (perhaps even neuters) Orientalist desire, a desire that is perceived as violent because the camera, like the phallus, can be used as a weapon. Sebbar's choice of vocabulary when Shérazade is being photographed indicates the potential danger of representation: Shérazade serves as a "cible à un oeil photographique" [target for a photographic eye] (*Carnets* 193).

In the colonial or postcolonial contexts, violence is inherent to the representational act, as Malek Alloula remarked in *Le Harem colonial*: "Le colonialisme est, entre autres choses, *l'expression parfaite de la violence du regard*" [Colonialism is, among other things, *the perfect expression of the violence of the gaze*] (84/131). Sebbar insists, even more than Alloula, that the colonial gaze is also a phallic gaze. Shérazade encounters several instances of the violence of photographic representation, including French military photographer Marc Garanger's collection of pictures of Algerian women, *Femmes algériennes 1960*. As opposed to the colonial postcards analyzed by Alloula (in which paid models were used to stand in for an absent subject, Algerian women), Garanger photographed Algerian women and men to establish identity cards for them during the Algerian war of liberation. As Shérazade leafs through that book, the narrator comments: "Ces Algériennes avaient toutes devant l'objectif-mitrailleur, le même regard, intense, farouche, d'une sauvagerie que l'image ne saurait qu'archiver, sans jamais la maîtriser ni la dominer. Ces femmes parlaient toutes la même langue, la langue de sa mère" [These Algerian women all had the same intense and savage stare in front of the shooting lens, a look so fierce that the image could only file it for posterity without ever mastering or dominating it. These women all spoke the same language, her mother's language] (*Shérazade* 220/237–38). The women's reaction to being forcefully photographed parallels Alloula's work, which attempts to "renvoyer à l'expéditeur cette immense carte" [return this immense postcard to its sender] (*Harem* 10/5). Alloula remarked that the women in the postcards, even though they were willing models, often returned a bored or empty gaze to the camera instead of projecting enjoyment and unbridled sexuality (65/98). Similarly, the women Garanger photographed resisted by returning what they perceived as a violent gaze to its sender. In his Introduction to the 1982 reprint of his book, Garanger described these women's eyes as powerful weapons: "J'ai reçu leur regard à bout portant" [I received their gaze at point-blank range] (*Femmes algériennes* n.p.). The photographs are, in both cases, representative of the general violence of the French colonization of Algeria.[10]

Sebbar's treatment of Garanger's photographs and Alloula's critique of the postcards bear testimony to the colonizer's inability to totally master or dominate the Algerian people. Decades later, Garanger's violent book allows Shérazade to establish a link to her roots because she connects these women to her mother through language. In this context, this violent photo album is made to serve a positive function for Shérazade. As Woodhull showed in her book, Shérazade comes across the picture book at a critical moment (121–22). Her encounter with Garanger's *Femmes algériennes* (a book whose direct violence covers the exotic potential of these new *Femmes d'Alger*) functions as a cautionary tale that allows her to reject the moviemaker's fantasy of the Oriental woman, in which she was getting entangled, and to leave his film project at that point.[11]

Hybrid Names

Sebbar illustrates the complexity of her characters' fragmented identities, not only through their masquerades as signs of resistance to Orientalism, but also through the multiplicity of names they assume. While their first names seem to proliferate, however, none of her teenage characters are ever endowed with a last name. Michel Laronde pointed out that "le nom de famille, le patronyme, a symboliquement une valeur sociale. La patronymie est la présence d'un 'modèle,' d'un 'protecteur' (le 'patron' ou 'père'/*pater*)" [the patronymic last name symbolically holds social value. It reveals the presence of a "model," a "protector" (the "patron" or "father"/*pater*)] (*Autour* 193). The absence of the last name can be interpreted in at least two ways. Sebbar once commented on the rejection of the patriarchal last name in the women's movement (in which she actively participated in the 1970s) and the sense of freedom this transgression brought (quoted in Achour, "Fatima" 180). Another possible interpretation is that it can also represent the disempowerment of male, working-class immigrants in France. Devalued culturally, individually, and economically, they find themselves stripped of their authority, even on the home front. Their attempts at salvaging that lost authority at home often result in their children feeling alienated and running away. Sebbar's teenage characters, as runaways, are creating their own identities and spaces in the in between.

Shérazade's first name embodies a hybridity that inscribes within itself the dynamics of loss and excess. As an Orientalist marker for the exotic woman, the name is too much—too good to be true: "Shérazade savait que son nom provoquait souvent des réactions bizarres, inattendues, incontrôlables" [Shérazade knew that her name often triggered strange, unexpected, and uncontrollable reactions] (*Carnets* 140). The first novel of the trilogy opens with a scene in which Julien, who is attracted to Shérazade precisely because she reminds him of Delacroix's green-eyed woman (in the painting *Femmes d'Alger dans leur appartement*), is stunned to find reality confirming his Orientalist fantasy in such a way (*Shérazade* 7/1). Shérazade, however, is not the sultana of *The Arabian Nights*. In the transcription of her name from spoken Arabic to the French birth certificate, the name loses what would be an excess syllable in French (because of the mute "h"), but it is "la syllabe la plus suave, la plus orientale" [the sweetest, most Oriental syllable] in Arabic, according to an old Lebanese woman whom Shérazade meets in the last book of the trilogy (*Fou* 164). Shérazade's name is a perfect metaphor for France's assimilation policy with regard to immigrants. What is most representative of other cultures must be cut off for the other to be accepted and assimilated into the fabric of French life. Thus what could be viewed as the richness of cultural difference is instead rejected as unnecessary excess.

The loss of the syllable, which is lost in the geographical, cultural, and linguistic trans-lation, marks Shérazade as a cultural métisse. Her name functions as a sign of in betweenness that metaphorically gives her some margin for maneuver. She takes on this new identity imposed on her by the French administrative system and uses it to avoid being confused with her namesake the sultana and thus to claim difference from her endangered model. As Gilles notes, the sultana Scheherazade "est une femme douce et souple, pas comme [Shérazade] . . . agressive" [is a gentle and flexible woman, not aggressive like Sherazade] (*Carnets* 104). Many of the men Shérazade encounters do not at first understand the difference between the two names and the two women, and Shérazade is always prompt to enlighten them. She claims her difference from Scheherazade by holding on to the unique spelling of her name whenever an Orientalist tries to impose his or her colonial fantasy on her. However, when the name is pronounced in the Arab way by an Arab, she accepts Scheherazade as her name (*Carnets* 269).

As part of the game of hide-and-seek that she plays with those who want to incorporate her into their colonial fantasy, Shérazade also uses aliases. When she first meets Michel Salomon, she plays with/anticipates his Orientalist fantasies by pretending to be named Balkis,

"[c]omme la reine de Saba" [like the Queen of Sheba] (*Carnets* 268).
However, when Nasser, the Tunisian scholar, joins them, she reveals
her real name (269). For those who cannot accept her name, she has
two alternatives to offer, sometimes Rosa (a name connoting an uncertain Latin origin—Italian or Spanish perhaps) and most often Camille
(*Shérazade* 87, 180, 187; *Carnets* 29, 169, 207; *Fou* 173). The choice
of the androgynous, traditional, French name Camille functions as yet
another disguise.[12]

In *Le Chinois vert d'Afrique*, Mohamed's name—yet another
overdetermined name—is, paradoxically, even more indicative of an identity that cannot be pinned down. The name of the Prophet (with one
missing letter), Mohamed is also the name that was used by many French
colonials to generically refer to all Arab men (the female equivalent being
Fatma, a variation on the name Sebbar chose as the title of her first novel,
Fatima ou les Algériennes au square). Almost every person who comes in
contact with Mohamed calls him by a different name. These variations on
his name symbolize the boy's elusive identity. He is on the run, both
literally—the seven parts of the novel are framed by short paragraphs which
all begin with "Il court" [He is running]—and symbolically, through the
metamorphoses of the name. Mohamed does not accept all the names he
is given. As opposed to Shérazade, he adamantly rejects French nomina-
tion, be it the othering nicknames the police use for him—"[le] Sauvage,
l'Indien, le Zoulou, le Samouraï" [Savage, Indian, Zulu, Samurai] (226)—
but more important, any French version of his name, such as Maurice
(52) or Mahom (75).

When he meets Myra, the young métisse who becomes his friend, he
writes her a message offering her all of the names he accepts as marks of
his fragmented identity:

> Mira,
> Je sais ton nom.
> Moi, c'est:
> Mohamed pour mon père
> Mehmet pour ma mère
> Madou pour ma soeur Mélissa
> Hammidou pour ma grand-mère Minh
> Momo pour les copains
> ou le Chinois
> ou le Chinois vert d'Afrique
>   M. (83)[13]

[Mira,
I know your name.
Mine is:
Mohamed for my father
Mehmet for my mother
Madou for my sister Melissa
Hammidou for my grandmother Minh
Momo for my buddies
or the Chinaman
or the green Chinaman from Africa
　　　M.]

The different names reveal the many facets of Mohamed's cultural identity: he is Arab through his father and Turkish through his mother. Like
Shérazade's first name, his name was transliterated into French with mistakes that reflect French pronunciation: "Je m'appelle Mohamed que je
devrais écrire Muhammad" [My name is Mohamed, which I should spell
Muhammad] (180). However, like Shérazade, he does not attempt to change
the spelling or the pronunciation, taking on his métissage rather than
trying to effect an impossible return to his origins. The nicknames given
by his sister and Vietnamese grandmother reflect love and tenderness,
whereas those given by his friends only increase the mystery of his multiple origins. Each of the people who name him only knows a facet of his
identity. No one can ever know him entirely.
 　 While Mohamed claims the nickname "Le Chinois vert d'Afrique" as
his own, it is interesting to note that even this composite description is
purposefully slippery: he is of Vietnamese rather than Chinese descent;
North Africa is often seen as an entity separate from sub-Saharan Africa
and is usually linked in geopolitical terms to the Middle East rather than
to the rest of Africa; as for "green," the term is polysemous. If taken as a
reference to Algeria (green is the color symbolic of Islam and of Algeria),
it is only partially representative, since Momo lives in France.[14] If taken, as
by Michel Laronde, as a possible reference to aliens (Martians as little
green men), the term emphasizes Momo's strangeness (*Autour* 67–68). No
name, however complex or multiple it may be, can really embody the
métis condition. This is further signified by the fact that, when signing his
message, Mohamed inscribes only his initial, letting Myra choose the name
she prefers: "C'est comme ça que je t'appelle: HAMI. Je l'ai choisi dans la
liste des noms que tu m'as envoyée" [This is how I name you: HAMI. I
chose the name from the list you sent me] (126). In fact, the name is *not*

on the list, but rather is a short version of Mohamed's grandmother's nickname for him. Myra, like all of Mohamed's loved ones, chooses a different version of his name, one that says more about their relationship than about anything else: Hami, pronounced the French way, is a homonym of "ami" [friend].

As a letter and message writer, Mohamed signs his name in different ways according to his addressee. To Myra, he is "M." or "M. le Chinois vert d'Afrique" (241). In his messages to his sister, he writes his name in Arabic calligraphy (139). In doing so, he is following his grandmother's practice of using a triple signature that is a sign of her multiple identity: once in French, once in Arabic, and once in Chinese ideograms. Rather than sign all his names at once, Mohamed lets his signature represent his fragmented identity. As Woodhull remarks about Sebbar herself, it is impossible for Mohamed to *decline* his identity, in both senses of the term: he can no more run through a full declension of his names—the list he gives Myra comes close, but, as Myra shows, it is not complete—than he can "flatly refuse (*decline*) a simple identity" (104).

Mohamed's identity is not fixed but must be constantly renegotiated with each relationship. His métis identity is marked by fluidity. Its boundaries are defined through relationships. By giving Myra the list of names, Mohamed allows her to gain more insight into his identity than any other character in the novel. Only she and the reader of the text can arrive at a wider perception of who Mohamed is while at the same time realizing that even the sum of all his names can never contain his identity. The proliferation of names is part of a very serious game in which Sebbar's characters engage as they navigate through representations that constitute them as objects at the same time as these representations reveal something about the characters' cultural identities.

In her article on Beur writer Azouz Begag, Samia Mehrez critiqued Deleuze and Guattari's concept of deterritorialized minor literatures by arguing for the necessity of reterritorialization in postcolonial minor literature: "[O]ur critical investigation should never stop at 'deterritorialization'" (Mehrez 28) because postcolonial "minor" literature, rather than glorifying exile, "seeks to acquire and legitimate territory" at the same time as it "deterritorializes the dominant" (27): "the crucial question is indeed one of territory, one of legitimate space that cannot afford to be nomadic, that can only counteract exile" (33). Mehrez linked the absence of a reflection on reterritorialization in Deleuze and Guattari's *Kafka* to the fact that, like Kristeva in *Etrangers à nous-mêmes* (Strangers to ourselves), Deleuze and Guattari appear to be more interested in the "depoliticized" implications of minor literature for native speakers of major languages (Mehrez 27). They investigate the possibility for such writers to carve their own space of difference within their language and culture. The difference in power position between such a situation and that of exiles or immigrants, especially Beurs in France, is too easily erased by Deleuze and Guattari and Kristeva, as both Mehrez and Woodhull have pointed out (Woodhull 88–94).

Members of exiled minority groups who are fragmented by conflicting allegiances and desires are confronted with the impossibility of using a nationalistic framework to further their cause. For exiles, the concept of belonging to a nation is often replaced by a desire to create an imagined territory for oneself and other exiles. In his "Reflections on Exile," Edward Said opposed exile to nationalism, and insists on exiles' "urgent need to reconstitute their broken lives" (360). Aware of the impossibility of effecting such reconstruction through the "triumphant ideology" of "a restored people," Sebbar and Djebar have chosen literature as a medium allowing them to work toward the construction of imagined communities and imagined territories (Said 360).

In Sebbar's works, writing is used as a locus for reterritorialization. Her purpose is to "donner un territoire (aux enfants de l'immigration) dans la littérature" [to give (children of immigration) a territory in literature] (quoted in Laronde, "Leïla Sebbar" 8). A group whose literal presence in France is denounced as excessive by too many French people, Beurs are extremely concerned with issues of territory. By weaving métissé texts, Sebbar attempts, not to reterritorialize at the nationalist level, but to create "imagined communities" that do not hark back to a common, mythical past.[15] Rather, they emerge through foregrounding a history of colonization and resistance. In an interview with Monique Hugon, she adds that she likes to "écrire dans la langue française . . . sur une réalité, qui n'est pas une réalité absolument française, et donner un droit de cité . . . dans la littérature française . . . à des arabes" [write in French . . . about a reality that is not exclusively French, and to give . . . Arabs a legitimate space . . . in French literature] (37). As Woodhull showed, this allows Sebbar to "productively alter the terms of debates about Frenchness," or, in other words, to reterritorialize the dominant by reappropriating, displacing, and challenging its self-definitions (106). It is in this context that Sebbar's assertion that she is a French writer must be understood: her project is to redefine Frenchness as métissage, in terms inclusive of people of Maghrebian descent living in France, by highlighting the performativity and instability of the categories of national identity. As Danielle Marx-Scouras rightly argues, why should Sebbar be "any

less 'French' than Samuel Beckett, Julien Green, or Eugene Ionesco?"
("Mother Tongue" 60).

For Sebbar, the French language is what allows her to "vivre l'exil
comme territoire," [experience exile as a territory] ("Langue" 10). Writing in French permits Sebbar to turn exile into a "productive" position
(quoted in Hugon 35). Exiled from her place of origin, she negotiates
her own location through the creative act: "Ecrire est le lieu privilégié, la
terre d'élection et d'adoption" [Writing is the privileged place, the chosen, adopted land] (quoted in Hugon 35). In other words, Sebbar finds
her imagined community in the space of writing. The lack of a land to
call her own, her home, makes her take writing as her territory, a territory inscribed in the French language. Sebbar would concur with Said's
assertion that "the only home truly available now, though fragile and vulnerable, is in writing," because "homecoming is out of the question" ("Reflections" 365, 361). This last remark is certainly true for the Beurs, as
exemplified by Shérazade's multiple journeys through Paris, France, and
the Middle East.

In the case of Sebbar's fiction, then, Mehrez's claim that postcolonial
"minor" literature seeks a "legitimate space that cannot afford to be nomadic" must be qualified (Mehrez 33). Because the space of
reterritorialization is marked by preexisting, overdetermined conditions and
borders, reclaiming such a territory must, of necessity, be at the same time
a grounded *and* a nomadic practice constantly negotiating between fixed
and objectifying representations. This is metaphorically represented by the
figure of Mohamed, who is on the run during the entire novel. As for
Shérazade, she travels in and out of Orientalist parameters, as an insider/
outsider, always on the border, in between, in flight. She reappropriates
representations of herself for what she can learn from them at the same
time as she returns the violent gaze to its sender by weaving her own
fragmented identity over and through these representations. For Woodhull,
it is a matter of both "dismantl[ing] fixed identities" and "affirm[ing] the
liberatory aspect of the *gatherings* of dispersed identities" (100). Mobility
can be understood precisely as what grounds Shérazade's and Mohamed's
relational, fragmented identities, what allows them to piece the different
parts of the mosaic together. The roots that Shérazade and Mohamed, the
nomadic Beur runaways, attempt to plant cannot be literal because they
are always in flight; rather, they are imagined, cultural and literary.[16]

Sebbar and Djebar both reclaim a possible u-topian territory in their
fiction. Djebar seeks to find a space of freedom for Algerian women within
Algerian society, a space that may finally be shared with men. Her fiction
works towards building bridges of solidarity between diverse women. The

utopian space can be realized only within the frame of the text because her narrators live separated from the women in their families. As for Sebbar, she appropriates writing as her territory, creating a utopian space of *métissage* for herself and the Beur community in her fiction. Whereas Djebar's imagined territory oscillates between Algeria and France, two countries on opposite sides of the Mediterranean, Sebbar's imagined territory extends to the entire Mediterranean region and beyond. If Djebar's fiction can be figured as a palimpsestic painting, Sebbar's works can be pictured as a Mediterranean mosaic.

Notes

1. It was only after developing these two concepts of mythologizing and reappropriation that I became familiar with a similar distinction made by Stuart Hall in "Cultural Identity and Diaspora." Hall considers two definitions of cultural identity. The first is based on an essential, fixed view of identity that must be unearthed from beneath the layers of colonial experience. The second presents identity in terms of mobile, shifting, historically contextual positionings, as a "production" constructed within representations (392–95). In an essay on the second book of the *Shérazade* trilogy, Françoise Lionnet developed an analogous model with respect to history, which, she asserts, can be suffered, acted on/inverted, or appropriated through discursive reconstruction ("Narrative Journeys" 174–75).

2. Shérazade, for instance, is descended from Abd el-Kader on her father's side (Sebbar, *Carnets* 221–24).

3. For an analysis of music in *Le Chinois*, see Caroline Clifford.

4. For a thorough treatment of Montagu's writings, see Lisa Lowe and Yegenoglu's response to her (45–80).

5. For a similar argument against the concept of "Orientalism in reverse," see Mani and Frankenberg (187).

6. In what follows, I am indebted to the analyses of Sebbar's *Shérazade* by Winifred Woodhull and Madeleine Van Strien-Chardonneau. For an analysis of identity and representation in Sebbar that parallels my own, see Anissa Talahite.

7. Bhabha calls these two impulses the "pedagogical" and the "performative," respectively (DissemiNation, 145–59). My own discussion of Sebbar's pedagogical tactics uses a very different meaning of the term than Bhabha's. Indeed, Sebbar's pedagogy, like her performative tactics, works to destabilize pregiven myths of French identity and of the absolute difference between the "French" and the "Arabs," which serve to conceal the fact that many Arabs are French citizens.

8. There is a way in which Shérazade's taste for masquerade and disguise parallels Sebbar's own interest in the subversive potentialities of gender inver-

sion, cross-dressing, and race inversion. For instance, Sebbar is fascinated with the figure of Isabelle Eberhardt, to whom she devoted an essay ("Isabelle Eberhardt"). A Russian woman writing in French who "went native," Eberhardt lived as an Arab man in Algeria, traveling around the country with a group of Algerian men. In his article on Isabelle Eberhardt, Hédi Abdel-Jaouad noted that, "Like Pierre Loti, . . . Isabelle had an irresistible attraction for masquerade and disguise" (106).

9. In *Les Alouettes naïves*, Djebar briefly dismisses Loti's novelistic world in similar terms, as a place "où l'Orient était sucré et multicolore" [where the Orient was sugary and many-colored] (72).

10. A much more critical approach to Alloula's book than Sebbar's or my own can be found in Mieke Bal ("Politics") and Rey Chow ("Where Have All the Natives Gone?").

11. It is interesting to note that Garanger produced another collection of photographs of Algerian women, also taken while he was doing his military service in Algeria during the war. Unlike his *Femmes algériennes 1960*, the pictures in *Femmes des Hauts-Plateaux* were taken when he was off-duty. The women were not photographed against their will, and the general impression given by the photographs is much less violent. Sebbar wrote the text accompanying the pictures.

12. Michel Laronde examines Shérazade's manipulations of these two pseudonyms in detail (*Autour du roman beur* 199–205). Shérazade's strategy is reminiscent of Sebbar's own tactic, as described in one of her rare autobiographical short stories, "Si je parle la langue de ma mère": young Leïla also had an alternative name to offer her curious schoolmates: "Je m'appelle aussi N. Je disais un prénom bien français que j'avais vu écrit près du mien sur un acte de naissance" [My name is also N. I would give a very French first name that I had seen written next to mine on a birth certificate] (1183). The vocabulary chosen, as well as the decision to reveal only the first letter of that middle name, indicate that the adult narrator does not really feel that the French name is hers: instead of accepting it as her middle name, she views it as a name that simply happens to be placed, almost arbitrarily, next to the only first name she recognizes as legitimately hers. Like Shérazade, the name Leïla is overdetermined because of the Orientalist tradition: it carries a "lyrisme obligé" [inevitable lyricism] (1185). The entire short story is a poignant meditation on identity through the interrogation of the name, as Sebbar prods it to explore the métissage it reveals and her multiple responses to it.

13. Laronde analyzes this message in *Autour du roman beur* (194–96). It is interesting that there, Mohamed also changes his friend's name slightly by replacing the *y* with an *i*, thus highlighting the unstable status of Myra/Mira's identity as well.

14. The significance of this color is mentioned in *Shérazade* 203/219. The entire phrase appears to have an autobiographical origin. In a 1997 short story published in a collection that Sebbar edited, on the theme of childhood

in Algeria, her narrator mentions the following: "L'ami de mon père a deux enfants, une fille, l'aînée, et un garçon qu'on appelle 'le chinois vert d'Afrique.' Il a les cheveux noirs et lisses de sa mère, eurasienne, et ses yeux verts" [My father's friend has two children, a daughter, the older, and a son nicknamed "the green Chinaman from Africa." His hair is black and straight like that of his mother, a Eurasian, and he has her green eyes] ("On tue" 191).

15. The words are Benedict Anderson's. I am following Chandra Talpade Mohanty's use of the term to describe nonessentialist, political bases for group alliances ("Cartographies" 4–5).

16. By being constantly in motion and constantly outside, the novels' characters inscribe themselves in a long Arabic tradition of nomadism and exile. As Gilles Kepel argued, "L'exil fonde l'islam" [Exile is at the foundation of Islam]. This is because the Muslim calendar begins with the Hijra, the Prophet Muhammad's exile to Medina (34). Nomadism continued to be a central feature of Muslim life through its long period of expansion and conquest (35). In a way, the Hijra continues nowadays through Maghrebian immigration (34).

Conclusion

In this book, I have proposed that postcolonial literature generally shares the following three characteristics: first, the fiction self-consciously positions itself as being both oppositional to, and complicit with, a variety of power structures, such as colonialism and patriarchy. Rejecting Manichean analyses of resistance, postcolonial literature often portrays subjects who negotiate hybrid identities through, and in spite of, multiple systems of exploitation. This is especially true of texts that take into account gender issues, since the patriarchal bases common to colonial and anticolonial politics make it difficult for women to embrace wholeheartedly monist ideologies that reinforce the principle of male firstness.

Second, postcolonial literature consistently seeks to reclaim a history written by the conqueror through engaging in complex rewritings of fractured colonial histories. Because the dominant narratives of the past inevitably display blanks and occlusions, writers seize fiction as a privileged medium with which to contend with hegemonic historiography. Postcolonial fiction exposes dominant history's ideological cover-ups and silences, while attempting to imaginatively flesh out its gaps. That these writers do not seek to create new master histories is evinced in the fragmentary, exploded nature of their narratives, which question and reopen the past more than provide rigid versions of it. Postcolonial feminist literature foregrounds the presence and voices of women silenced by a history that discounts them and fails to consider their agency.

Finally, even when postcolonial texts are not written in as experimental a manner as Djebar's *Fantasia*, Condé's *Heremakhônon*, or Maximin's *L'Isolé soleil*, they typically refer to a complex intertextual matrix that provides a historical, cultural, and literary genealogy. This intertextual matrix allows writers to position their texts within diverse traditions that they contest, reclaim, and reinvent. The retrieval and recasting of powerful female figures in history, literature, and culture is a particularly important strategy of postcolonial feminist literature, as it establishes a *géné/elle/logie* [female genealogy] of solidarity between women across time and space.

In *Recasting Postcolonialism*, I have used the model of postcolonial literature summarized here as a lens through which to analyze the fiction of two Francophone women writers from one specific geographical context, Algeria, which is a site of multiple production of meaning for postcolonial studies. Further avenues of research include the application of this model to postcolonial contexts beyond Algeria and the study of two other major characteristics of postcolonial literature, multilingualism and the creation of hybrid, autobiographical genres.[1] When written in European languages, postcolonial literature subverts and incorporates linguistic diversity into these languages. This literature reterritorializes colonial languages by using words and concepts that are foreign to them and by reshaping them according to the syntax of indigenous languages. Once imposed on colonized peoples, the language of the former colonizer now stretches out of its own limitations in order to be appropriated into postcoloniality. Moreover, because postcolonial literature tends to plot the process of negotiation of diverse hybrid subjectivities, it often breaks generic boundaries by mixing autobiography, fiction, and historical narrative in highly experimental forms. Some postcolonial writers (Djebar, El Saadawi, Mernissi) explicitly write in the autobiographical mode. Others (Sebbar, Maximin, Condé) attribute personal experiences to fictional characters. In what follows, I map out these further directions for research through several specific examples.

While it is beyond the scope of the present work to extend this model to other geographical, linguistic, and literary contexts in the postcolonial world, my frequent references to Caribbean literature in the introduction to *Recasting Postcolonialism* indicate that this area is a particularly fruitful site for such investigation. The Guadeloupean writer Daniel Maximin's *L'Isolé soleil* (1981) is an exemplary postcolonial text. In this polyphonic novel, historical chronology is disturbed, narrators and literary genres overlap, women's voices are retrieved, and the liberation movements of Afro-Caribbean and African-American peoples are foregrounded historically. Maximin's novel evinces strong parallels with Djebar's *Fantasia*, not least of all in the focus on women's voices. Maximin rises beautifully to the challenge of "writing like a woman" and "writing-with the woman"

(Scharfman 238), seeking out traces of and reinscribing Caribbean people of both genders into their history and landscape. The presence of various intertexts, literary, historical, and fictional, highlights the necessarily constructed nature of any historical or narrative enterprise in the colonial context.

Maximin positions his text at the point of convergence of African, European, African-American, and Caribbean traditions. According to VèVè Clark, these four cultural traditions serve as the reference points of Caribbean literature. Caribbean influences are present in *L'Isolé Soleil,* not only through the towering presence of Aimé Césaire, but also in the focus on contributions of his wife, Suzanne, to Antillean thought (one of the many ways in which Maximin highlights the occluded participation of women to Caribbean history and culture). Maximin also foregrounds the influence of folkloric music, proverbs, tales, art, and Creole language. He rewrites Louis Delgrès's historical resistance to the French in Martinique. The European connection is developed not only because several characters live in France, or between France and the islands, but also through intertextual references to William Shakespeare, Arthur Rimbaud, and Surrealism. The African influence is expressed through the importance of masks, music, religion, and literature. Finally, both recent and older aspects of the African American tradition are foregrounded through the presence of the Coleman Hawkins' jazz piece *Body and Soul,* the Harlem Renaissance writers, and the radical activism of Angela Davis and the Soledad brothers, George and Jonathan Jackson.

Another text that can be fruitfully analyzed along such parameters is Maryse Condé's 1976 novel *Heremakhônon,* which openly rejects a male Caribbean writers' master narrative of Caribbean literature that demands Marxist-based, social realist, Manichean depictions of collective, cultural, and political resistance. Texts such as Jacques Roumain's *Gouverneurs de la rosée* present a male redeeming figure leading the rebellion of poor farmers on Caribbean soil.[2] In this perspective, *Heremakhônon* operates as a fragmented narrative focusing on sexual and racial politics seen through the eyes of Véronica Mercier, a Caribbean woman living in Africa. The novel can be read as the antithesis of *Gouverneurs de la rosée.* Condé rejects the prescriptive ideologies concerning committed writing.

Condé's project includes an attempt to rewrite black women into Caribbean literary history by underscoring the ambivalent nature of her project and by rejecting Manichean certainties. *Heremakhônon* also provides a forceful response to Fanon's searing indictment of Mayotte Capécia's novel, *Je suis martiniquaise,* through an ironic rewriting of that novel (Andrade 219–

22). Irony is *Heremakhônon*'s main narrative mode. Véronica's extreme lucidity allows her to critique Manichean thought systems and to realize the extent of her own alienation and the paradoxes of her romanticized search for the "wrong" history, one that would not be marred by the stigma of Caribbean slavery and enforced métissage. Véronica foregrounds her own complicity in perpetuating neocolonialism through her job as teacher of Western philosophy in Africa and through her internalization of stereotypes, which she both underscores and undermines in a complex and ambivalent narrative.

There is an urgent need for more studies of postcolonial literature focusing specifically on the texts' many strategies of multilingualism.[3] Theorizing postcoloniality as subversion rather than binary opposition is a fruitful point of departure for detailed analyses of the presence of indigenous languages breaking through the strictures of a text written in what Djebar calls the language of yesterday's enemy. For example, Arabic vocabulary abounds in Djebar's entire literary production, especially her post-1980 work. The presence of Arabic words defamiliarizes the French language for a French audience. Conversely, Djebar's French texts become more hospitable to native speakers of Arabic. As opposed to more conventional uses where indigenous vocabulary is consistently explained in footnotes, translations within the body of the text, or glossaries, Djebar's incorporation of Arabic into her French texts is not always in the service of transparency to a French reader.

Although she sometimes provides a translation—what Zabus calls "cushioning" (158)—she uses this mostly when referring to very specialized concepts (many of which are of Turkish or Farsi origin) in her historical rewriting of the beginnings of French colonization in *Fantasia*. In this case, Arabic words either indicate traditional myths or cultural concepts or give the reader an insight into the meaning of the characters' proper names. Djebar uses many Arabic words that have become part of the specialized vocabulary of Orientalism, placing them in quotation marks or in italics. When she does not provide translations for these words, she contextualizes them so that readers can roughly understand their general meaning. She also uses Arabic words that have become fairly common in French, such as terms for titles and ranks, traditional clothing, and geographical places, thus suggesting that colonization also changes the colonizing power's culture and language. She highlights the epistemic violence of colonialism by staging the struggle for dominance between different factions through linguistic battle such as that between "les Frères" [the Brothers] versus "des *fellaghas*" [a derogatory term used by the French to refer to the freedom fighters during the Algerian war] (232, 234/207–8).

Finally, Djebar uses unmarked French words to render Arab concepts such as shame [*hichma*], thus stretching the French language and pushing it beyond conventional usage. These insertions of Arabic allow her to reterritorialize French by staging alternative linguistic spaces in and through literature.[4]

In *Fantasia*, Djebar amply demonstrated how problems of autobiography were linked to language, especially for an Arab woman. One fruitful area for further research will be a comparative study of different Arab women writers' narrative and linguistic strategies to write autobiographical works. Whereas Djebar reveals herself in the language of yesterday's enemy, Egyptian feminist Nawal El Saadawi lives and writes in her mother tongue, Arabic. As with Condé, El Saadawi's husband of many years translates her works into English. She is a medical doctor, a self-described feminist activist, and an acclaimed author, many of whose novels are partly autobiographical. Even in her scholarly essays and books, El Saadawi refuses to shrink from having recourse to autobiographical testimony to drive home her point. This is particularly evidenced in the chapter of *The Hidden Face of Eve* in which she graphically recounts her own clitoridectomy at age six (7–11). The English translation of her autobiography, *A Daughter of Isis* (originally written in Arabic), was published in June 1999.

Two other influential Arab feminists, an Egyptian, Leila Ahmed, and a Moroccan, Fatima Mernissi, also published autobiographies at the turn of the century (Ahmed's *A Border Passage* in April 1999, Mernissi's *Dreams of Trespass* in 1994). Both writers are well-known scholars. Ahmed teaches Women's Studies at the University of Massachusetts—Amherst; her work is historical and sociological. Mernissi is a sociologist at the Université Mohammed V in Rabat, Morocco. Although neither had written strictly in the autobiographical mode prior to these recent memoirs, both women, like El Saadawi, have connected their scholarly works to their own experiences as Arab women. Ahmed's scholarly career has taken her from Egypt to the United Kingdom and then to the United States, and her language of writing (including that in *Border Passage*) is English. Mernissi holds an American Ph.D., which explains why her first book (originally her Ph.D. dissertation), *Beyond the Veil* (1975), was written and first published in English. However, all of her subsequent works were written and first published in French, Morocco's second official language after Arabic (Moroccan children are schooled in both languages). Interestingly, when she wrote more directly about the self, Mernissi chose English as the language of writing.

Does the choice of the language of writing (Arabic, French, English) entail a concomitant adjustment of narrative strategies? Does one highlight different aspects of one's life based on which language one uses? To the extent that the language of writing implies a different target audience, it is bound to have an impact on the events one chooses to recount and how they are presented. For example, although Mernissi lives and works in Morocco, her memoir's target audience is international due to her choice of writing in English (although the book was translated into Arabic in 1997 and French in 1996). Her knowledge of English allows her to bypass the dangers of writing about the self in the language of the former colonizer. In that context, English is a more neutral language, one that may allow writers to distance themselves from the text and possibly reveal certain things that may be difficult to say, and even more to write, in Arabic, the language of the sacred text.

Yet, whether written in Arabic (El Saadawi), French (Djebar) or English (Mernissi and Ahmed), what is clear in all of these autobiographical narratives is that the reader learns precious little about actual personal events occurring in the women's lives. This is especially true of Mernissi's book (which only covers the years of her childhood between the ages of four and nine) and of Djebar's. Both Mernissi and Djebar present a "collective autobiography" (Geesey) foregrounding the importance of the community of women and inserting themselves into a female tradition and a group of secluded women from whom life separated them. In contrast, Ahmed's memoir, like *Out of Place*, Edward Said's 1999 memoir, provides a greater sense of the growth of a solitary, individual self. At the same time, she comments on not finding it appropriate to discuss her relationships with men. This reticence to write about sexuality and desire in directly autobiographical ways is common to many Arab women writers. Djebar's works evince an interesting evolution with respect to this issue. While writing female sexuality has been at the center of her literary project since her first novel, *La Soif* in 1957, it was only with her breakthrough 1995 autobiographical narrative *Vaste est la prison*, that she was finally able to write about desire in a directly autobiographical fashion. Perhaps because she is a doctor who sees her pen as a scalpel, Nawal El Saadawi has been more directly autobiographical much earlier—and in Arabic—than these other Arab women writers.

The choice of writing in a language unfamiliar to the majority of Moroccan people puts certain constraints on Mernissi's memoir. Because an international audience would not be familiar with many of the realities Mernissi depicts, she finds herself obligated to provide detailed explanations. For example, her use of a large corpus of Arabic vocabulary, in contrast to Djebar's innovative incorporations of Arabic into French, remains constantly within the parameters of translation, as each word is either immediately translated within the body of the text or footnoted with extensive cultural explanation. Further, since she is describing certain practices that are on the wane now but in which women used to engage in the 1940s, her sociological training leads her to describe and explain these practices (such as beauty rituals) at great length, both so that such knowledge will not disappear entirely and so that her non-Moroccan target audience will understand everything. All of these factors have led some Moroccan scholars to be extremely critical of what they perceive as Mernissi's pandering to the Orientalist tastes of a Western audience (Lebbady).

The rather conventional beginning of Mernissi's memoir, "I was born in a harem in 1940 in Fez, a ninth-century Moroccan city some five thousand kilometers west of Mecca, and one thousand kilometers south of Madrid, one of the dangerous capitals of the Christians," can first be read as highlighting the focus on an international audience that needs to be told where Fez is located (*Dreams* 1). This conventional beginning can be contrasted with Djebar's words, "Fillette arabe allant pour la première fois à l'école, un matin d'automne, main dans la main du père" [A little Arab girl going to school for the first time, one autumn morning, walking hand in hand with her father] in her autobiographical novel, *Fantasia* (11/3). Djebar's narrative begins in the third person, indicating a reticence about using "I" in French that allows her to universalize a rather unique experience (only a few dozen Arab girls went to French school in 1940s colonial Algeria). The autobiographical novel opens with the narrator's first day of attending a French school and the historical narrative begins with the moments before the French attack on Algiers in 1830. In both cases, what is highlighted is the dawn of colonization, perceived as both new and dangerous. The motif of the child's hand in her parent's recurs at the end of the first chapter, when the adult narrator leaves, her hand in her daughter's hand. The image of the father holding his daughter's hand is repeated toward the end of the novel, in the chapter "La Tunique de Nessus" ("The Tunic of Nessus"). Finally, in the closing chapter, a surrogate father figure, Fromentin, metaphorically hands the writer-narrator the severed hand of an Algerian woman so that Djebar can bring her to writing/into the text. The image of the child holding the father's hand at the opening and the close of the novel encapsulates Djebar's writing project in *Fantasia*: to account for the father figures who preceded and brought her into the French language, and also for the female *géné/elle/logie* of personal and national history. The recurrence of the image is one example of the consummate artistry of the novel's structure and narrative technique.

It would be both unfair and poor reading to dismiss Mernissi's autobiography, which presents itself on the surface as an easy-to-read text but, like the works of many other postcolonial writers, such as Ousmane Sembène or Ken Bugul, is actually very carefully wrought. The memoir is organized according to the structure of the *Arabian Nights*. Mernissi's use of this intertext is consistent with usage by other postcolonial Arab women writers, who frequently include in their texts early examples of proto-feminist heroines from their own literary tradition (such as Scheherazade). Unlike Djebar, who highlights the solidarity between the storyteller and her sister, Dinarzade, waking her under the bed, Mernissi foregrounds Scheherazade's powerful use of language to defy death, which provides her with a model for dreaming and writing about women's liberation. Mernissi makes use, not only of the framing device of the *Arabian Nights*, but also of some of the stories told by Scheherazade, such as that of Princess Budur and the tale of the birds and beasts.

Mernissi creatively incorporates the *Arabian Nights* model of storytelling and deferral to frame her own chapters. Just as Scheherazade interrupts her story at a climactic moment before dawn, Mernissi begins telling a story at the end of a chapter, only to take it up again at greater length in the next chapter. Like Djebar in the first part of *Fantasia*, she ends one chapter and begins the next with similar vocabulary. Mernissi's use of pictures of traditional Arab women from the upper class, taken by Ruth V. Ward, to both separate each chapter and create a thematic connection, reflects a highly crafted choice, in which the pictures serve the role of threshold, both marking the limit and allowing passage from one chapter to another. This metaphorically reflects the text's emphasis on *hudud*, the sacred frontiers that little Fatima is constantly trying to understand in the text. At the same time, however, the presence of these pictures can also be viewed as problematic in that they may correspond to Orientalist stereotypes held by Westerners of harem women (whose eyes are either averted from the camera or hidden by curtains or veils; they are shown indoors, behind gates and doors, and with one exception, are dressed in traditional ways).

The second half of Mernissi's opening sentence highlights the dual system of address embedded in the memoir: she positions Fez in terms of its distance from Mecca, the Muslim reference point, and Madrid, the capital of Spain, one of Morocco's colonizing powers. Whereas the first part of the sentence reads like a textbook example of the autobiographical pact's claim to truth through the identical nature of author, narrator, and protagonist, the end of the sentence introduces narrative subjectivity through the judgment that Madrid was "one of the dangerous capitals of the Christians" (*Dreams* 1). This statement positions the narrator as non-Christian and in an adversarial position to the center of colonial power. From the very first sentence, the reader encounters the inscription of Mernissi's dual target audience, both Moroccan and international. Mernissi's memoir continually enacts the ambivalent nature (both oppositional and complicit) of postcolonial literature.

I situate the oppositional nature of Mernissi's memoir in that it reads as a powerful response to two discourses that have overdetermined Arab feminism. The first is the conservative Islamic view that feminism is a Western imposition and that the Koran dictates different roles for men and women. The second is the imperialist feminist ideology according to which Arab women are so oppressed that they need Western feminists to provide them with intellectual frameworks to liberate themselves from "backward" Arab men. Between these two discourses, Arab feminism can easily be pronounced an oxymoron. Mernissi's autobiography belies both discourses by focusing on several topics, some of which she had already addressed in her earlier works. These include the fact that Moroccan nationalists of the 1940s insisted on making the education of women a part of their political platform, as well as the existence of a radical version of Islam that foregrounds the search for justice and belief in equality for all. She also highlights the presence of strong, active, feminist and nationalist role models in her family, literature and history, as well as the writings and lives of famous Egyptian feminists such as Huda Shaarawi, a major nationalist and feminist leader in the early twentieth century. By the end of the memoir, Mernissi has indissolubly linked feminism and anticolonialist nationalism in the Arab world, in a powerful response to convenient positionings of feminism as the handmaiden of imperialism. She radically reformulates feminism as Maghrebian, Arab, and Islamic, in order to call on the modern nation-state of Morocco to actualize the original feminist vision of its founders and Arab countries to return to what she sees as the original egalitarianism of Islam.[5]

I have briefly sketched a few of the many avenues for further research using the framework developed in *Recasting Postcolonialism*. One of its advantages is that it is flexible enough to account for a variety of postcolonial texts that foreground the nexus of complicity/opposition, provided the analysis takes into account the cultural and historical specificity of the context of production. Taking my cue from Maximin's *L'Isolé soleil*, I end this book by returning to its beginning: Said's suggestions about the need for "studies in contemporary alternatives to Orientalism" (*Orientalism* 24). The works of Djebar, Sebbar, and many other postcolonial feminist writers participate in the "new kind of dealing with the Orient" that Said called for over two decades ago (28). As such, their literary reformulations deserve to be further highlighted and critically examined.

Notes

1. John Erickson also highlights four of the five characteristics of postcolonial literature in *Islam and Postcolonial Narrative:* multilingualism, oppositionality, intertextuality, and genre mixing. He does not focus on rewriting history. He also foregrounds the importance of storytelling, dialogic literature, the play of language, and ends up underscoring the affinity between postcolonial and postmodern literature to a much higher degree than I do (perhaps due to the fact that his corpus, except for Djebar, is based on male writers) (7–36).

2. See Condé's own descriptions of this master narrative and of Caribbean women's literature in "Order, Disorder, Freedom, and the West Indian Writer."

3. See, for example, Ashcroft, Griffiths, and Tiffin; Zabus.

4. For a more detailed analysis, see my essay, "Multilingual Strategies of Postcolonial Literature."

5. For a more detailed analysis, see my essay, "Portrait of a Maghrebian Feminist as a Young Girl."

Bibliography

Abdel-Jaouad, Hédi. "*L'Amour, la fantasia*: Autobiography as Fiction." *CELFAN Review* 7.1–2 (1987–88): 25–29.

———. "Isabelle Eberhardt: Portrait of the Artist as a Young Nomad." *Yale French Studies* 83 (January 1993): 93–117.

Abu-Haidar, Farida. "Language, Innovation and Imagery in the Novels of Paul Smaïl." Paper given at the fifty-second annual Kentucky Foreign Language Conference, Lexington, KY, April 1999.

Accad, Evelyne. "Assia Djebar's Contribution to Arab Women's Literature: Rebellion, Maturity, Vision." *World Literature Today* 70.4 (Autumn 1996): 801–12.

———. *Sexuality and War: Literary Masks of the Middle East.* New York: New York University Press, 1990.

Achour, Christiane. "Fatima ou les Algériennes au square (1981)." *Diwan d'inquiétude et d'espoir: La Littérature féminine algérienne de langue française.* Ed. Christiane Achour. Algiers: ENAG, 1991. 180–87.

Ahmad, Aijaz. *In Theory: Classes, Nations, Literatures.* London: Verso, 1992.

Ahmed, Leïla. *A Border Passage: From Cairo to America—A Woman's Journey.* New York: Farrar, Straus and Giroux, 1999.

———. "Western Ethnocentrism and Perceptions of the Harem." *Feminist Studies* 8.3 (Fall 1982): 521–34.

Al-Azmeh, Aziz. *Ibn Khaldun: An Essay in Reinterpretation.* London: Frank Cass, 1982.

———. *Ibn Khaldun in Modern Scholarship: A Study in Orientalism.* London: Third World Centre for Research and Publishing, 1981.

"L'Album de la 'Nostalgérie.'" *Paris-Match* (July 9, 1992): 92–93.

Alloula, Malek. *The Colonial Harem.* Trans. Myrna Godzich and Wlad Godzich. Minneapolis: University of Minnesota Press, 1986.

―――. *Le Harem colonial: Images d'un sous-érotisme*. Geneva: Slatkine, 1981.

Amrane, Djamila. *Les Femmes algériennes dans la guerre*. Paris: Plon, 1991.

Amrouche, Taos. *Jacinthe noire*. Paris: Charlot, 1947.

Anderson, Benedict. *Imagined Communities: Reflections on the Origin and Spread of Nationalism*. London: Verso, 1983.

Andrade, Susan Z. "The Nigger of the Narcissist: History, Sexuality and Intertextuality in Maryse Condé's *Heremakhonon*." *Callaloo* 16.1 (1993): 213–26.

Appiah, Kwame Anthony. "The Postcolonial and the Postmodern." *In My Father's House: Africa in the Philosophy of Culture*. New York: Oxford University Press, 1992. 137–57.

Apter, Emily. "Female Trouble in the Colonial Harem." *Differences: A Journal of Feminist Cultural Studies* 4.1 (Spring 1992): 205–24.

Ashcroft, Bill, Gareth Griffiths, and Helen Tiffin. *The Empire Writes Back: Theory and Practice in Post-Colonial Literatures*. London: Routledge, 1989.

Assouline, David, and Mehdi Lallaoui, eds. *Un Siècle d'immigrations en France: Troisième période, 1945 à nos jours: Du Chantier à la citoyenneté?* Paris: Syros, 1997.

Baali, Fuad, and Ali Wardi. *Ibn Khaldun and Islamic Thought-Styles: A Social Perspective*. Boston: G. K. Hall, 1981.

Bacqué, Raphaëlle. "La guerre d'Algérie n'est plus une 'guerre sans nom.'" *Le Monde* (June 11, 1999): 40.

Bal, Mieke. "The Politics of Citation." *Diacritics* 21.1 (Spring 1991): 25–45.

Begag, Azouz, and Abdellatif Chaouite. *Ecarts d'identité*. Paris: Seuil, 1990.

Bekri, Tahar. "Leïla Sebbar: Les Nouvelles de l'entre-deux" (interview). *Notre Librairie* 111 (October–December 1992): 55–57.

Benayoun, Catherine. "Photopsie d'un massacre." *Hommes et migrations* 1219 (May–June 1999): 65–67.

Ben Jelloun, Tahar. *Hospitalité française: Racisme et immigration maghrébine*. Paris: Seuil, 1984.

Bensmaïa, Réda. "Nations of Writers." Trans. Touria Khannous. *Studies in Twentieth-Century Literature* 23.1 (Winter 1999): 163–78.

―――. "*La nouba des femmes du Mont Chenoua*: Introduction to the Cinematic Fragment." Trans. Jennifer Curtiss Gage. *World Literature Today* 70.4 (Autumn 1996): 877–84.

Bergner, Gwen. "Who Is That Masked Woman? or The Role of Gender in Fanon's *Black Skin, White Masks*." *PMLA* 110.1 (January 1995): 75–88.

Berstein, Serge. *La France de l'expansion: I—La République gaullienne 1958–1969*. Paris: Seuil, 1989.

————. "Une Guerre sans nom." *La France en guerre d'Algérie: Novembre 1954–Juillet 1962.* Ed. Laurent Gervereau, Jean-Pierre Rioux, and Benjamin Stora. Paris: Musée d'histoire contemporaine–BDIC, 1992. 34–39.

Bhabha, Homi K. "DissemiNation: Time, Narrative, and the Margins of the Modern Nation." *The Location of Culture.* London: Routledge, 1994. 139–70.

————. *The Location of Culture.* London: Routledge, 1994.

————. "Of Mimicry and Man: The Ambivalence of Colonial Discourse." *The Location of Culture.* London: Routledge, 1994. 85–92.

————. "The Other Question: Stereotype, Discrimination and the Discourse of Colonialism." *The Location of Culture.* London: Routledge, 1994. 66–84.

Boehmer, Elleke. "Stories of Women and Mothers: Gender and Nationalism in the Early Fiction of Flora Nwapa." *Motherlands: Black Women's Writing from Africa, the Caribbean and South Asia.* Ed. Susheila Nasta. London: The Women's Press, 1991. 3–23.

Boudjedra, Rachid. *Les 1001 années de la nostalgie.* Paris: Denoël, 1979.

Brahimi, Denise. "*L'Amour, la fantasia*: Une Grammatologie maghrébine." *Itinéraires et contacts de cultures* 11.2 (1990): 119–24.

————. "Orientalisme et conscience de soi." *Littérature maghrébine d'expression française de l'écrit à l'image.* Ed. Guy Dugas. Meknes, Morocco: Faculté des Lettres et des Sciences Humaines de Meknes (Morocco), Université Sidi Mohamed Ben Abdellah, 1987. 29–36.

Braudel, Fernand. *L'Identité de la France: Les Hommes et les choses.* Paris: Arthaud-Flammarion, 1986.

Bugul, Ken. *The Abandoned Baobab: The Autobiography of a Senegalese Woman.* Trans. Marjolijn de Jager. New York: Lawrence Hill Books, 1991.

————. *Le Baobab fou.* Dakar: Nouvelles éditions africaines, 1984.

Butler, Judith. *Gender Trouble: Feminism and the Subversion of Identity.* New York: Routledge, 1990.

Césaire, Aimé. 1939. *Cahier d'un retour au pays natal.* Paris: Présence africaine, 1983.

————. *Discourse on Colonialism.* Trans. Joan Pinkham. New York: Monthly Review Press, 1972.

Cheddadi, Abdesselam. "Lectures d'Ibn Khaldun." *Le Voyage d'Occident et d'Orient.* Paris: Sindbad, 1980. 14–22.

Chikhi, Beïda. "Histoire et stratégie fictionnelle dans les romans d'Assia Djebar." *Ecrivains maghrébins et modernité textuelle.* Ed. Naget Khadda. Paris: L'Harmattan, 1994. 17–30.

————. *Les Romans d'Assia Djebar.* Alger: Office des publication universitaires, 1990.

Chow, Rey. "The Politics of Admittance: Female Sexual Agency, Miscegenation and the Formation of Community in Frantz Fanon." *The UTS Review: Cultural Studies and New Writing* 1.1 (1995): 5–29.

————. "Violence in the Other Country: China as Crisis, Spectacle, and Woman." *Third World Women and the Politics of Feminism.* Ed. Chandra Talpade Mohanty, Ann Russo, and Lourdes Torres. Bloomington: Indiana University Press, 1991. 81–100.

————. "Where Have All the Natives Gone?" *Writing Diaspora: Tactics of Intervention in Contemporary Cultural Studies.* Bloomington: Indiana University Press, 1993. 27–54.

Chrisman, Laura, and Patrick Williams. "Colonial Discourse and Post-Colonial Theory: An Introduction." *Colonial Discourse and Post-Colonial Theory: A Reader.* Ed. Patrick Williams and Laura Chrisman. New York: Columbia University Press, 1994. 1–20.

Cixous, Hélène. "The Laugh of the Medusa." Trans. Keith Cohen and Paula Cohen. *Feminisms: An Anthology of Literary Theory and Criticism.* Ed. Robyn R. Warhol and Diane Price Herndl. New Brunswick, NJ: Rutgers University Press, 1991. 334–49.

————. "Le Rire de la Méduse." *L'Arc* 61 (1975): 39–54.

Clair, Jean. "The Adventures of the Optic Nerve." *Bonnard: The Late Paintings.* Ed. Sasha M. Newman. London: Thames and Hudson, 1984. 29–50.

————. *Bonnard: Le peintre et l'homme.* Paris: Henri Scrépel, 1975.

Clark, VèVè A. "Developing Diaspora Literacy and *Marasa* Consciousness." *Comparative American Identities: Race, Sex, and Nationality in the Modern Text.* Ed. Hortense J. Spillers. New York: Routledge, 1991. 40–61.

Clifford, Caroline. "The Music of Multiculturalism in Leïla Sebbar's *Le Chinois vert d'Afrique.*" *French Review* 86.1 (October 1994): 52–60.

Cogniat, Raymond. *Bonnard.* Trans. Anne Ross. New York: Crown Publishers, n.d.

Collins, Patricia Hill. 1990. *Black Feminist Thought: Knowledge, Consciousness, and the Politics of Empowerment.* New York: Routledge, 1991.

Condé, Maryse. *Heremakhônon.* Paris: Union Générale d'Editions, 1976.

————. "Order, Disorder, Freedom, and the West Indian Writer." *Yale French Studies* 83.2 (1993): 121–35.

Cooke, Miriam. "Ibn Khaldun and Language: From Linguistic Habit to Philological Craft." *Ibn Khaldun and Islamic Ideology.* Ed. Bruce B. Lawrence. Leiden, Netherlands: E. J. Brill, 1984. 27–36.

————. *War's Other Voices: Women Writers on the Lebanese Civil War.* New York: Cambridge University Press, 1987. Reprint. 1988.

Daeninckx, Didier. *Ecrire en contre: Entretiens.* Vénissieux, France: Paroles d'aube, 1997.

———. *Meurtres pour mémoire*. Paris: Gallimard, 1984.

Debêche, Djamila. *Leïla, jeune fille algérienne*. Algiers: Imprimerie d'Alger, 1947.

Deleuze, Gilles, and Félix Guattari. *Kafka: Pour une littérature mineure*. Paris: Minuit, 1975.

Derrida, Jacques. "Freud et la scène de l'écriture." *L'Ecriture et la différence*. Paris: Seuil, 1967. 293–340.

Dib, Mohammed. *Le Métier à tisser*. Paris: Seuil, 1957.

Dine, Philip. *Images of the Algerian War: French Fiction and Film, 1954–1992*. New York: Oxford University Press, 1994.

Djebar, Assia. *Les Alouettes naïves*. Paris: Julliard, 1967.

———. *L'Amour, la fantasia*. Paris: J.-C. Lattès, 1985.

———. *Le Blanc de l'Algérie*. Paris: Albin Michel, 1996.

———. Comments made at the Postkolonialismus und Autobiographie conference at Würzburg University, Würzburg, Germany, June 1996.

———. Comments made at the roundtable on Djebar's films during the Colloque sur l'écriture des femmes migrantes en français en France et au Canada at Concordia University, Montreal, Quebec, May 1994.

———. Comments made on *La Zerda* at the Icono-Graphies Colloquium at Louisiana State University, Baton Rouge, LA, March 1996.

———. *Fantasia: An Algerian Cavalcade*. Trans. and intro. Dorothy S. Blair. London: Quartet Books, 1989.

———. *Femmes d'Alger dans leur appartement*. Paris: des femmes, 1980.

———. *Loin de Médine*. Paris: Albin Michel, 1991.

———. *The Mischief*. Trans. Frances Frenaye. New York: Simon and Schuster, 1958.

———. *Les Nuits de Strasbourg*. Arles, France: Actes Sud, 1997.

———. *Ombre sultane*. Paris: J.-C. Lattès, 1987.

———. "Rétablir le langage des femmes." Interview with C. Bouslimani. *El Moudjahid* (March 8, 1978): 7.

———. "Le Romancier dans la cité arabe." *Europe* 474 (October 1968): 114–20.

———. *A Sister to Scheherazade*. Trans. Dorothy S. Blair. London: Quartet Books, n.d.

———. *La Soif*. Paris: Julliard, 1957.

———. *Vaste est la prison*. Paris: Albin Michel, 1995.

———. *Women of Algiers in Their Apartment*. Trans. Marjolijn de Jager. Charlottesville: Caraf Books and University Press of Virginia, 1992.

Djebar, Assia, dir. *La Nouba des femmes du Mont Chenoua*. 1978.

———. *La Zerda ou les chants de l'oubli*. 1982.

Doane, Mary Ann. "Dark Continents: Epistemologies of Racial and Sexual Difference in Psychoanalysis and the Cinema." *Femmes Fatales: Feminism, Film Theory, Psychoanalysis*. New York: Routledge, 1991. 209–48.

Donadey, Anne. "Between Amnesia and Anamnesis: Re-Membering the Fractures of Colonial History." *Studies in Twentieth Century Literature* 23.1 (Winter 1999): 111–16.

———. "The Multilingual Strategies of Postcolonial Literature: Assia Djebar's Algerian Palimpsest." *World Literature Today* 74.1 (Winter 2000): 27–36.

———. "Portrait of a Maghrebian Feminist as a Young Girl: Fatima Mernissi's *Dreams of Trespass.*" *Edebiyât: The Journal of Middle Eastern Literatures* 11.1 (Spring 2000): 85–103.

Dumay, Jean-Michel. "Maurice Papon a fui la justice de son pays." *Le Monde* (October 21, 1999): 1, 10.

Einaudi, Jean-Luc. *La Bataille de Paris: 17 octobre 1961*. Paris: Seuil, 1991.

Elliott, James. "Bonnard and His Environment." *Bonnard and His Environment*. Ed. James Thrall Soby, James Elliott, and Monroe Wheeler. New York: Museum of Modern Art, 1964. 22–29.

Elshtain, Jean Bethke. *Women and War*. New York: Basic Books, 1987.

Enan, Mohammad Abdullah. *Ibn Khaldun: His Life and Work*. Kashmiri Bazar, Lahore: Shaikh Muhammad Ashraf, 1946.

Erickson, John. *Islam and Postcolonial Narrative*. New York: Cambridge University Press, 1998.

Etcherelli, Claire. *Elise ou la vraie vie*. Paris: Denoël, 1967.

Fanon, Frantz. "Algeria Unveiled." *A Dying Colonialism*. Trans. Haakon Chevalier. New York: Grove Weidenfeld, 1965. 35–67.

———. "L'Algérie se dévoile." 1959. *Sociologie d'une révolution: L'An V de la révolution algérienne*. Paris: Maspéro, 1968. 16–50.

———. *Black Skin, White Masks*. Trans. Charles Lam Markmann. New York: Grove Weidenfeld, 1967.

———. *Les Damnés de la terre*. 1961. Reprint. Paris: La Découverte, 1985.

———. *Peau noire, masques blancs*. Paris: Seuil, 1952.

———. *The Wretched of the Earth*. Trans. Constance Farrington. New York: Grove Weidenfeld, 1963.

Faulkner, Rita A. "Assia Djebar, Frantz Fanon, Women, Veils, and Land." *World Literature Today* 70.4 (Autumn 1996): 847–55.

Feagin, Joe R., and Hernán Vera. *White Racism: The Basics*. New York: Routledge, 1995.

Fermigier, André. *Pierre Bonnard*. New York: Harry N. Abrams, 1984.

Fischel, Walter J. *Ibn Khaldun in Egypt: His Public Function and His Historical Research (1382–1406). A Study in Islamic Historiography*. Berkeley: University of California Press, 1967.

Freud, Sigmund. *Beyond the Pleasure Principle*. 1922. Reprint. New York: Liveright Publishing, 1950.

———. "The Uncanny." Trans. Alix Strachey. *Collected Papers*. London: Hogarth Press and the Institute of Psychoanalysis, 1934. 4:368–407.

Fromentin, Eugène. *Une Année dans le Sahel.* Paris: Le Sycomore, 1981.
—————. *Un Eté dans le Sahara.* Paris: Le Sycomore, 1981.
Fuss, Diana. "Interior Colonies: Frantz Fanon and the Politics of Identification." *Diacritics* 24.2–3 (Summer–Fall 1994): 20–42.
Gafaiti, Hafid. "The Blood of Writing: Assia Djebar's Unveiling of Women and History." *World Literature Today* 70.4 (Autumn 1996): 813–22.
—————. "Ecriture autobiographique dans l'oeuvre d'Assia Djebar: *L'Amour, la fantasia.*" *Itinéraires et contacts de cultures* 13 (1991): 95–101.
—————. *Les Femmes dans le roman algérien: Histoire, discours et texte.* Paris: L'Harmattan, 1996.
Gallissot, René. "La Guerre et l'immigration algérienne en France." *La Guerre d'Algérie et les Français.* Ed. Jean-Pierre Rioux. Paris: Fayard, 1990. 337–47.
Garanger, Marc. *Femmes algériennes 1960.* Reprint. Paris: Contrejour, 1982.
—————. *Femmes des Hauts-Plateaux: Algérie 1960.* Text by Leïla Sebbar. Paris: Boîte à Documents, 1990.
Gates, Henry Louis, Jr. "Critical Fanonism." *Critical Inquiry* 17 (Spring 1991): 457–70.
Geesey, Patricia. "Collective Autobiography: Algerian Women and History in Assia Djebar's *L'amour, la fantasia.*" *Dalhousie French Studies* 35 (Summer 1996): 153–67.
Genette, Gérard. *Palimpsestes: La Littérature au second degré.* Paris: Seuil, 1982.
—————. *Seuils.* Paris: Seuil, 1987.
Gervereau, Laurent, Jean-Pierre Rioux, and Benjamin Stora. "Conclusion." *La France en guerre d'Algérie: Novembre 1954–Juillet 1962.* Ed. Laurent Gervereau, Jean-Pierre Rioux, and Benjamin Stora. Paris: Musée d'histoire contemporaine–BDIC, 1992. 304.
Gervereau, Laurent, Jean-Pierre Rioux, and Benjamin Stora, eds. *La France en guerre d'Algérie: Novembre 1954–Juillet 1962.* Paris: Museé d'histoire contemporaine–BDIC, 1992.
Ghaussy, Soheila. "A Stepmother Tongue: 'Feminine Writing' in Assia Djebar's *Fantasia: An Algerian Cavalcade.*" *World Literature Today* (Summer 1994): 457–62.
Ghazoul, Ferial. "The Metaphors of Historiography: A Study of Ibn Khaldun's Historical Imagination." *In Quest of an Islamic Humanism: Arabic and Islamic Studies in Memory of Mohamed al-Nowaihi.* Ed. A. H. Green. Cairo: American University in Cairo Press, 1984. 48–61.
Girard, René. *Violence and the Sacred.* Trans. Patrick Gregory. Baltimore: Johns Hopkins University Press, 1977.
—————. *La Violence et le sacré.* Paris, Grasset, 1972.
Giudice, Fausto. *Arabicides: Une Chronique française 1970–1991.* Paris: La Découverte, 1992.

Gracki, Katherine. "Writing Violence and the Violence of Writing in Assia Djebar's Algerian Quartet." *World Literature Today* 70.4 (Autumn 1996): 835–43.

Griffin, Susan. *A Chorus of Stones: The Private Life of War*. New York: Doubleday, 1992.

Guyot-Bender, Martine. "Harmony and Resistance in *L'Amour, la fantasia*'s Algerian Women's Communities." *Homemaking: Women Writers and the Politics and Poetics of Home*. Ed. Catherine Wiley and Fiona R. Barnes. New York: Garland, 1996. 175–99.

Hadj-Moussa, Ratiba. "Le Difficile surgissement de la mémoire." *Littérature et cinéma en Afrique francophone: Ousmane Sembène et Assia Djebar*. Ed. Sada Niang. Paris: L'Harmattan, 1996. 198–208.

Hall, Stuart. "Cultural Identity and Diaspora." *Colonial Discourse and Post-Colonial Theory: A Reader*. Ed. Patrick Williams and Laura Chrisman. New York: Columbia University Press, 1994. 392–403.

Hamm, Jean-Jacques. "Le Regard de l'objet: Sur l'oeuvre d'Assia Djebar." *Mises en scène d'écrivains: Assia Djebar, Nicole Brossard, Madeleine Gagnon, France Théoret*. Kingston, Canada: Trait d'union, 1993. 37–48.

Hamon, Hervé, and Patrick Rotman. *Les Porteurs de valises: La résistance française à la guerre d'Algérie*. Paris: Albin Michel, 1979.

Hannouche, Dalila. "Quand les Maghrébines ré-écrivent Scheherazade: *Ombre sultane* d'Assia Djebar." Paper given at the meeting of the Midwest Modern Language Association, Chicago, IL, November 1991.

Hargreaves, Alec G. "Language and Identity in Beur Culture." *French Cultural Studies* 1 (1990): 47–58.

Harlow, Barbara. *Resistance Literature*. New York: Methuen, 1987.

Herzberg, Nathaniel. "Archives: Trente-cinq ans de mensonge officiel sur les crimes policiers de 1961." *Le Monde* electronic edition (Friday, July 13, 1999). Available at <http://www.lemonde.fr>

hooks, bell. "Choosing the Margin as a Space of Radical Openness." *Yearning: Race, Gender, and Cultural Politics*. Boston: South End Press, 1990. 145–53.

———. "Feminist Scholarship: Ethical Issues." *Talking Back: Thinking Feminist, Thinking Black*. Boston: South End Press, 1989. 42–48.

Hugon, Monique. "Leïla Sebbar ou l'exil productif" (interview). *Notre librairie* 84 (July–September 1986): 32–37.

Huston, Nancy. *L'Empreinte de l'ange*. Arles, France: Actes Sud, 1998.

Hutcheon, Linda. "The Post Always Rings Twice: The Postmodern and the Postcolonial." *Textual Practice* 8.2 (Summer 1994): 205–38.

Huughe, Laurence. "'Ecrire comme un voile': The Problematics of the Gaze in the Work of Assia Djebar." *World Literature Today* 70.4 (Autumn 1996): 867–76.

Imache, Tassadit. *Une fille sans histoire*. Paris: Calmann Lévy, 1989.

Irigaray, Luce. "Pouvoir du discours, subordination du féminin." *Ce Sexe qui n'en est pas un*. Paris, Minuit, 1977. 65–82.

———. "The Power of Discourse and the Subordination of the Feminine." *This Sex Which Is Not One*. Trans. Catherine Porter. Ithaca, NY: Cornell University Press, 1985. 68–85.

JanMohamed, Abdul. "The Economy of Manichean Allegory: The Function of Racial Difference in Colonialist Literature." *"Race," Writing, and Difference*. Ed. Henry Louis Gates Jr. Chicago: University of Chicago Press, 1985. 78–106.

Jeyifo, Biodun. "The Nature of Things: Arrested Decolonization and Critical Theory." *Research in African Literatures* 21.1 (Spring 1990): 33–48.

Kalisa, Marie-Chantal. "'Geographies of Pain.'" Chapter in "Violence, Memory and Writing in Francophone African and Caribbean Women's Fiction." Ph.D. Dissertation, University of Iowa, 1999. 1–60.

Kandiyoti, Deniz. "Identity and Its Discontents: Women and the Nation." *Colonial Discourse and Post-Colonial Theory: A Reader*. Ed. Patrick Williams and Laura Chrisman. New York: Columbia University Press, 1994. 376–91.

Katrak, Ketu H. "Decolonizing Culture: Toward a Theory for Postcolonial Women's Texts." *Modern Fiction Studies* 35.1 (Spring 1989): 157–79.

Kelley, David. "Assia Djebar: Parallels and Paradoxes." *World Literature Today* 70.4 (Autumn 1996): 844–46.

Kepel, Gilles. "Islam: L'Exil sans fin." *Magazine littéraire* 221 (July–August 1985): 34–35.

Kettane, Nacer. *Le Sourire de Brahim*. Paris: Denoël, 1985.

Khaldun, Ibn. *Le Voyage d'Occident et d'Orient*. Trans. Abdesselam Cheddadi. Paris: Sindbad, 1980.

King, Deborah K. "Multiple Jeopardy, Multiple Consciousness: The Context of a Black Feminist Ideology." *Feminist Theory in Practice and Process*. Ed. Micheline R. Malson, Jean F. O'Barr, Sarah Westphal-Wihl, and Mary Wyer. Chicago: University of Chicago Press, 1990. 75–105.

King, Ynestra. "Healing the Wounds: Feminism, Ecology, and Nature/Culture Dualism." *Gender/Body/Knowledge: Feminist Reconstructions of Being and Knowing*. Ed. Alison M. Jaggar and Susan R. Bordo. New Brunswick, NJ: Rutgers University Press, 1992. 115–41.

Kolodny, Annette. "Dancing through the Minefield: Some Observations on the Theory, Practice, and Politics of a Feminist Literary Criticism." *The New Feminist Criticism: Essays on Women, Literature, and Theory*. Ed. Elaine Showalter. New York: Pantheon Books, 1985. 144–67.

Kristeva, Julia. *Etrangers à nous-mêmes.* Paris: Fayard, 1988.
———. *La Révolution du langage poétique. L'Avant-garde à la fin du XIXe siècle: Lautréamont et Mallarmé.* Paris: Seuil, 1974.
Lacoste, Yves. *Ibn Khaldun: The Birth of History and the Past of the Third World.* Trans. David Macey. London: Verso, 1984.
Lahbabi, Mohamed Aziz. *Ibn Khaldun: Notre contemporain.* Rabat and Paris: OKAD-L'Harmattan, 1987.
Lallaoui, Mehdi. *Les Beurs de Seine.* Paris: L'Arcantère, 1986.
Laronde, Michel. *Autour du roman beur: Immigration et identité.* Paris: L'Harmattan, 1993.
———. "Leïla Sebbar et le roman 'croisé': histoire, mémoire, identité." *CELFAN Review* 7.1–2 (1987–88): 6–13.
Lawson, Alan, and Chris Tiffin. "Conclusion: Reading Difference." *De-Scribing Empire: Post-colonialism and Textuality.* Ed. Chris Tiffin and Alan Lawson. London: Routledge, 1994. 230–35.
Lazarus, Neil. "Disavowing Decolonization: Fanon, Nationalism, and the Problematic of Representation in Current Theories of Colonial Discourse." *Research in African Literatures* 24.4 (Winter 1993): 71–98.
Lazreg, Marnia. *The Eloquence of Silence: Algerian Women in Question.* New York: Routledge, 1994.
———. "Gender and Politics in Algeria: Unraveling the Religious Paradigm." *Signs: Journal of Women in Culture and Society* 15.4 (Summer 1990): 755–80.
Lebbady, Hasna. "Fatima Mernissi's *Dreams of Trespass*: Self Representation or Confinement within the Discourse of Otherness." Paper given at the African Literature Association Conference, Fes, Morocco, March 1999.
Lebovics, Herman. *True France: The Wars over Cultural Identity, 1900–1945.* Ithaca, NY: Cornell University Press, 1992.
Le Clézio, Marguerite. "Assia Djebar: Ecrire dans la langue adverse." *Contemporary French Civilization* 9.2 (Spring–Summer 1985): 230–43.
Leulliette, Pierre. *Saint Michel et le dragon.* Paris: Minuit, 1961.
Leymarie, Jean. "Préface." *Bonnard dans sa lumière.* Paris: Maeght Editeur, 1978. 11–22.
Lionnet, Françoise. *Autobiographical Voices: Race, Gender, Self-Portraiture.* Ithaca, NY: Cornell University Press, 1989.
———. "Narrative Journeys: The Reconstruction of Histories in Leïla Sebbar's *Les Carnets de Shérazade.*" *Postcolonial Representations: Women, Literature, Identity.* Ithaca, NY: Cornell University Press, 1995. 167–86.
Loomba, Ania. "Overworlding the 'Third World.'" *Colonial Discourse and Post-Colonial Theory: A Reader.* Ed. Patrick Williams and Laura Chrisman. New York: Columbia University Press, 1994. 305–23.

Lorde, Audre. "Age, Race, Class, and Sex: Women Redefining Difference." *Sister Outsider: Essays and Speeches.* Freedom, CA: The Crossing Press, 1984. 114–23.

Lowe, Lisa. *Critical Terrains: French and British Orientalisms.* Ithaca, NY: Cornell University Press, 1991.

Mahdi, Muhsin. *Ibn Khaldun's Philosophy of History: A Study in the Philosophic Foundation of the Science of Culture.* Chicago: University of Chicago Press, 1971.

Mammeri, Mouloud. 1965. *L'Opium et le bâton.* Paris: La Découverte, 1992.

Mani, Lata and Ruth Frankenberg. "The Challenge of *Orientalism.*" *Economy and Society* 14.2 (May 1985): 174–92.

Marrouchi, Mustapha. "Mémoire d'Algérie: Écrire l'histoire." *Contemporary French Civilization* 14.2 (Summer/Fall 1990): 245–53.

Marx-Scouras, Danielle. "The Mother Tongue of Leïla Sebbar." *Studies in Twentieth-Century Literature* 17.1 (Winter 1993): 45–61.

———. "Muffled Screams/Stifled Voices." *Yale French Studies* 82 (January 1993): 172–82.

Mattei, Georges M. *La Guerre des gusses.* Paris: Balland, 1982.

Maximin, Daniel. *L'Isolé soleil.* Paris: Seuil, 1981.

McClintock, Anne. "The Angel of Progress: Pitfalls of the Term 'Post-colonialism.'" *Colonial Discourse and Post-Colonial Theory: A Reader.* Ed. Patrick Williams and Laura Chrisman. New York: Columbia University Press, 1994. 291–304.

———. *Imperial Leather: Race, Gender, and Sexuality in the Colonial Conquest.* New York: Routledge, 1995.

———. "'No Longer in a Future Heaven': Gender, Race, and Nationalism." *Dangerous Liaisons: Gender, Nation, and Postcolonial Perspectives.* Ed. Anne McClintock, Aamir Mufti, and Ella Shohat. Minneapolis: University of Minnesota Press, 1997. 89–112.

Mehrez, Samia. "Azouz Begag: Un di zafas di bidoufile or the Beur Writer: A Question of Territory." *Yale French Studies* 82 (January 1993): 25–42.

Memmi, Albert. 1965. *The Colonizer and the Colonized.* Trans. Howard Greenfeld. Boston: Beacon Press, 1967.

———. *Le Désert, ou la vie et les aventures de Jubair Ouali El-Mammi.* Paris: Gallimard, 1977.

———. 1957. *Portrait du colonisé, précédé de portrait du colonisateur.* Paris: Gallimard, 1985.

Merad, Ali. "L'Autobiographie d'Ibn Khaldûn." *IBLA* 19 (1956): 53–64.

Mermet, Gérard. *Francoscopie 1993.* Paris: Larousse, 1992.

Mernissi, Fatima. *Beyond the Veil: Male-Female Dynamics in Modern Muslim Society.* 1975. Reprint. Bloomington: Indiana University Press, 1987.

————. *Dreams of Trespass: Tales of a Harem Girlhood*. Reading, MA: Addison-Wesley, 1994.

————. *Le Harem politique: Le Prophète et les femmes*. 1987. Reprint. Paris: Complexe, 1992.

————. *The Veil and the Male Elite: A Feminist Interpretation of Women's Rights in Islam*. Trans. Mary Jo Lakeland. Reading, MA: Addison-Wesley, 1991.

Les Mille et Une Nuits. Trans. Antoine Galland. 3 vols. Paris: Garnier, 1881.

Miller, Nancy K. "Arachnologies: The Woman, the Text, and the Critic." *The Poetics of Gender*. New York: Columbia University Press, 1986. 270–95.

Mishra, Vijay, and Bob Hodge. "What is Post(-)colonialism?" *Colonial Discourse and Post-Colonial Theory: A Reader*. Ed. Patrick Williams and Laura Chrisman. New York: Columbia University Press, 1994. 276–90.

Mohanty, Chandra Talpade. "Cartographies of Struggle." *Third World Women and the Politics of Feminism*. Ed. Chandra Talpade Mohanty, Ann Russo, and Lourdes Torres. Bloomington: Indiana University Press, 1991. 1–47.

————. "Under Western Eyes: Feminist Scholarship and Colonial Discourses." *Third World Women and the Politics of Feminism*. Ed. Chandra Talpade Mohanty, Ann Russo, and Lourdes Torres. Bloomington: Indiana University Press, 1991. 51–80.

Mortimer, Mildred. "Assia Djebar's *Algerian Quartet*: A Study in Fragmented Autobiography." *Research in African Literatures* 28.2 (Summer 1997): 102–17.

————. "Entretien avec Assia Djebar, écrivain algérien." *Research in African Literatures* 19.2 (Summer 1988): 197–205.

————. *Journeys through the French African Novel*. Portsmouth, NH: Heinemann Educational Books, 1990.

————. "Language and Space in the Fiction of Assia Djebar and Leïla Sebbar." *Research in African Literatures* 19.3 (Fall 1988): 301–11.

Mowitt, John. "Algerian Nation: Fanon's Fetish." *Cultural Critique* 22 (Fall 1992): 165–86.

Murdoch, H. Adlai. "Rewriting Writing: Identity, Exile and Renewal in Assia Djebar's *L'Amour, la fantasia*." *Yale French Studies* 83 (January 1993): 71–92.

Naïr, Sami. *L'Immigration expliquée à ma fille*. Paris: Seuil, 1999.

Nash, Stephen A. "Tradition Revised: Some Sources in Late Bonnard." *Bonnard: The Late Paintings*. Ed. Sasha M. Newman. London: Thames and Hudson, 1984. 19–28.

Nelson, Terri J. "La Thématique du nu chez Pierre Bonnard." Unpublished essay, 1988.

Newman, Sasha M., ed. *Bonnard: The Late Paintings*. London: Thames and Hudson, 1984.

"1962–1992: 30 ans après . . ." *Paris-Match* (July 9, 1992): 92–93.

Nnaemeka, Obioma. "Bringing African Women into the Classroom: Rethinking Pedagogy and Epistemology." *Borderwork: Feminist Engagements with Comparative Literature*. Ed. Margaret R. Higonnet. Ithaca, NY: Cornell University Press, 1994. 301–18.

———. "Feminism, Rebellious Women, and Cultural Boundaries: Rereading Flora Nwapa and Her Compatriots." *Research in African Literatures* 26.2 (Summer 1995): 80–113.

Noiriel, Gérard. *Le Creuset français: Histoire de l'immigration XIXe-XXe siècle*. Paris: Seuil, 1988.

———. *The French Melting Pot: Immigration, Citizenship, and National Identity*. Trans. Geoffroy de Laforcade. Minneapolis: University of Minnesota Press, 1996.

Nora, Pierre. "Entre Mémoire et Histoire: La Problématique des lieux." *Les Lieux de mémoire*. Paris: Gallimard, 1984. 1:xv–xlii.

Norindr, Panivong. "Mourning, Memorials, and Filmic Traces: Remembering the *Corps étrangers* and Unknown Soldiers in Bertrand Tavernier's Films." *Studies in Twentieth Century Literature* 23.1 (Winter 1999): 117–41.

Oyono, Ferdinand. *Une Vie de boy*. Paris: Juillard, 1956.

Page, Andrea. "Rape or Obscene Copulation? Ambivalence and Complicity in Djebar's *L'Amour, la fantasia*." *Women in French Studies* 2 (Fall 1994): 42–54.

Parry, Benita. "Problems in Current Theories of Colonial Discourse." *Oxford Literary Review* 9.1–2 (1987): 27–58.

Patai, Daphne. "U.S. Academics and Third World Women: Is Ethical Research Possible?" *Women's Words: The Feminist Practice of Oral History*. Ed. Sherna Berger Gluck and Daphne Patai. New York: Routledge, 1991. 137–53.

Peltier, Josiane. "Didier Daeninckx's *Meurtres pour mémoire*: The Detective as Historian." In "(En)quêtes d'identité: Novels of Detection in France and the U.S., 1830–1990." Ph.D. Diss., University of Iowa, 1998. 161–93.

Pervillé, Guy. "Historiographie de la guerre." *La France en guerre d'Algérie: Novembre 1954–Juillet 1962*. Ed. Laurent Gervereau, Jean-Pierre Rioux, and Benjamin Stora. Paris: Musée d'histoire contemporaine–BDIC, 1992. 308–9.

Renan, Ernest. "Qu'est-ce qu'une nation?" *Oeuvres complètes*. 1882. Reprint. Paris: Calmann-Lévy, 1947. 1:887–906.

———. "What Is a Nation?" Trans. Martin Thom. *Nation and Narration*. Ed. Homi K. Bhabha. London: Routledge, 1990. 8–22.

Rezzoug, Simone. "Ecritures féminines algériennes: Histoire et société." *Maghreb Review* 9.3–4 (May–August 1984): 86–89.

Rich, Adrienne. "Notes toward a Politics of Location." *Blood, Bread and Poetry: Selected Prose 1979–1985.* New York: Norton, 1986. 210–31.

———. "Resisting Amnesia: History and Personal Life." *Blood, Bread and Poetry: Selected Prose 1979–1985.* New York: Norton, 1986. 136–55.

Rioux, Jean-Pierre. *La France de la IVe République. 2: L'expansion et l'impuissance, 1952–1958.* Paris: Seuil, 1983.

Rose, Wendy. "The Great Pretenders." *The State of Native America: Genocide, Colonization, and Resistance.* Ed. M. Annette Jaimes. Boston: South End Press, 1992. 403–21.

Rosenthal, Franz. "Ibn Khaldun in His Time (May 27, 1332–March 17, 1406)." *Ibn Khaldun and Islamic Ideology.* Ed. Bruce B. Lawrence. Leiden, Netherlands: E. J. Brill, 1984. 14–26.

Rothe, Arnold. "L'Espace du harem dans *Ombre sultane.*" *Mises en scènes d'écrivains: Assia Djebar, Nicole Brossard, Madeleine Gagnon, France Théoret.* Kingston, Canada: Trait d'union, 1993. 49–60.

Roumain, Jacques. *Gouverneurs de la rosée.* Paris: Editeurs français réunis, 1946.

Roumani, Judith. "Memmi's Introduction to History: *Le Désert* as Folktale, Chronicle and Biography." *Philological Quarterly* 61.2 (Spring 1982): 193–207.

Rousso, Henry. *Le Syndrome de Vichy (1944–198 . . .).* Paris: Seuil, 1987.

El Saadawi, Nawal. *A Daughter of Isis.* Trans. Sherif Hetata. London: Zed Press, 1999.

———. *The Hidden Face of Eve: Women in the Arab World.* Trans. and ed. Sherif Hetata. London: Zed Press, 1980.

Said, Edward W. *Orientalism.* New York: Pantheon Books, 1978.

———. *Out of Place: A Memoir.* New York: Alfred Knopf, 1999.

———. "Reflections on Exile." *Out There: Marginalization and Contemporary Cultures.* Ed. Russell Ferguson, Martha Gever, Trinh T. Minh-ha, and Cornel West. New York: New York Museum of Contemporary Art, 1990. 357–66.

Salien, Jean-Marie. "L'Ironie du métissage dans *Le Chinois vert d'Afrique* de Leïla Sebbar." Paper delivered at the eighth annual Conference on Foreign Literature, Wichita State University, Wichita, KS, April 1991.

Sandoval, Chela. "U.S. Third World Feminism: The Theory and Method of Oppositonal Consciousness in the Postmodern World." *Genders* 10 (Spring 1991): 1–24.

Sangari, Kumkum. "The Politics of the Possible." *The Nature and the Context of Minority Discourse.* Ed. Abdul JanMohamed and David Lloyd. Oxford: Oxford University Press, 1990. 216–45.

Schalk, David L. *War and the Ivory Tower: Algeria and Vietnam.* New York: Oxford University Press, 1991.

Scharfman, Ronnie. "Rewriting the Césaires: Daniel Maximin's Caribbean Discourse." *L'Héritage de Caliban.* Ed. Maryse Condé. Pointe à Pitre, Guadeloupe: Editions Jasor, 1992. 233–45.

Schnapper, Dominique. *L'Europe des immigrés.* Paris: François Bourin, 1992.

Scullion, Rosemarie. "Vicious Circles: Immigration and National Identity in Twentieth-Century France." *SubStance* 76–77 (1995): 30–48.

Sebbar, Leïla. *Les Carnets de Shérazade.* Paris: Stock, 1985.

———. *Le Chinois vert d'Afrique.* Paris: Stock, 1984.

———. *Fatima ou les Algériennes au square.* Paris: Stock, 1981.

———. *Le Fou de Shérazade.* Paris: Stock, 1991.

———. "Isabelle Eberhardt. Isabelle, l'Algérien." *Cahiers du GRIF* 39 (Fall 1988): 97–102.

———. *J. H. cherche âme soeur.* Paris: Stock, 1987.

———. "La Langue de l'exil." *La Quinzaine littéraire* 436 (March 16–31, 1985): 8, 10.

———. "La Littérature 'beur' n'existe pas." *Actualité de l'émigration* 80 (March 11, 1987): 27.

———. "On tue des instituteurs." *Une Enfance algérienne.* Ed. Leïla Sebbar. Paris: Gallimard, 1997. 187–97.

———. *La Seine était rouge.* Paris: Thierry Magnier, 1999.

———. *Shérazade, 17 ans, brune, frisée, les yeux verts.* Paris: Stock, 1982.

———. *Sherazade, Missing: Aged 17, Dark Curly Hair, Green Eyes.* Trans. Dorothy S. Blair. London: Quartet Books, 1991.

———. "Si je parle la langue de ma mère." *Les Temps modernes* 379 (February 1978): 1179–1188.

———. *Le Silence des rives.* Paris: Stock, 1993.

———. *Soldats.* Paris: Seuil, 1999.

Sebbar, Leïla, and Nancy Huston. *Lettres parisiennes: Autopsie de l'exil.* Paris: Bernard Barrault, 1986.

Sembène, Ousmane. *Xala.* Paris: Présence africaine, 1973.

Sharp, Joanne P. "Gendering Nationhood: A Feminist Engagement with National Identity." *BodySpace: Destabilizing Geographies of Gender and Sexuality.* Ed. Nancy Duncan. London: Routledge, 1996. 97–108.

Shatzmiller, Maya. *L'Historiographie mérinide: Ibn Khaldun et ses contemporains.* Leiden, Netherlands: E. J. Brill, 1982.

Shohat, Ella. "Notes on the 'Post-Colonial.'" *Social Text* 31–32 (1992): 99–113.

Silverman, Maxim. *Deconstructing the Nation: Immigration, Racism and Citizenship in Modern France.* London: Routledge, 1992.

Smaïl, Paul. *Vivre me tue.* Paris: Balland, 1997.

Spivak, Gayatri Chakravorty. "Acting Bits/Identity Talk." *Critical Inquiry* 18.4 (Summer 1992): 770–803.

———. "Echo." *New Literary History* 24.1 (Winter 1993): 17–43.

———. "Examples to Fit the Title." *American Imago* 51.2 (1994): 161–96.

———. "Imperialism and Sexual Difference." *Oxford Literary Review* 8.1–2 (1986): 225–40.

———. "Three Women's Texts and a Critique of Imperialism." *Feminisms: An Anthology of Literary Theory and Criticism.* Ed. Robyn R. Warhol and Diane Price Herndl. New Brunswick, NJ: Rutgers University Press, 1991. 798–814.

Stasiulis, Daiva K. "Relational Positionalities of Nationalisms, Racisms, and Feminisms." *Between Woman and Nation: Nationalisms, Transnational Feminisms, and the State.* Ed. Caren Kaplan, Norma Alarcón and Minoo Moallem. Durham, NC: Duke University Press, 1999. 182–218.

Stora, Benjamin. *La Gangrène et l'oubli: La mémoire de la guerre d'Algérie.* Paris: La Découverte, 1991.

———. "La Guerre d'Algérie en livres." *La Bibliothèque des deux rives: Sur la Méditerranée occidentale.* Ed. Thierry Paquot. Paris: Lieu commun, 1992. 155–72.

———. *Ils venaient d'Algérie: L'Immigration algérienne en France (1912–1992).* Paris: Fayard, 1992.

———. *Imaginaires de guerre: Algérie, Viet-Nam, en France et aux Etats-Unis.* Paris: La Découverte, 1997.

Talahite, Anissa. "Odalisques et Pacotille: Identity and Representation in Leïla Sebbar's *Shérazade, 17 ans, brune, frisée, les yeux verts.*" *Nottingham French Studies* 37.2 (Autumn 1998): 62–72.

Thomas, Nicholas. *Colonialism's Culture: Anthropology, Travel, and Government.* Princeton, NJ: Princeton University Press, 1994.

Trinh T. Minh-ha. "Not You/Like You: Post-Colonial Women and the Interlocking Questions of Identity and Difference." *Making Face, Making Soul: Haciendo Caras. Creative and Critical Perspectives by Feminists of Color.* Ed. Gloria Anzaldúa. San Francisco: Aunt Lute Books, 1990. 371–75.

———. *Woman, Native, Other: Writing Postcoloniality and Feminism.* Bloomington: Indiana University Press, 1989.

Tristan, Anne. *Le Silence du fleuve: Ce Crime que nous n'avons toujours pas nommé.* Bezon: Au nom de la mémoire, 1991.

Vaillant, Annette. *Bonnard.* Trans. David Britt. Greenwich, CT: New York Graphic Society, 1965.

Van Strien-Chardonneau, Madeleine. "De la quête d'une patrie à la découverte de l'écriture: les enfants de l'immigration dans deux romans de Leïla Sebbar." *CRIN (L'Etranger dans la littérature française,* Ed. Danièle de Ruyter-Tognotti) 20 (1989): 26–54.

Verthuy, Maïr. "Histoire, mémoire et création dans l'oeuvre d'Assia Djebar." *Mises en scènes d'écrivains: Assia Djebar, Nicole Brossard, Madeleine*

Gagnon, France Théoret. Kingston, Canada: Trait d'union, 1993. 25–36.

Woodhull, Winifred. *Transfigurations of the Maghreb: Feminism, Decolonization, and Literatures*. Minneapolis: University of Minnesota Press, 1993.

Yacine, Kateb. *Nedjma*. Paris: Seuil, 1956.

Yegenoglu, Meyda. "Supplementing the Orientalist Lack: European Ladies in the Harem." *Inscriptions* 6 (1992): 45–80.

Young, Robert. *White Mythologies: Writing History and the West*. London: Routledge, 1990.

Zabus, Chantal. *The African Palimpsest: Indigenization of Language in the West African Europhone Novel*. Amsterdam: Rodopi, 1991.

Zimra, Clarisse. "Afterword." *Women of Algiers in Their Apartment*. Charlottesville: Caraf Books and University Press of Virginia, 1992. 159–211.

———. "Disorienting the Subject in Djebar's *L'Amour, la fantasia*." *Yale French Studies* 87 (1995): 149–70.

———. "Not So Far from Medina: Assia Djebar Charts Islam's 'Insupportable Feminist Revolution'." *World Literature Today* 70.4 (Autumn 1996): 823–34.

Index

About the Author

ANNE DONADEY is Associate Professor, Comparative Literature and
Women's Studies, The University of Iowa.